Leadership, Greatness & Servanthood

"He that would be great among you,
let him be the servant of all."

Leadership, Greatness & Servanthood

PHILIP GREENSLADE

BETHANY HOUSE PUBLISHERS
MINNEAPOLIS, MINNESOTA 55438
A Division of Bethany Fellowship, Inc.

Originally published in England by Marshall, Morgan, and Scott Publications LTD. under the title *Leadership*, ISBN 0–551–01135–1

NB: Unless otherwise stated Scripture references are from 'The New International Version' Hodder.

Abbreviations used are as follows:–
JBP The New Testament in Modern English. J. B. Phillips. Geoffrey Bles 1960.
JB The Jerusalem Bible. Darton, Longman & Todd 1974.
NASB The New American Standard Bible. Holman 1977
TEV The Good News Bible (Today's English Version). Collins 1976.
NEB The New English Bible. Oxford/Cambridge 1970.
LB The Living Bible Paraphrased. Tyndale 1971.
Moffatt The Moffatt Translation of the Bible. Hodder 1957.
Barclay The New Testament. A new translation by William Barclay. Fontana/Collins 1969.

Published by Bethany House Publishers
A Division of Bethany Fellowship, Inc.
6820 Auto Club Road, Minneapolis, MN 55438

Printed in the United States of America

Library of Congress Cataloging in Publication Data

Greenslade, Phillip.
   Leadership, greatness, and servanthood.

   Published in Great Britain in 1984 under title: Leadership.
   1. Christian leadership.   I. Title.
BV652.1.G74   1986   262'.1   85-30667
ISBN 0-87123-871-3 (pbk.)

To Mary

After training for the Baptist ministry at Spurgeons College,
Philip Greenslade spent 13 years in pastoral ministry.
He is now a part of the team ministry of The King's Church,
based at The King's Centre, Aldershot, Hants.

Contents

PART FOUR   LEADERSHIP TODAY

Foreword

The state of leadership in the church of Jesus Christ is a spiritual barometer. Leaders are gifts of the ascended Christ to his 'body' – gifts that he may withhold for certain reasons, or gifts that he may freely bestow. Spiritual decline invariably results in a leadership shortage. In his day Isaiah declared that the Lord Almighty was about to act in judgement by taking from Jerusalem and Judah 'the hero and warrior, the judge and prophet, the captain of 50 and man of rank'. On the other hand, repentance and a fresh turning to God brings a release of these vital gifts.

Apart from the spiritual state of a nation world wars tend to cut down the flower of a nation's manhood. It is not, therefore, surprising that in the wake of World War II there was a dearth of leadership in general, and the church of Jesus Christ was no exception. But since the movement of the Spirit that broke out in the mid-sixties, there has been a significant acceleration in the bringing forth of leaders. If there is to be any lasting church growth, there must be equivalent leadership growth. One must be thankful for the new emphasis that has come on the training and developing of leaders.

The author is no theorist in this realm. In addition to his several years experience in the shepherding of a flock, he has brought to his task considerable experience derived through the Towards Leadership Training Programme with which he has been involved. I have personally benefited from the bi-monthly bulletin TOWARDS LEADERSHIP of which he is a Co-editor, and consider it the most significant publication on leadership that is being issued regularly in this country.

Philip Greenslade is thoroughly biblical in the treatment of his subject. There is a depth and quality in his writing that comes from the discipline of his theological training and the anointing of the Holy Spirit that he has subsequently received. He has not been content simply to stay with a 'renewal' emphasis but has pressed on into the fuller revelation that God has given him concerning God's purposes for his church and his kingdom. This has supplied a prophetic edge to his message, so that here we have a 'now' word for the aspiring leaders of tomorrow. To some readers much of what is contained here will seem to be new, but it is only new because we have not drunk deeply enough of the wells of truth found in the New Testament.

The author has taken it for granted that all the vital ingredients of spiritual leadership are found in principle and example in the New Testament. He has rightly assumed that God has etched there all he wants his people, leaders or followers, to be and to do.

What I like most about this book is that the writer, rather than giving us techniques, methodology, or psychological insights has instead taken us to the heart of the matter by unfolding *the character* of the leader God is wanting, illustrating his points from the example of our Lord, of Paul and of other great saints in scripture and history. This is just where the New Testament puts the emphasis. The qualifications of the elders that Paul gives us in Timothy and Titus are concerned overwhelmingly with the issue of character rather than gift. Leadership tragedies are almost entirely caused by character breakdown rather than gift deficiency.

If a leader picks up this book, whether he be an aspiring one, a perspiring one, or even in danger of becoming an expiring one, it will not surprise me if he finds it necessary to pause in his reading, drop on his knees and call on the Lord to bring him into the good of what he is reading.

We are surely moving into a phase of spiritual activity, the most exciting and demanding that we have ever known. Our problem will not be that of empty nets, but nets breaking with the weight of the catch. Many churches would be swamped by a sudden intake of even a dozen new converts. What will they do with a couple of hundred? Any church not involved in a thorough comprehensive scheme to train the leaders of tomorrow, will find that the coming wave of revival blessing will pass them by and leave them high and dry. I believe that this book will play a valuable part in the preparation of young leaders for the coming day of visitation.

ARTHUR WALLIS

Preface and Acknowledgments

This book has been written on the assumption that patterns of ministry and leadership in the Church are changing and is, therefore, to be regarded only as a provisional statement drawn up 'on the way'.

Its aim is the modest one of giving clues to that biblical standard of leadership which we are all 'towards'.

What it is

Part ONE assumes that leadership is a good thing, asks why it is important, and suggests ways of overcoming resistance to it.

Part TWO looks at how leadership emerges and functions, the difficulties it faces, the dangers it is prone to, and the safeguards available to it.

Part THREE looks first at the kind of leadership Jesus repudiated and then at the leadership he endorsed by his own example and teaching and bestowed as his own legacy to the Church.

Part FOUR surveys some of the ways in which leadership operates today and seeks to encourage the restoration of more biblical structures to the Church's life and ministry.

What it is not

Three disclaimers.

(i) It is not the literary equivalent of 'painting by numbers' for leaders. This is more a 'what' book than a 'how-to' book.

(ii) It is not an identikit-picture of the ideal leader. Apart from the Lord Jesus there is no such person. It is a suggestive rather than an exhaustive treatment of the theme. I regret here it does not deal specifically, for example, with the subject of women's ministry, though this should not be taken as denying countless ways in which women are called and gifted to serve in the body of Christ.

(iii) It is not a colouring book for leaders to be filled in with whatever shades of ecclesiastical opinion one prefers. Any readers of this book are welcome from whatever backgrounds and traditions they come, and I hope they will find it useful. Nevertheless, it clearly implies the need for radical change in the wineskins the Church is currently occupying. So often, as Alvin Toffler notes, 'leaders – even the "best" – are cripples because the institutions they must work through are obsolete'.

I realise now that certain themes, even passages of Scripture recur throughout this book. I trust that this is not vain repetition but, as in a symphony, the resurgence of an underlying motif which says something slightly different whenever it occurs and which serves to hold the whole thing together.

I gladly give acknowledgement to many people. I am especially grateful for the support and loving help of my wife, Mary, who has tirelessly checked the product at every turn. I record my indebtedness to Derek Brown, whose friendship and counsel, often while travelling together, have made this book almost as much his as mine. I have appreciated also the backing of Mike Pusey and my other colleagues in ministry at Farnborough. Looking further back down the road, I express my thanks to Harold Owen for his counsel in the earlier stages of renewal; and, even further back to A. J. Tugwell and Andrew McKie for their help in my formative years. My thanks are due to my friends Dacre and Coral Wicks for the use of their home in which to begin writing: to Stuart Reid for his constant encouragement; and to all the other members of Antioch Ministries – Garth Moody, Trevor Martin, Ken Humphries, Hugh Clark – with whom I have learned and unlearned so much, usually with good humour. Particular thanks must go, too, to Sandra Stockwell who gave up much free time to type and re-type the manuscript. To all the saints among whom I minister and to all the men on the Towards Leadership Training Courses whose fellowship has proved so invigorating, I express my thanks. You are the front line troops.

Finally, to every aspiring leader wondering where he fits into the picture I offer my encouragement. As the original 'square peg', I urge you not to let definition cramp your style or quench the Holy Spirit.

Part One
Why Leadership

1. First Service

Jesus must be the first word in this book. He is the leader of the leaders, Lord of lords, King of kings. Before Abraham was, he was; the pioneer and perfecter of faith, a prophet eclipsing Moses, a priest superior to Aaron, David's Lord as well as son, a greater than Solomon, the Chief Shepherd of all shepherds. Going ahead of his disciples in a way that amazes and overawes us, he puts our own leadership in its proper perspective. 'They were on their way up to Jerusalem, with Jesus leading the way, and the disciples were astonished, while those who followed were afraid. Again he took the Twelve aside and told them what was going to happen to him' (Mark 10.32). Clearly Jesus must *have* the first and last word on this subject.

'Do not be called leaders' is his starting point, a shot across the bows of this book that might have stopped it being written! Seemingly it makes for as unpromising a start to it as you could find.

Thankfully, Jesus does not leave it there but opens up our theme by adding: 'for one is your leader, even Christ; and the greatest among you shall be your servant' (Matt. 23. 10–11 NASB). Here Jesus is not decrying leadership but redefining it. He is recasting the pattern of leadership into the shape of his own. From the outset we remind ourselves that any move towards leadership is a move towards the Lord Jesus Christ. 'To lead is to serve.' This is our basic premise, first lesson and chief ambition. We first learn to be leaders by learning to be servants. 'Before honour comes humility' (Proverbs 15.33).

It hardly needs saying that this is an unfashionable note to strike. As I write, a high-powered, road show is touring the country's conference centres, sponsored by the Institute of Sales and Marketing no less! 'Give John Fenton your sales team', business firms are urged, 'and achieve all these targets by March next year.' 'These targets' include everything from improving profits by 100 per cent to reducing selling costs by 15 per cent; from eliminating negative thinking to eliminating courtesy telephone calls! One newspaper described the event as 'like having a private interview with Billy Graham'.

Now no one doubts that the Church could do with an improved efficiency drive or even a dose of the right kind of positive thinking. The sales road show might conceivably be a useful finishing school for Christian leaders. But it is definitely not where we start. Ours is a service industry not a sales industry.

Upstairs-downstairs

Undeniably 'service' is a word that has fallen on hard times recently. It has a rather fusty smell about it, suggestive in progressive minds of rather old-fashioned, untrendy, even illiberal attitudes. In an age where there is more talk of rights than of obligations 'service' is almost regarded as demeaning.

It has come to describe work that cannot be done without, but which attracts few volunteers. Everyone wants to receive it; few to give it. Usually it is assigned by default to the poor or underprivileged, to the under-educated or those with few choices. Service industries are poor relations of production industries.

In my previous church we ran a social gathering for over-60s where the senior citizens could relax in a friendly atmosphere. Often if asked, the elderly ladies would describe to me their days 'in service'. In those days, as young women, they served 'below stairs' as chambermaids or parlour maids in the large houses of early Edwardian England. For their part, the old men, fewer in number, survivors of the Great War, still stiffened with pride as they recounted their days in the 'services' as comrades in arms. Clearly 'service' is a concept in need of rehabilitation.

Biblically we find the concept of servanthood transformed by the prophetic vision. Isaiah dignifies for ever the idea of service in his moving prophecies of the suffering servant of God, the model for the Messiah. And when Messiah came he took the form of a servant in which to express himself. He anticipated his coming into the world in the words of a previous servant of God (Heb. 10.5f, Ps. 40) – 'therefore when he comes into the world, he says: "Sacrifice and offering thou has not desired; but a body hast thou prepared for me. Then I said behold I come; (in the volume of the book it is written of me) to do thy will, O God"' (NASB).

'I am among you as one who serves.'
'I have come not to be ministered unto but to minister.'

In a radical fashion Jesus, by example and word, establishes servanthood as the way in which his men are to lead others. He expressly repudiates every secular model of leadership in favour of servanthood. His men are not to be like the Pharisees, whose leadership was spoiled by hypocrisy, misuse of authority, ostentation and blatant professionalism (Matt. 23.1–7). They are not to act like gentile rulers who 'lord it over' those under them (Mark 10.32). No category, whether social, cultural, ecclesiastical or political, will fit his vision of leadership without drastic alteration in style and attitude. His 'not so among you' thwarts any attempt to institutionalise worldliness in the leadership structures of his Church.

This raises a question mark against those many current leadership manuals which are weighted almost exclusively towards goal setting, public relations techniques and management methods. Needful correctives as they are to the habitual sloppiness and inefficiency of the Church, they do not touch the mainspring of motivation in the Kingdom of God. As we shall see again later, it was the form of servanthood that the Son of God chose to pour his divine life into. And Father didn't break the mould when he sent him.

For this reason the apostles never stray far from this theme in describing their own calling and that of their readers. Paul, a 'bond-servant of Jesus Christ' writes to the Romans. It is as bond-servants that Peter, James, Jude and John record their testimony. The New Testament writers ransack the vocabulary of servanthood, as if to show that to be a servant is not to be a robot or automaton, but a friend and confidant and partner. Servanthood enlarges, not shrinks, our horizons, as the original words suggest.[1]

- 'diakonos' is a servant viewed in relation to his *work*, so stressing his *activity*
- 'doulos' is a servant in relation to his *master*; underlining his *accountability*.
- 'huperetes' is a servant in relation to his *superior*, thus emphasising the *authority* he is under.
- 'leitourgos' is a servant in relation to the *organisation* that employs him, so highlighting the *administration* he is part of.

Then the whole range of words associated with 'oikos' (i.e. 'house') draw the commercial and domestic worlds much closer together than we are used to. In the household is where we belong with the Father and his Son. Ever since the Son and Heir came downstairs, serving has been something entirely different. And below stairs is where Jesus looks for his potential leaders. When Jesus looks for leaders he looks for men with a servant heart and a serving spirit. These men will serve Jesus by serving his Body. 'For we do not preach ourselves but Jesus Christ as Lord and ourselves as your bond-servants for Jesus' sake' (2 Cor. 4.5).

Serving Instructions

We look to the same source as the Lord Jesus for clues to this servant spirit and attitude. Psalm 40.6–8 shows us a little of what it means to be a servant. 'Sacrifice and offering you did not desire, but my ears you have pierced; burnt offerings and sin offerings you did not require. Then I said, "Here I am, I have come – it is written about me in the scroll. To do your will, O my God, is my desire; your law is within my heart" ' (NASB).

(1) Get to know what God desires not just what he requires. The laws of sacrifice were not the total expression of His will. He was looking beneath the offering for obedience. A true servant will look for what pleases his Lord. Our Puritan forefathers, in contrast to ourselves, rarely bothered with the problem of guidance. They merely looked each day for fresh ways of glorifying God. If this is our attitude as leaders, we shall begin to satisfy his desires not just meet his requirements.

(2) Be wholly committed to the Lord. The pierced ear was an ancient sign of belonging (cf. Ex. 21.1–6). Bought with a price, no believer, no spiritual leader is his own man. My leadership is not the path to emotional fulfilment for my insecure ego. I am in it for his sake first.

(3) Pay attention to what the Lord is saying. When God has got me by my ears he's got all of me! It's a poor servant who is deaf to his master's voice. Don't try to begin as a great prophet; begin as Samuel did by being awake to the smallest whisper.

(4) Be available! Then I said: 'Behold, I come'. 'Here I am for you called me' is the servant spirit. Redeemed from being a slave to sin and unrighteousness, I now serve in newness of the Spirit and bring my life to attention to be of use to righteousness (Romans 6.17–19).

(5) Be confident about your usefulness to the Lord. 'I come' into the Master's presence because when called I have a right to be there. You are needed in his Kingdom. You are not redundant. You are not second reserve for the third

team. Sadly there is still much unused potential in the Body of Christ because people are waiting for their name to be called or their bell to ring. What is true of them is true of their leaders, many of whom develop rapidly just as soon as someone, usually another leader, helps them to know their name and place and to identify their true gift and calling.

(6) Do the will of God from the heart. Once you know your destiny is written in the book, you can embrace it with joy. Soon the book is written into you and the law of God is etched on your heart. Duty hardly comes into it for such leaders. They delight to do the will of God. In this way fresh challenges will not deter but inspire us as leaders. If we make love our aim and earnestly desire the spiritual gifts, we will surprise ourselves by what we are able to achieve and be amazed at where we travel to as leaders in God's Church.

'You've not made much out of all these years' said an affluent merchant to an impoverished fellow Devonian who had voyaged with Drake to the new World. 'Maybe not', was the reply, 'but I've been with the greatest captain who's ever sailed the seas'.

Full-time Service

Being a servant is then deeper and greater than doing a job for God. The call to 'full-time' service has nothing essentially to do with quitting one's secular work in order to study at Bible College and enter the ministry in a clerical sense. Simply by calling men to be his disciples in training for leadership, Jesus revises all ambitions and ruins many careers.

In one of his books, that sensitive Methodist preacher of an earlier era, A. E. Whitham muses on the possibility of there being a museum in heaven, exhibiting tokens of spiritual leadership. It's an intriguing thought. In such a museum would surely be Moses's staff and Aaron's rod – the one that budded. Alongside these, among many others, we might reasonably expect to find the inkpot that Luther threw at the devil, John Wesley's saddle and stirrups, not to mention praying Hyde's knee patches and Billy Graham's air-line tickets. But two items would surely be conspicuous by their absence. The towel and basin would not be there; for the good reason that they are still in use!

2. Double Fault

Nothing could be wiser for a leader, as I have discovered for myself, than to decide not to be the saviour of the world! This spares you many headaches, much heartache and not a few nervous breakdowns.

As a young man with a tendency to manage other people said to E. Stanley Jones at one of the latter's retreats, 'I have resigned as general manager of the universe'. This is a word in season for leaders if for no other reason than that it may release us from the self-important activism that we are prone to. In the evangelical hustle and bustle of my youth, the patron saint appeared to be St. Vitus and he led us an unmerry dance. The treadmill of meetings and activities, of clubs and organisations, of efforts and campaigns, seemed unstoppable. We had yet to learn that perspiration does not guarantee inspiration. We should never mistake a messianic complex for the messianic anointing!

Stanley Jones concludes from all this that the training of leaders is too dangerous and should be left well alone. He writes, 'we have classes for leadership in our churches – a mistake. This does not produce leaders – it only produces fussy managers of other people'.[1] Point taken! In fact I make a point of reading out this statement at the start of each of our Towards Leadership training programmes. I do this because to take such a remark on the chin without being knocked out by it will help us to come to our senses and at least stop us from losing the fight for leadership on points of complacency. In fact, Jones's comment helps us to identify the first of two opposite errors made about leadership which I now want to look at.

Superstars

The first error made about leadership is the tendency to *over-glamorise it*. It is one of the dangers of special books about it like this one. Other recent books on this theme do seem to me to have fallen into this trap. They give the impression that the ideal

Christian leader can be cloned. He emerges as a cross between Abraham Lincoln and Napoleon; a composite of Montgomery with his meticulous preparation for battle and Patton with his daring initiatives in it. Throw in bits of the Angel Gabriel and Martin Luther King, the Pied Piper and the Bionic Man and you just about have the right blend! You have only to read about Paul Yonggi Cho as you drift off to sleep and your mind goes into the fifth dimension of total fantasy. Such images of myself as a leader tend to last no longer than it takes to get up the next morning! These romantic images are, however, unwittingly reinforced by much of the admirable material published by the Church Growth School in America. Reading of the latest high-powered success story I am presented with a picture of leadership which prompts in me an unholy mixture of envy and self-condemnation. In these illustrated success stories the Senior Pastor is usually shown ensconced in managerial splendour, oozing charm and self-assurance from a black-leather, swivel chair in his lavishly-appointed executive suite. Around him in the well-equipped church office, are his bevy of eager colleagues. As a picture of leadership this is as impressive as it is intimidating. Rather than rejecting this image outright or rejecting ourselves in the light of it, we might do well to pull it back from a never-never land of unfulfilled dreams into the everyday world where most of us are.

In pondering the dearth of able leaders in the Church, Howard Snyder has recently questioned the concept of ministry implicit in the glamour view of leadership. 'Is the problem really a lack of ecclesiastical superstars? Thank God for the superstars. But the Church of Jesus Christ cannot run on superstars and God never intended that it should. But he does promise to provide all necessary leadership through the gifts of the Spirit (Eph. 4.1–16)'.[2] All this is good news for those churches which are open to hear what the Spirit is saying to them today. Already it is bringing release and development to whole areas of evangelicalism both inside and outside the mainline denominations. It has yet to penetrate other sections of Christendom quite different from the one we have described where an exclusive clerical monopoly still prevails. There the priest, father, dominie or minister still stands apart or on high, on pedestal or pulpit, six feet above contradiction.

But where the Spirit has blown through our concepts of ministry to renew us in biblical principles of leadership, we have all begun to breathe again. There is a romance and a glorious dignity about true spiritual leadership to satisfy every dream, as we shall see later. But we need to approach leadership from underneath, as it were, with a healthy recognition that we are servants and that at best we make a modest contribution to the overall victory of the Kingdom. The crowns and rewards are well worth waiting for.

Reverend Dogsbody

There is an opposite error to the one we have outlined which is, if anything, even more harmful to the Church. This is the tendency to *denigrate leadership*.

A number of factors have contributed to this trend.

(i) There has been a decline in the status of the Christian ministry

This is especially true in post-war Britain where leadership in the Church has had a distinctly 'fly-blown' image. The men from the ministry all too often have been the ones wearing the shabby suits and driving the secondhand cars. This down-at-heel mentality has been unwittingly reinforced by church structures which have left the minister with the feeling that he is the underpaid employee of a far-from-successful business. True servanthood has degenerated into servility with the minister hard pressed to believe that he has any self-worth. Tied to a church-owned cottage or Manse he has little room for maneouvre.

Such a system has been a recipe for anxiety and insecurity among Christian leaders, cramping prophetic courage. His faithfulness exploited, the pastor has too often been the doormat rather than the door to the fold. Professionalism has been the only refuge for such vulnerable men. This helps to account for the fact that ministers' fraternals have often had more than their fair share of unbelief, cynicism and competitiveness.

Treat a man as a hireling and you can scarcely complain if he does not prove a good shepherd. The Church gets the ministry it deserves. That this is changing in many places is a tribute to the revolution in our thinking the Holy Spirit has inspired.

(ii) Christians have for long had a love-hate relationship with leadership

Notable voices have gone on record as playing down the whole idea. 'To tell a man', says Bishop Stephen Neill, 'that he is called to be a leader, or that he is being trained to be a leader, is the best way of insuring his spiritual ruin, since in the Christian world ambition is more deadly than any other sin'.[3]

Bishop Neill, a far-sighted missionary statesman, is unlikely to endorse mediocrity as the pattern for the Church. But his warning reflects a double-mindedness about leadership that reaches down to every level of the church's life. I profoundly disagree with his statement as it stands. This book would not have been attempted if I had not been sure of Paul's commitment to the truth that 'to aspire to leadership is an honourable ambition' (1 Tim. 3.1 NEB).

One of the very positive gains of the Church Growth movement is that we are now less shy of talking not only of success and efficiency but also of dynamic and effective leaders as needed in the Body of Christ. Here, as elsewhere, the sons of darkness have a glimmer of wisdom that the sons of light do well to notice. Throughout this book I presuppose that leadership is a good thing, a blessed necessity, not a blessed nuisance. Key scriptures like Ephesians 4.11 and Romans 12.3ff have behind them the whole history of God's guidance of his people through his appointed and anointed servants. Clearly leadership is a gift to the Church not an imposition on it.

Our double-mindedness will even confuse us here if we're not careful. Many people idolise the past and yearn for some great preacher of yesteryear to be reincarnated. Evangelicals have a pantheon of saints every bit as large as Catholics. Stirred by nostalgia, fervent saints will pray for some trumpet voice again to be raised to rally the Church and recall the world. No sooner does he arise among them saying uncomfortable things than they wish he was somewhere else altogether. Recognition has usually been posthumous. A. W. Tozer is now revered as a prophet by many of the very people who deny that the Ephesians 4 ministries are valid for today.

No one wants to return to the bad old days when the Church was a creepy mutual admiration society. Then two hours of back-slapping at the Annual General Meeting was deemed adequate compensation for eleven and a half months of back-biting. Then the best thing that could be said about a man's ministry was said at his memorial service or reserved for his obituary notice. But Jesus who gave us in his ascension someone to look up to also expects us to honour and appreciate those he has delegated to represent him. 'We ask you my brothers, to get to know those who work so hard among you. They are your spiritual leaders . . . hold them in high esteem' (1 Thess. 5.12, JBP).

(iii) A third factor contributing to the denigrating of leadership in the church is egalitarianism

The pressure for equal rights so strong in secular society has been felt in the Church. Disrespect for authority figures has obscured the biblical basis of leadership. The spirit of the Women's Rights movement has infiltrated the minds of traditional churchmen with a resultant pressure for women's ordination. Much of this is quite frankly the spirit of the world.

This is not the place to dwell at length on the role of women in the Body of Christ. A whole book could be written on the infinite variety of God-given ministries and functions Spirit-filled women can perform in the Kingdom of God. But I am quite convinced that authoritative, directive leadership is not one of them. To my mind there is clear biblical authority for placing governmental, spiritual authority in male, not female hands. But the Holy Spirit's re-emphasis on this has been against a wave of egalitarian thinking that has threatened the integrity of so-called Bible-believing churches.[4]

Even to talk the language of authority, direction and government is itself to go against the prevailing secular tide. In recent years Hebrews 13.17 has dropped like a bombshell into many nonconformist churches, especially those which are congregational in order and government. 'Obey your leaders and submit to them for they keep watch over your souls' (NASB). Blurring these distinctions does not build the Church.

(iv) The fourth factor I would mention as a threat to proper recognition of leadership is one which apart from this is altogether positive and welcome. That is the renewed experience of the Church as the Body of Christ in which every member has a gift to give and a role to play. What the Holy Spirit is doing here is one of the most exciting aspects of his work today.

For this reason it would be especially tragic if this release of the potential of every member was at the expense of leadership. We do not up-grade the role of membership by down-grading the place of leaders.

The priesthood of all believers is more widely practised now in churches renewed by the Holy Spirit than ever before, whatever the denominational creeds claimed. It would be wrong, however, if the priesthood of all believers was taken to mean the leadership of none.

In fact, as many of us in leadership are experiencing, the release of the gifts and ministries of all the members of Christ's Body calls for more and better leadership, not less. As the gifts of the Spirit through the members express his *body* so the gifts of leadership express the *headship* of Jesus over it. The more prolific and varied the gifts and ministries, the more clear and respected does the leadership have to be. God's necessary order and direction, control and sensitivity is clearly to be safeguarded, not by liturgy or written constitution but by men at every level who have God's anointing to lead.

So we are neither superstars nor dogsbodies! Like Paul we cherish no exaggerated ideas of our own importance – 'I am the least of the apostles'. Like Paul we can be free of the burden of an inferiority complex – 'but I laboured even more than all of them'! Like him we can rest easy in the grace of God which enables us to be just what we are and to become just what we are meant to become. Paul never minimised his calling, nor was he reticent when it came to describing it. 'Paul an apostle and preacher and teacher' is his unabashed assessment. For him it was not a status symbol but rather the brand-mark of a slave. His apostleship was etched not on a brass plate outside an imposing front door but in the scars he carried and in the hearts of the saints who loved him.

He asserted his leadership when he had to for the sake of truth. He magnified his ministry in order to provoke Israel to jealousy. There is no higher dignity than to be the servant of Christ. 'It is enough for the student to be like his teacher, and the servant like his master' (Matt. 10.25). Doubts about our status are dispelled when we know that our leadership is by royal appointment to the glorified Man beside the throne of God. We need not be hesitant or double-minded about what we are called to do.

After all our service is to the right-hand court.

3. Undercover Agents

Every servant needs to be sure of his commission because sooner or later he will be asked for his credentials. 'Hey! what do you think you're doing? Leave that donkey alone! who do you think you are anyway?' One can sympathise with the owners of the animal so boldly requisitioned by Jesus. The disciples had their answer ready in advance. 'If anyone asks you 'Why are you untying it?' tell him, 'The Lord needs it" (Luke 19.31)!

Before long the master himself was being asked similar questions. 'By what authority are you doing these things, who gave you this authority?' It is still *the* question behind many questions.

In my own experience of a church undergoing renewal by the Holy Spirit, I discovered this to be the question at issue in whatever changes were taking place.

Should we allow speaking in tongues into our neat Baptist worship? Was it right to let people raise their hands or clap in praise to God? Should elders supplant the church meeting as the main focus of God's rule in the church? Whatever the matter in hand it became clear to me that the underlying issue was one of spiritual authority, or, to put it in the terms in which it was expressed to me: 'What right have you got to introduce these changes among us?'

An effective answer to this rests on a number of important considerations.

Firstly, we need to understand that spiritual leadership is part of God's kingdom rule.

There has been of late a heartening rediscovery of the nature and impact of the kingdom of God. The restoration of this truth of the kingdom is to my mind the most important feature to emerge from the current charismatic renewal of the Church. There has come an appreciation of both the power of the kingdom – its dynamic aspect – and the authority of the kingdom – its governmental aspect. Some have denied one or both of these aspects. Dispensationalist writers minimise both, by relegating the Kingdom to the dim-distant past or projecting it into the far-away future. Charismatic dispensationalists, while affirming the power of the kingdom as operative today, postpone its governmental aspects to a coming millenium. While all our experience of the kingdom is a foretaste, a down-payment in the Holy Spirit of what is yet to come, nevertheless, what we do see now is a real representation of every aspect of the kingdom.

The same movement of the Spirit therefore that has brought a widespread recovery of spiritual gifts, the powers of the age to come, has at the same time brought a renewed interest in spiritual authority, the rule and order of the age to come. Our growing concern for leadership in the church is to be seen then, I believe, as a direct consequence of our re-awakening to the kingdom dimension of our life in Christ.

One implication of this for today's leader is that he is given, as never before, a foundation and framework for his leadership which transcends all current church practice and traditions. He derives his spiritual authority directly from his commitment to this unshakeable kingdom. This gives him a vision and inspiration larger than his present role, larger than his own competence, bigger than his own brand of churchmanship, wider than his calling to any particular sphere or locality. The true spiritual leader is a kingdom man. He is, in the end, the servant of no particular church, nor does he owe his allegiance to any sect or denomination. He is not a functionary concerned to keep any particular institution alive; he is a propagandist for no particular party line; he is compromised by no special vested interest that would maintain the status quo. He can cope when every conventional view of ministry is called into question because he is dependent on none for his security.

This gives to any leader a sense of proportion and immense staying power. He is throne-centred not man-centred. Like the Psalmist, his heart is steadfast because his God is exalted. Like Jeremiah, when the deceitfulness of the human heart seeks to stifle the prophetic voice, he looks to a glorious throne set on high. This is to know with Stephen that when earth's doors close heaven's doors open. This is apostles singing hymns in prison; this is Paul shouting 'I believe God' on a sinking ship; this is Luther's 'Here I stand I can do no other'. This is convenanters asserting the 'crown rights of the Redeemer'; this is Corrie ten Boom confessing in Ravensbruck that there 'is no pit so deep that He has not gone deeper still'.

For a leader to sense a little of this is not to have illusions of grandeur. It is to embrace the indispensable romantic and heroic element in true spiritual leadership. This is kingdom iron for the soul of every leader.

The Empire Strikes Back

The Kingdom of God then is making such a comeback in our day that we begin to suspect it never went away. Further implications of this fact for leaders need to be spelt out.

What needs to be recognised, secondly, is that *spiritual leadership arises within the framework of God's structure of authority in his created order.*

Traces of this order remain unobliterated, if often defaced, by the fall, and are repeatedly affirmed in Scripture. Such an order is claimed for the angelic sphere, so that even fallen spirits, though to be resisted, are not to be reviled (Jude 8–10). Submission to the State is a clear part of apostolic teaching though one which has caused endless discussion amongst believers.

Sound theological reasons are given to explain why we respect civil rules and pay our taxes to them. Where the State oversteps its own God-given bounds, citizens of God's kingdom have the duty to obey God rather than men (Acts 5.29).

Both the business and family areas have their own appropriate pattern of authority or headship, as does the Church. 'Obey your leaders and submit to their authority' (Heb. 13.17).

Obviously the dynamics of submission is vastly different in the areas of family and church than in the areas of State and business. On the one hand we move in the realm of institutions – the Government or our employers; on the other we move in the realm of relationships. A wife's submissive response to her husband is obviously altogether different from a servant's to his master. But this needs to be said, if only because the nature of this relationship is so often abused or parodied.

In fact, as John Yoder has shown, the 'household rules' enshrined in apostolic teaching (e.g. Eph. 5.21 – 6.9, Col. 3.18 – 4.1, 1 Peter 2.13 – 3.7 etc) represent quite revolutionary counsel. These rules which show us how to 'behave in the household of God' (1 Tim. 3.15) constitute what Yoder calls 'revolutionary subordination'. What is startling in them is that the seemingly 'subordinate' partner is summoned to be a moral agent, responsible for his or her attitudes and reactions in the situation.[1] In this climate only the fruits of the Holy Spirit can flourish. In it the emphasis is once again on servanthood, humility, and the voluntary foregoing of one's own rights. The only precedent for this is the Son's submission to his Father. He can say both 'I and my Father are one' and also 'My Father is greater than I'. We learn from Jesus, if from no one else, that subordination is not inferiority.

James Lee Beall has summed up well what is happening. 'Accompanying the widespread outpouring of the Holy Spirit is a restoration of obedience to delegated authorities. God is restoring the truth that he is behind all authority . . . Answers about delegated authority and respect will first come in the community of the redeemed where true leadership comes from the Holy Spirit.'[2]

Delegated Authorities

Taking this further we need to state clearly a third important principle. *God rules and directs his people through delegated spiritual authorities not democratic consensus.*

To say this is to run counter to the tide. But it is a vital principle to establish if God-given leadership is ever to thrive in the Church.

At once we need to counteract distortions of this view which would immediately jump to the conclusion that a dangerous authoritarianism is being advocated.

Acts 6 is familiar ground for those who have walked this way of spiritual authority in recent years. What is recorded has the ring of truth for any one attempting to put into practice what I am now describing. Luke records for us the emergence and recognition of those leaders from the Hellenistic side of the Jerusalem church who were needed to give the whole church greater balance and maturity, and to release the apostles for wider ministry.

We find here a wonderful interaction of apostolic ministry and the people's assent. The apostles stated the need, the number and the nature of the new leaders required: the people made their choice of men with the right qualifications and brought them to the apostles for their endorsement. Here leadership is neither elected nor imposed. In the dynamic of the Spirit and in the security of godly relationships, apostolic initiatives are not blunted, nor congregational feelings over-ridden.

This mutual recognition of what God was doing and saying about leadership brought a release to the church that a purely democratic process would have thwarted.

Our American friends in the Church Growth School have been quicker to see this than we have. Few would endorse everything Robert Schuller says or does, but his careful observations on this matter deserve to be heard. 'Those churches', he writes, 'with a strong congregationalism allow no major thinking, planning, or promoting to be done without congregational approval. I have yet to see a church with such a system of government that is really roaring ahead with fantastic success'.[3] Peter Wagner, more soberly, has given his assessment. 'Pastoral authority, earned through a loving relationship with the Family of God, is thus an important ingredient for growth. To some it might appear as dictatorship or totalitarianism, but it is not. It is the recognition and exercise of God-given spiritual gifts in the Body of Christ.' He goes on to add a pertinent comment. 'Some congregational-type churches oppose strong pastoral leadership on principle. Congregationalism was developed along with American democracy and strong pastoral authority seems undemocratic to some Christians. Where this feeling persists, it will be overcome if the church wants to move into a pattern of growth.'[4]

If then there is no Scriptural basis for democracy in the local church, its leadership must be entrusted only to safe and honourable hands.

This leads us to a fourth, very important principle. *To exercise spiritual authority a leader must be under authority himself.* 'Your rulers are rebels' (Is. 1.23) is the ultimate indictment of leadership as well as being a contradiction in terms.

(a) A leader must be fully submitted to the written word of God.

Unfortunately, this cannot be taken for granted even amongst those who profess to be evangelical in their view of the Bible. What is normative for doctrine or spiritual life sometimes, surprisingly, becomes relative and advisory for matters of church structure and government. Yet these are the very areas where a leader will have to stay faithful to the Scriptures if he is to lead his people forward into more godly ways. As the great German scholar, Adolph Schlatter once said, 'he will not stand on the Word; he will stand under the Word'.

I well remember a crucial church meeting some years ago when I and others faced a vote of confidence over the direction in which I was leading the people. Changes are seldom introduced without trouble and this was no exception. At one point a leading critic intervened in a tense debate, waving a copy of our denominational handbook. It was implied that I had forsaken the rubrics of the green book in favour of the black, leather-bound book open on the lectern in front of me! In all good faith I could only confess that I undoubtedly had and undoubtedly would continue to do just that. No doubt too with the ebullience of youth, I waved the good book back at my critic!

The fact remains that whatever the situation – in the family, in the house group, in the youth programme, in church affairs and worship – a leader has no solid ground beneath his feet except he trusts implicitly in the authority of God's Word.

And when it comes to submitting to another man in leadership, I know that in the last resort what I am prepared to submit to in a man is the authority of the Word of God in his life and ministry.

(b) A leader must be able to control himself and his own household. (1 Tim. 3.1–7).

His own self-control qualifies him for leadership. He is above reproach, moderate, gentle and uncontentious because he has taken himself in hand by the power of the Spirit. 'Better a man who controls his temper than one who takes a city' (Prov. 16.32). This is reflected in his leadership in the home which is a microcosm of the church. 'For if anyone does not know how to manage his own family, how can he take care of God's church?' (1 Tim. 3.5).

So much has been written and said on these subjects in recent years that now is not the time to go over the ground. Suffice it to say that the leader himself is not above the principle of mutual submission set out in apostolic teaching. 'Submit yourselves to one another in the fear of the Lord' when practised between brothers in leadership can be the very means of grace to a leader who needs help either to manage himself or his family or both!

Put positively, our principle makes encouraging reading. To be under spiritual authority is to have spiritual authority! Such authority is more often linked with the power of the kingdom in the gospels. It is the authority which legitimises us to use the power of the kingdom to heal and preach and cast our demons.

When a Roman centurion came to Jesus for the healing of his servant, he recognised that Jesus needed merely to speak the word for healing to take place. The explanation he gave for his confidence is very significant. 'For I too am a man under authority, with soldiers under me; and I say to this one, "Go!" and he goes, and to another, "Come!" and he comes, and to my slave, "Do this!" and he does it' (Matt. 8.5–13 NASB). As a representative of the Roman Empire, the centurion knew that he was part of a chain of command stretching back ultimately to the Emperor himself. Every command he gave to a soldier or a servant in effect carried with it the authority of the Emperor. His insight was to acknowledge this same principle of authority in the ministry of Jesus. Because Jesus represented his Father and was completely submissive to him, his every word was invested with his Father's authority.

Jesus was thrilled and amazed at what this soldier was seeing by faith. For in saying 'I also am a man under authority' the centurion was touching on the biblical basis for all true authority. The authority a man exercises is dependent on the authority he is under. And to be under spiritual authority is to have spiritual authority.

Such credentials make room for charisma to operate. And to this we now turn.

4. Charisma

Charisma is a fashionable commodity at present. Even bottles of perfume bear the word as a label. Anyone who makes a startling public impression is said to have it! But when I hear that Hitler had it and that John McEnroe has it, I'm not sure that I want it! Charisma is currently as much in vogue as servanthood and authority are not. For this reason our starting point for discovering what it really is must be elsewhere.

Biblically, it is clear that a natural personality, however colourful and impressive, is not the source of true charisma. Nor does the charisma of God's servants come from ecclesiastical training, clerical ordination, ritual or role-playing. For the servant of God charisma is a direct gift of the Holy Spirit. It comes from the Spirit's anointing or 'unction' – to use the Latinised form of the word beloved of older writers. Its first impression is felt rather than understood. Charisma in a man of God is that indefinable 'plus' factor which gives weight to his words and force to his actions. Its absence is something we notice as much as its presence. It is not the projection of personality and yet it releases personality, investing it with power and freshness. It is an unmistakeable aura which draws and holds us to some men rather than to others who may be equally eloquent or gifted. The charisma of Jesus, as James Dunn puts it, is that 'mysterious ability to inspire fear and awe; confidence and trust.'[1] This is the first clue in experience to the fact that the anointing of the Holy Spirit is the indispensable requirement for leaders of God's people.

Indispensable Requirement

The Church is in the middle of an energy crisis. Her habitual reliance on merely natural resources is being ruthlessly exposed. As John Taylor has pointedly said 'I have not heard recently of committee business adjourned because those present were still awaiting the arrival of the Spirit of God. I have known projects abandoned for lack of funds but not for lack of the gifts of the

Spirit.'[2] Thankfully times are changing. With a recognition that even the Church's natural resources are fast running out, there has come a renewed desire for the powers and resources which only the Holy Spirit can bestow. His supernatural endowment or charisma, and his spiritual gifts or charismata are now widely being seen and sought as indispensable to the Church's life and mission. We recognise now as never before that natural talents cannot build the Church; that the charisms cannot be rationalised away and equated simply with natural abilities. Accountants no longer automatically become church treasurers!

At the same time we need to be clear that what the Holy Spirit is doing is not suppressing but releasing truly human potential. Grace does not destroy nature but redeems it. Supernatural endowments do not therefore override normal capabilities; rather they extend and enhance them. An older writer Samuel Chadwick puts this well. 'The spirit of power sanctifies, vitalises, energises the natural faculties, and makes possible things beyond their most perfect development. The gifts of the Spirit give a supernatural power to the work of sanctified natural endowments so that men are challenged to see and consider cause and effect, and find there is nothing in natural man to account for what is manifestly of God.'[3] More recently Arnold Bittlinger has added his endorsement of this view by defining a charism as 'a gratuitous manifestation of the Holy Spirit working in and through, but going beyond, the believer's natural ability for the common good of the people of God.'[4]

In a redeemed and restored humanity such 'supernatural' abilities might well be normal functions. Meanwhile, we are often still amazed by what we have said and done and achieved when under the anointing of the Holy Spirit.

The roots of this understanding of charisma are in the Old Testament. By the Spirit Bezalel was equipped to oversee the construction of the tabernacle. 'And I have filled him with the Spirit of God, with skill, ability and knowledge in all kinds of crafts' (Ex. 31.3). Judges too felt the impact of the Spirit as he prepared them for their tasks. So the Spirit 'came upon' Samson (Judges 3.10, 6.34, 14.6).

Prophets, priests, and kings were consecrated for their role in a similar way, often in a dramatic ceremony involving an anointing with oil. This anointing with oil was not an empty ritual but was a true, external symbol of an internal grace. 'So Samuel took the horn of oil and anointed him in the presence of his brothers, and from that day on the Spirit of the Lord came upon David in power' (1 Sam 16.13). To David, his anointing with the Spirit was an indispensable requirement. In the wake of a self-inflicted crisis of leadership, David confesses that he can neither live nor rule without it: 'Do not take your Holy Spirit from me' (Psalm 51.11).

Zerubbabel, overseeing the morale-sapping business of rebuilding Jerusalem, is reassured by personal prophecy of the presence of the anointing as the one thing needful to him: '"Not by might nor by power, but by my Spirit," says the Lord' (Zech. 4.6). Whether consecrated, commissioned or crowned, no leader in Israel could do without this.

Furthermore, the Spirit is the only guarantee of a living continuity. Without him new leaders, while seeking faithfully to preserve their predecessors' position, merely perpetuate a dead tradition. Principles soon become legalism when implemented by men of lesser gift and anointing than the originators of the vision.

For this reason it is imperative that the seventy men deputed to assist Moses receive a portion of the Spirit resting on him and do not merely attempt to duplicate his methods. Moses can confidently recommend Joshua as his successor because he recognises that the younger man is 'a man in whom is the Spirit;' (Num. 27.18). Joshua's impressive 'ordination' did not bestow this anointing but only confirmed it in a public way.

When Elijah's successor Elisha received his mantle it was to set a precedent, not in clerical dress, but in desiring and needing a double portion of the prophet's spirit. Vestments are a thin disguise for the absence of an anointing which only the investiture of the Holy Spirit can give.

The Charismatic Christ

A leader's need for the charisma of the Spirit is highlighted when we look at the significance of the Holy Spirit in the life of the Lord Jesus himself. Without the Spirit the Messiah could not have lived up to his name as the Anointed One.

Accounts of his baptism and endowment with the Spirit are too full and consistent for us to minimise this. Unfortunately, for fear of adoptionist-type heresies, the Church has often underplayed the role of the Spirit in the life and ministry of the Lord Jesus. Yet it is not untrue to say that Jesus did all by the power of the Holy Spirit. He accomplished the work the Father had given him to do not by the inherent powers of deity but by the imparted powers of deity. The eternal Son of God, incarnate, chose to fulfil his redemptive mission by the resources of the Holy Spirit in a sinless humanity. These same resources are available to us in our, as yet, far from sinless but redeemed humanity.

He was the 'manifested Son' on whom the Spirit had come and remained (John 1.31f). He was led by the Spirit into the wilderness and full of the Spirit was sustained for forty days there until he returned to Galilee in the power of the Spirit (Luke 4.1,14). He embarked on his great 'Jubilee Year' of salvation activity because, he said, 'the Spirit of the Lord is upon me, for he anointed me to preach the gospel to the poor' (Luke 4.18). He cast out demons by the Spirit of God, bringing the freedom of the kingdom into men's lives (Matt. 12.18). He 'rejoiced greatly in the Holy Spirit' as he saw the disciples sharing in the revelation of the Kingdom (Luke 10.21). He was strengthened to offer himself as a sacrifice for sin by the 'eternal Spirit' (Heb. 9.14). Peter's marvellous picture of him as the 'great Itinerant' captures perfectly this charismatic dimension to the Lord's ministry. 'You know of Jesus of Nazareth, how God anointed Him with the Holy Spirit and with power, and how He went about doing good and healing all who were oppressed by the devil; for God was with Him' (Acts 10.38 NASB).

When we turn to our own ministry and leadership we must surely seek to be as charismatic in our measure as he was in his. Recent New Testament studies have confirmed that leadership in the early church was essentially charismatic not institutional. In James Dunn's words 'The authority of leadership . . . was the charismatic authority of the Spirit'.[5] Because leadership itself is a gift of grace from the ascended Lord by his Spirit to the Church, it immediately becomes obvious where the source of its power lies (Eph. 4.11, Romans 12.8). The Christian leader derives his authority and weight not from any title or office, but from his function, role and gift. No man is a pastor because his church noticeboard or headed writing paper says so, but because he has a shepherd heart, can feed sheep, and is someone sheep will follow. As in the New Testament, true leaders cannot pull rank because they do not have any. Certainly Paul appealed to his apostolic ministry to give weight to his admonition but this was precisely an appeal to his tremendous spiritual authority, felt, in fact, as much in his absence and at a distance, as in his presence! (1 Cor. 5.3f, 2 Cor. 13.10).

The sixth chapter of the Acts of the Apostles shows that the fullness of the Spirit was the common factor to be looked for in emerging leaders, the one credential that could not be done without. 'But select from among you, brethren, seven men of good reputation, full of the Holy Spirit and wisdom whom we may put in charge of this task' (Acts 6.3 NASB). Out of an overflow or surplus of faith, grace and power, a man like Stephen, full of the Spirit, ministered in a way that others found irresistible (Acts 6.5,10).

Such leaders have an abundance that makes them a source of supply to others. They are not mere deacons, but men with an already proven ministry in the Hellenistic section of the church in Jerusalem, who are now called to be elders or apostolic delegates administering a large-scale operation of pastoral care. And all this without detriment to their powerful preaching and healing ministries! (Acts 6.8, 8.5ff). Of them it could be said as of the elders at Ephesus that 'the Holy Spirit has made you overseers, to shepherd the Church of God ' (Acts 20.28 NASB).

The laying on of hands was an important feature of this release of ministry in the New Testament Church, but one which took place in a very dynamic context. To equate this with our current practice of ordination is to confuse rather than clarify the issue. Here was no formal, ritualised or perfunctory act of ecclesiastical machinery. Rather in the context of prayer, men clearly recognised as apostles gave their endorsement of the Spirit's gifts and calling in others by laying their hands upon them (cf. Acts 6.6).

The strategic thrust from Antioch began in the same way (Acts 13.1–4). Here was a gathering of charismatic leaders, both prophets and teachers, meeting to fast and worship the Lord together. In this atmosphere the Holy Spirit spoke, presumably through prophecy, to indicate that the time was right for the setting apart of Barnabas and Saul for the work to which he had already called them. After further fasting and prayer, the laying on of hands occurred. As if to leave us in no doubt as to the source of their commission, Luke adds that the two men were 'sent out by the Holy Spirit' (13.4).

Timothy too was 'ordained' in a dynamic context with his ministry shaped and impelled by prophetic utterance and quickened by the impartation of fresh gifts. 'Do not neglect your gift, which was given you through a prophetic message when the body of elders laid their hands on you' (1 Tim. 4.14 cf. 2 Tim. 1.6). 'This is what is meant by charismatic leadership' says Howard Snyder, ' – leadership inspired by God's Spirit, endowed with needed graces or charisms and appropriately recognised by the believing community.'[6]

Gifts With Graces

It is at this point that a worthwhile distinction can be made between the 'ministries' in the Body and the 'gifts' in the Body. (e.g. cf 1 Cor. 12.28 and Eph. 4.11 with 1 Cor. 12.7ff and Romans

12). For example, prophecy is both ministry and gift. As a ministry, prophecy is an 'appointment' which all do not have (1 Cor. 12.28) whereas, as a gift, prophecy is a 'manifestation' each can receive (1 Cor. 12.7). This distinction is a functional, not a formal one, which has to do with a person's calling, measure of faith and place in the Body. There is clearly a functional difference between a ministry gifted to enable others to serve in the body and those gifted and enabled by it to serve the body.

In either case we need to stress the given-ness of these abilities. It is 'giving' the gift, not 'possessing' the gift that is important in the kind of body-life envisaged in 1 Cor. 12–14, and this is as true for the leader as the led. No one can pride himself that he 'has' a gift when the emphasis is on delivering the gift to others. This is as true of the gift of leadership itself. For this reason the apostolic stress is on an exhortation to 'exercise the gifts', to 'employ them' for the benefit of others, without thinking either too highly or too lowly of oneself (Rom. 12.3–8, 1 Peter 4.10f, 1 Cor. 15.10). The release and confidence this gives is priceless. Many leaders would share Howard Snyder's testimony. 'When I identified and named my spiritual gifts, it seemed as if all the contradictory pieces of my life suddenly fell into place. I found the key to what God was doing in and through my life.'(7)

All this is further proof of our reliance on the indispensable requirement of the Holy Spirit. Without him we have wood without fire however 'contemporary' our grasp of the principles of body-life. Apollos is a New Testament case in point. Learning, eloquence, enthusiasm – he had everything short of the anointing. Lacking this himself he produced disciples in the same condition who expressed bewilderment when asked if they had received the Holy Spirit when they believed. Having been shown the way of Jesus more clearly, Apollos is later said to have exercised a profitable 'watering' ministry in the church at Corinth (Acts 18–19, 1 Cor. 3.6). Anointed teachers water the church: unanointed teachers merely dry out the church. The urgent appeal made by Dr. Martyn Lloyd-Jones to preachers in his great book on preaching, might well be applied to all Christian leaders. 'This "unction", this "anointing" is the supreme thing. Seek it until you have it. Be content with nothing less.'(8)

Timothy too is urged to stir up the gift in him in order to fulfil his ministry (2 Tim. 1.6). If the fire of the Spirit cools, Timothy will inevitably give way to his natural reticence and fail to take up his God-given responsibilities. But by kindling afresh the charisma within him, Timothy realises that he has not been given a spirit of timidity but of power and love and self-control. In short he has been given, with the charisma, the grace needed to be a leader. By the Spirit he has the ability to dominate any situation with moral authority, to give himself in love to the brethren whatever their reaction, and to maintain the necessary self-discipline that will help him keep his head in any crisis (2 Tim. 1.7). Receiving the Spirit of God in this way does not mean 'that the servant of God must of necessity be a powerful personality, but that he has strength of character to be bold in the exercise of authority.'(9)

Timothy's example is encouraging if only because it frees us from the idea that the Spirit indwelling leaders conforms to a narrow 'macho'-stereotype. In fact his style is often altogether different.

Sensitivity is a mark of the anointing. The anointed servant of God has a light touch and is not heavy-handed. The Spirit-anointed servant of God will more than likely 'not shout or cry out, or raise his voice in the streets. A bruised reed he will not break, and a smouldering wick he will not snuff out' (Is. 42.1–4). This charismatic style characterised the healing ministry of the Lord Jesus (Matt. 12.15ff).

That the root meaning of the word 'charis' is charm is not insignificant. The English poet Laurie Lee has defined charm as a 'generosity that makes no demands . . . which can't withhold but spends itself willingly on young and old alike, on the poor, the ugly, the dim, the boring, on the last fat man in the corner.'(10)

So the Spirit will transfigure our style of leadership, opening us more to God at one end and to people at the other. Ungracious charismata are a contradiction in terms which is the point Paul is making to the Corinthians in the thirteenth chapter of his first letter.

Biblically the root of 'charisma' is in the 'charis' or grace of God. New Testament leaders view their ministry as an expression and measure of this one 'charis'-gift of Jesus (Eph. 4.11f). So Paul says that from Christ he has 'received grace and apostleship' (Romans 1.5). He was made a minister, he tells us, 'according to the gift of God's grace which was given me according to the working of his power' (Eph. 3.7). Paul's testimony was that the call to ministry carried with it a sense of undeserved privilege, of uncaused ability, of unusual freedom. The very grace of God in leadership bestows a sense of mastery, of spaciousness, of inner confidence and external boldness. All this is token of the fact that our leadership is carried out as servants of the new covenant, as servants of the Spirit who gives life (2 Cor. 3.6). Knowing this we can lead with an adequacy that is not of ourselves but from God (2 Cor. 3.5).

Knowing that God's calling is not burdensome, we can, like Timothy stir up the Spirit's gifts within us and with gladness of heart take up the yoke of responsibility laid on us.

5. Where The Buck Stops

'Taking responsibility' sounds altogether more prosaic than 'exercising leadership' and it is. Responsibility does not come in glossy packaging and therefore has few immediate takers. I am reminded of the classic story of the police recruit given an interesting scenario for his initiative test. Called to the scene, he arrives to be jostled by a panic-stricken, nearly incoherent man and to find a crowd gathered round two other men clearly intent on killing each other. Behind them a burglar is obviously breaking into the house of one of the spectators. The panic-stricken man has by now managed to get through to him that his wife is about to give birth to a baby, that the ambulance men are on strike, and that his own car has broken down! The recruit can hardly take this in before he notices that across the street a fire is rapidly spreading through a block of flats and a woman is already shouting for help from a top-floor window! Asked what to do in such a situation the confused recruit is alleged to have written: 'take off uniform and merge with the crowd'.[1]

At some time every leader, I suspect, would like to do just that. Under the pressure of conflicting demands, in the confusion of competing priorities, every leader has been tempted to opt out of his responsibilities. So the phone always rings on your much needed day-off when you've promised to take the children out or when you've just started that extra-special, intimate, dinner-for-two with your wife. Blessed is the man who can answer the phone without impatience or leave it off the hook without guilt.

In fact in the current renewal of the Church it's very difficult to take off your uniform and merge with the crowd. The reason for this is not, as might once have been true, that the leader cannot afford to let his mask of professionalism slip for a moment – though sadly for some this may still be the case. Nor is it to say that a leader can never relax, be off-duty, or 'unstring his bow', as Bob Mumford puts it. Thankfully, and not before time, we are all learning that God-given discipline of rest and recreation which keeps our humanity in good shape. What makes it well-nigh impossible to take off one's uniform to merge with the crowd is precisely the nature of life in the body of Christ. Having taught the people of God that each has a God-given role, gift and function to contribute to the body, the leader finds it hard to make himself the exception to the rule. We cannot shed our uniform of ministry and gift in order to merge with them because they're all in uniform anyway! Nothing looks sillier or indeed more conspicuous than a leader misguidedly attempting to recede into the background. It is false pride to claim the best seat at the feast as Jesus made clear. It must surely be false modesty however for a man with the gift of leadership to take the back seat!

I have tried to sit in the back row of our worship meetings only to find a sense of disquiet and unease rising within me. This I found was not, as I first thought, a sign of pride but clear evidence that I was meant to be a leader. I could not skulk in the background for whatever high and holy motives without denying my gifts and calling in God. No man called to be a frontman can sit easy in the back row. 'The buck stops here' was how Harry S. Truman felt from behind his Presidential desk. And where the buck stops is where leadership begins. Within hours of President Reagan being critically wounded by an assassin's bullet, Alexander Haig, then Secretary of State, was asked by anxious newsmen: 'Who's in charge at the moment?' 'I am,' Haig replied. It is a sad sign of the times that for this admission he was almost universally criticised rather than commended. The heart of a true spiritual leader is a readiness to accept God-given responsibility. In Elizabeth Elliot's words 'He is a take-charge man'.[2] For the man called to be a leader this is as much an instinct as a duty and certainly not a burden he wants to discard. For all the pains and pressures of his apostolic calling, Paul showed no inclination to join Apostles Anonymous.

Abdication Crisis

People of my parents' generation still recall the day in 1936 when in a poignant radio broadcast to an awe-struck nation the King of England announced his abdication from the throne. For love of Mrs. Simpson, Edward the Eighth passed up his crown. It's not hard to feel sympathy for him. Equally it is not difficult to conclude as you read the story of the sad later years of increasing ignominy, self-indulgence and wasted potential, that here was a man who saved his common life but lost his kingly soul.

This is an apt parable of the plight of every man, the root cause of which is man's failure to take responsibility. Since original sin shows up more clearly in leadership than anywhere else, the leader needs to know more than anyone his roots and raison d'être in the grace and calling that is more original than sin. There is much to be said for the view that in Genesis 3 man's original sin is not pride but *sloth*. Leaving it to one's wife or to the snake is our great Adamic mistake. Our rebellion is less an aggressive coup d'état, more a passive abdication, a stubborn refusal to rise to our royal calling. Our tragedy as men is not that we usurp a throne but that we settle for less than our kingly destiny. What the Mediaevals called 'accidie', the sin of withdrawing into passivity, is really our chief temptation and the one most to be blamed for the dearth of spiritual leadership in the family and in the church. Resignation in a leader is more dangerous than over-ambition. He is more likely, however busy, to die of boredom than over-exertion.

Yet if a man shirks his responsibility it does not disappear; it simply reverts to someone else – his wife, his employer, the government. [3] 'All my best men are women' William Booth is reputed to have said. This is not an endorsement of Women's Lib. but an indictment of male apathy. Brave and incredibly heroic women saints once outnumbered men on the mission field because men failed to rise to the challenge of their calling. Strong women are often said to be the bane of the church. They are not. Weak men are the bane of the church. Weak kings who abdicate in favour of divorced socialites have their parallel in the history of God's people. Even the most prophetic leader at times of self-pity and defeatism can, like Elijah, want to withdraw from ministry under the oppression of the spirit of Jezebel that still stalks the church.

So, as Steve Clark puts it, the first area in the character formation of a leader, is that of 'training men to take social responsibility'.[4]

'Dominion-havers'

Our training of men to take responsibility in the kingdom of God has its roots in Genesis 1 and is a recognition of our renewal by the Holy Spirit into the image of God (cf. Colossians 3.10–25). In Leonard Verduin's inelegant but telling phrase, man is meant to be a 'dominion-haver'. He is called to share in God's rule as God's co-regent.[5] He is invited by grace to reproduce his kind, peopling the earth with obedient children, walking with God. He is called to replenish the earth, to fill up its lack, to add to life not merely subtract from it. He is further commissioned to restore

the earth by subduing it, bringing it back under its original rule
to its true order and arrangement. This is where spiritual leadership takes its rise. Our prospectus for leadership comes from the
creation order not the careers' office. This is why 'to aspire to
leadership is an honourable ambition' (1 Tim. 3.1 NEB).

Realising this, a leader can resist the temptation to pass up his
responsibilities and settle for an easy life. When the house group
lapses into deadly silence and no one knows what to do or say, it
is the house-group leader who has to make a move – even if his
decision is that there is no more to be said! In doing so he will,
on a small and homely scale, be exercising dominion. 'To exercise
dominion in the given situation is to fasten one's will upon that
situation'.[6] Insignificant as it seems the leader has found the lever
that lifts a world. On the basis of redemption and in the renewal
of the Holy Spirit we can break out from the paralysing effects of
original sloth.

This freedom obliges us of course to be much more open and
honest in our confession of weakness. Original sloth puts up a
clever smokescreen to mask its work; it's called 'rationalisation'.
This tendency to explain away is one of sin's deepest scars. Every
insurance company has a long litany on file of excuses people
have made for accidents they have been responsible for.

'I collided with a stationary truck coming the other way.'
'The guy was all over the road. I had to swerve a number of
times before I hit him.'
'I had been driving for 40 years when I fell asleep at the wheel
and had an accident.'
'My car was legally parked as it backed into the other vehicle.'
'The pedestrian had no idea which direction to run, so I ran
over him.'

'But they all alike began to make excuses' was how Jesus pictured
men in his parable as they tried to evade the responsibility of
deciding for or against his kingdom. Refusing to make excuses, a
Christian leader today can face squarely the situations which call
for the fastening of the will upon them.

Withdrawal Symptoms

'Sustain me with a willing spirit' (Psalm 51.12 NASB) is a leader's
prayer when he feels the pressure to withdraw. The opposite of
a willing spirit is a withholding spirit and it shows up in many
different situations faced by a leader. 'I have had enough, I can't

be bothered' is how it talks. Sometimes this is the direct result of sin, as in Psalm 51. Often it is the consequence of overwork, tiredness and strain.

We may find ourselves *withholding in worship*. Listless and heavy, we find it hard to lift up our hearts. We let others do it whose emotional resources seem more adequate. This may be the time for various moods to be expressed in the body of Christ. More often than not it reveals a refusal to pay the price of worship, to make the sacrifice of praise. Worship is first explicitly mentioned in the Bible in connection with the supreme offering of Abraham, who gained God's favour, as God told him, 'because you did not withhold your only son'.

Withholding in the ministry of the word is a temptation that comes to every preacher. Dogged by criticism or fear or tedium, we may hold back as we give the word. We check our spirits so that though the words go out we don't give of ourselves in speaking them. They go out without power or passion because we are not putting our heart into them.

In the same way that Peter 'began to withdraw' (Gal. 2.12) from the Gentiles, so may we tire in pressing through with relationships. Maybe we fear being misunderstood or being hurt again, or what others might think. Whatever the reason a subtle cooling off of our affections takes place. We begin to 'stand aloof' *withholding in relationships*. We need especially as leaders to replenish our emotional reservoirs if we are not to succumb to this spirit. Once our affections become regularly restrained worse dangers befall us. 'We have spoken freely to you, Corinthians, and opened wide our hearts to you. We are not withholding our affection from you, but you are withholding yours from us ' (cf. 2 Cor. 6.11–12). Even the stimulus to action is lost. 'If anyone has material possessions and sees his brother in need but has no pity on him, how can the love of God be in him?' (1 John 3.17). *Withholding in good deeds* may be the start of a process of decline that ends with hypocrisy and satanic deception (cf. Acts 5.3). A heart which is at the secret source of every precious thing can be different. 'One man gives freely, yet gains even more; another withholds unduly but comes to poverty' (Prov. 11.24).

So this pressure to withhold is another symptom of the original sloth and the points where it arises are danger points for leaders. 'Watch the things you shrug your shoulders over' was Oswald Chambers' word of wisdom. This is the Sargasso sea of leadership. Here a leader finds himself unwilling to begin things, or finish things or face things. The sluggishness of the sluggard paralyses him. And the proverbial sluggard, in Derek Kidner's words, is usually an 'ordinary man who has made too many excuses, too many refusals and too many postponements. It has all been as imperceptible and pleasant as falling asleep'.(7)

Response Ability

Alert to the danger of failing to take up our God-given responsibilities, we can be reassured as leaders about the built-in safeguards of doing so. God does not make impossible demands upon us, nor impose unrealistic responsibilities beyond our capacity to bear. His commands bring his enablings, as the old adage goes.

The leader who knows the safeguards is less likely to take on more than he can cope with. He will have a realistic estimate of himself. 'For by the grace given me I say to every one of you; Do not think of yourself more highly than you ought, but rather think of yourself with sober judgment, in accordance with the measure of faith God has given you' (Rom. 12.3). Knowing his measure of faith he will know too when the moment has come to increase his faith and venture into ground never taken before. But he will not over-reach himself. Although we will have cause to return to this point later, it is right to make it here. For a leader needs to know that although he is called to bear others' burdens (gk. 'baros') he is not required to share their unique load (gk. 'phortion') of responsibility (Gal. 6.2,5). 'What shall this man do?' is not always my concern. 'Mind your own business' is liable to be the Lord's reply!

Instead every leader is given with his calling special gifts of the Holy Spirit. These give him the ability to respond to the grace of God that can equip him for his tasks.

Filled with the Holy Spirit a leader can take responsibility without being overwhelmed by it. If you have the gift of leadership you know you can 'exercise it with enthusiasm' (Rom. 12.8 Barclay). As a Spirit-filled leader you can be told to 'exert yourself to lead' (NEB). Stimulated and strengthened by God the Holy Spirit you can react with zest to the responsibilities of leadership. Sustained with a willing spirit, you will not grow weary in well-doing. Even though you are a pressed-man you will still be able to maintain the enthusiasm of a volunteer. If you as a leader refuse to pass the buck, those you lead will imitate you and will become a responsive and responsible people.

Part Two
Looking at Leadership

6. The Music and the Call

Great music is a great inspiration. It can take us out of ourselves and strangely at the same time deeper into ourselves. Music, in P. T. Forsyth's words, 'opens the fountains of a greater deep and bathes us in a world of victory.'[1] So it was with Isaiah. Caught up in heaven's worship, he is made conscious of heights in God and depths in himself previously unknown to him. In this experience he finds the call to his life's work.

His heart leaps to a melody that soars above the plainsong of sinners. His heart beats to the eternal rhythm of a higher order than time. He finds himself lifted above earth's discords into the ultimate harmony of heaven. He realises, in contrast, how out of step he is, how out of tune the world is, how offbeat its response, how sullen its song and radical its rebellion. Awe-struck, he is summoned to share in the ministry of reconciliation this realisation demands. Ruined and restored, cleansed and claimed, he becomes a chosen instrument of God.

This is heady stuff but is not so far a cry as it may seem from visiting the widows and caring for the fatherless. For as George Maloney has it, prophetic leaders are those who 'offer a reason for living because they have seen and experienced for themselves the Fatherhood of God.'[2] This is what is happening to Isaiah. He is touching the one who works for good in everything with those who love him. He is absorbing the scale of the symphony and, in doing so, is making sense of all the parts of which it is made up, including his own.

The Composer

There is then an ultimate calling; what might be described as the *call of the Father*. It is a call to serve God first of all in his big world not my little one! This stops me at once being a big fish in a small pond. The Father's call, like a tidal wave, submerges my pettiness and sweeps me out into larger seas. From fishing for fish in the local lake, men are called to fish for other men in the ocean of the world. This is the call to share the Father's heart, to feel what he feels, to identify with his interests, to be committed to what Le is committed to, to see with his eyes. To look at leadership with this wide-angle lens is vital in order to set it in its true perspective. Looked at this way, my service for God takes on a new grandeur and dignity. A veteran missionary to China is said to have been asked to take up a post with a large business firm. Well-qualified by his knowledge of the country's language and culture, he was certain to be well-paid for his work. When each successive salary offer was refused, the exasperated business man asked the missionary how much it would take to secure his services. 'Oh' said the missionary, 'your first offer was more than enough. The salary is fine but your job is too small!'

A sense of our ultimate calling not only gives scale to our leadership but also security. A call from God to be a leader is the mere outcrop of a very big rock. 'Before I formed you in the womb, I knew you' (Jer. 1.5) gives Jeremiah the timid prophet great confidence. Paul finds his security in being an apostle not in any human decision but in him 'who set me apart from birth and called me by his grace' (Gal. 1.15). This is what it means to know the call of the Father. It is to realise that the call of God to serve him in ministry only highlights the mysterious election that has long preceded it. What makes a man a minister of God is part of what makes him a man of God in the first place.

Knowing where our leadership stems from should in turn help us to see where the credit is to go. From him by grace alone; back to him in glory and praise. This is the order of things for leaders.

Many famous composers have in fact been plagiarists. In their finest masterpieces we can detect a snatch of someone else's melody, or a variation on someone else's theme. So it is with us as leaders. No one gets the credit but the original composer.

Whenever I lose my way, the call of the Father, like the call of the sea, draws me back. Deep calls to deep, usually in worship, and the clarity of my calling comes home afresh.

The Great Conductor

It is an amazing privilege that this ultimate call becomes an intensely personal call. The Father's claim on my life comes home to me as the *call of the Son*. He calls me by name. And Jesus only calls the men he wants! 'Jesus went up into the hills and called to him those he wanted' (Mark 3.13). A leader who is truly called of God has the privilege and satisfaction of being wanted. He did not volunteer for this. Nor on the other hand was he press-ganged into it as if anyone would do for the job. Here we move in the realm of friendship rather than recruitment. Jesus wants me; he wants my heart, he wants my company. He wants me to come in close to him before I go out from him. Communion comes before commission. 'He appointed twelve that they might be with him' (Mark 3.14). Any ministry I may have is born and nourished in fellowship with him.

Here, too, I find myself alongside fellow-workers. I discover that the call of God is the call to serve the Son of God in the fellowship of his body. There is really no place for the free-lance ministries that strew the scene in today's church. Our calling is in the context of one body (Col. 3.15) and our ministry is meant to be an expression of it. I am part of an orchestra responding to the conductor. If at any time I play a more prominent role it is not without the backing and support of the other players. It is a concerto but not a sonata. The ministries of Ephesians chapter four, prominent as they seem, are nonetheless 'for the body', meant to equip others to play their part and know their place. A leader's personal relationship with Jesus is the key to his fulfilment here. We take our timing from him too. If the tempo slackens we do not lose heart for there are slow movements in the work. If we have to wait for recognition we can be patient for he will cue us in at the right time.

The Spirit of the Piece

Most of our minor failures in leadership are due to inattention to detail, lack of concentration, moodiness and day-dreaming on the one hand; and impulsiveness and presumption on the other.

This does not make you a total failure as a leader. As P. T. Forsyth points out 'Beethoven was not troubled when a performer struck a wrong note, but he was angry when he failed with the spirit of the piece.' So it is with a leader's God. Even when our hearts condemn us he is greater than our hearts and he knows that we love him (1 John 3.20 and John 21.17). 'The final judgement is not whether we have at every moment stood, but whether having done all we stand'.[3]

Our calling can further be described as the *calling of the Spirit*. We are called as leaders to serve God the Holy Spirit in the flexibility and variety of his ways. The Holy Spirit pinpoints the call of God for us. 'This not that' is what you are to do; 'here not there' is where you are to go; 'now not then' is when you are to do it. Because the Spirit is interested in the small-scale things I find greater joy in attending to details; I concentrate more even in the dull moments so as not to miss his presence. He lights up my moodiness by his freshness and jolts me out of day-dreaming to find Christ in the immediate need before me. He stills my over-eagerness and calms my fevered brow. He puts colour into the drabness of ordinary days. He puts variety into the sameness of my work. Filled with the Spirit I do not treat every one who comes to me in the same way. I give up stock answers and learn to wait for his words of wisdom. I begin to discover unexpected delights in mundane events. Even in the slow movements or when waiting my cue I find I am humming the tune and am gripped by the spirit of the piece.

His ways are all the more interesting for being so elusive. Peter knew the call of the Father and had heard the commission of the Son but it took the Spirit to bring him, dazed with his own bravado, to the house of Cornelius. What the Spirit showed him in a vision pushed back the walls of Peter's closed mind, exposing him to startling new possibilities. He had only one defence for his action – 'The Spirit told me to have no hesitation about going with them' (Acts 11.12).

Again, the Spirit articulates what till then has been a felt but unspoken call of God. 'The Holy Spirit said: "Set apart for me Barnabas and Saul for the work to which I have called them." ' (Acts 13.2). Ordination, over which so much controversy still rages, is simply our recognition of the gifts and calling made manifest by the Spirit in another man. 'So after they had fasted and prayed, they placed their hands on them and sent them off' (Acts 13.3).

The Spirit makes specific what is only general. He focusses the overall call of God on the particular point of need. So going into all the world to preach the gospel, the apostolic team is prevented from entering Bithynia and diverted by vision to Macedonia (Acts 16.6ff) where God is already at work laying the basis of their success.

The Spirit's dazzling variety of gifts, ministries and effects gives scope for every leader to find his place and function with great joy. He need not envy others or compete with them. He can fulfil his calling however minor because he is filled and fired by the spirit of the piece.

Chosen Instruments

What the call of God can do to a man is graphically illustrated in the life of Abraham. Its first effect is *obedience*.

(a) 'By faith Abraham, when called, obeyed.' (Heb. 11.8).
There is no alternative when God calls. The old advice to
those thinking of entering the full-time ministry 'if you can
do anything else do it' had this understanding of the call of
God behind it. The leader who knows his calling confesses
the constraint on his life. Necessity is laid on him and he
has no choice.

(b) The call issues in *movement*. Obeying the call, Abraham
'went out' (Heb. 11.8). Taking off his slippers, he put on
his walking shoes again. The call of God often uproots us,
raises many eyebrows, ruins many a career. It leaves fishing
businesses managerless and hangs 'situations vacant' signs
in tax-office windows.

(c) God sets in motion a great adventure in our lives. Abraham
went out *'though he did not know where he was going'* (Heb.
11.8). A call which is too well-defined too soon is suspect.
The call of God is open-ended, unconditional, trading on
our trust. 'The life of Jesus', said F. B. Meyer, 'was planless'. Not aimless of course but planless, he relied on
hearing what the Father was saying and working where he
was working at every turn of the road. 'It has cost the writer
much to find his way so far. And he has yet a long way to
go. But he believes he has found the true and magnetic
North. And a voice is in his ears.'[4] Obedience is a mobile
home, you can park it anywhere.

(d) All this implies *progress and change*. The man called to be
a leader is caught up in a 'momentum apart from himself',
to use D. T. Niles' words. This keeps us going. We feel
ourselves to be part of a great continuity of leaders of God's
people. 'As I said to David . . . as I was with Moses so I
will be with you' – become personal reassurances to us of
our ability to be of use and to rise to the next challenge.
The 'upward call of God' fascinates and attracts us and we
press on eager to see the face behind the voice.

(e) The goal of this calling is an *inheritance* (Heb. 11.8).
Leadership of God's people has uncertain prospects as a
career but ultimate rewards as a vocation. Moses disdained
the riches of Egypt because he was looking to the reward.
Abraham owned not one inch of the promised land but
owning nothing he possessed all things. For this is a
heavenly calling (Heb. 3.1) whose rewards lie beyond carnal
horizons.

Watching a nun dressing the revolting wounds of a leper, a traveller said: 'I wouldn't do that for 10,000 dollars'. 'I wouldn't either' was her reply.[5] The call of God will make us enigmas, strangers and exiles on the earth like our fathers in the faith.

We can take heart in facing the challenges of this by remembering that the 'gifts and calling of God are without repentance'. Entranced by the Piper at the Gates of Dawn, Rat turns to his friend Mole. " 'It's gone," sighed Rat. "So beautiful and strange and new! Since it was to end so soon, I almost wish I had never heard it. For it has roused a longing in me that is pain, and nothing seems worthwhile but just to hear that sound once more and go on listening to it for ever. No! There it is again! Now it passes on and I begin to lose it", he said presently. "O Mole! The beauty of it! The merry bubble and joy, the thin, clear, happy call of the distant piping! Such music I never dreamed of, and the call in it is stronger than even the music is sweet! Row on Mole, row! *For the music and the call must be for us*" '.[6]

7. The Vision and The Dream

Revelation is vital to leadership. God's view of things not man's has been the starting point for all great movements of God in history. It is not enough to have a call from God. We need to know who God is, and where he wants to take his people. 'I have a dream' has set things off in God's direction from Joseph to Martin Luther King. And 'not disobedient to the heavenly vision' has been the resolve of men determined to see things through once they have begun. When God's chosen instrument has seen God's plan and purpose he can stir and motivate the people of God, keeping them on course when the going gets rough as it usually does. It was long after I had studied First Corinthians in the original Greek that the vision of the Body of Christ with its varied gifts and functions dawned on me by spiritual revelation. I felt as if I had never read the New Testament before. My eyes were opened to new truth which fired my heart and shaped my ambitions in leading God's people. As Watchman Nee puts it, 'The start of a true work of God with us is not when we consecrate ourselves to Him, but when we *see*. Consecration should result from spiritual vision; it can never take its place'.[1]

To miss this is to court disaster. For 'where there is no vision the people perish' (Prov. 29.18). The 'vision' which this much-quoted text speaks of, is to be taken in its exact sense of the revelation a prophet receives.[2] This gives a rendering: 'where there is no *prophetic vision (among the leaders)* the people whom they lead become confused, disorganised and rebellious'.

To say 'I have no clear vision for this church' is the saddest thing any pastor can say. Without revelation, today's leaders can easily succumb to ungodly pressures from both inside and outside the church. From within is the pressure which says 'we want more of this' or 'we must cater for that.' From the outside comes the pressure of other men's teaching, principles from the latest best-seller, or trends from the latest Bible-week and conference. Some men in today's church are opportunists – adopting ideas simply because they are fashionable or endorsed by men they respect.

This is not to deny that pressure is often good for us, nor, of course, that God speaks to us through others. But if we are to avoid the fatal trap of legalism we cannot afford slavishly to copy others. We need leaders who by the Spirit's revelation of truth to their own hearts *have seen for themselves* the purpose of the Living God. Borrowed ideas and techniques will make us feel as overwhelmed and as heavy-footed as David in Saul's armour.

This ought not to deter us from having big visions. A British Ambassador in Washington was once asked by a television reporter sometime before the event what he would like for Christmas. Modestly, courting no favours or inducements, he declined to say. When pressed he eventually said he would be happy with a small box of crystallised fruit. Months later on Christmas Eve the programme came on screen. The French Ambassador, when asked what he would like for Christmas, said that he would like peace in the world and new agreements between nations; the German Ambassador said he wanted a new upsurge in international trade; the British Ambassador that he would like a small box of crystallised fruit! Beware your small ambitions!

The Ministry of Glory

A revelation of God himself is the first essential for a leader. 'The God of glory', we are told, 'appeared to our father Abraham' (Acts 7.1). And in some measure this has been true for all who have significantly affected the lives of God's people. Judson Cornwall notes this as a special feature of the great revivalists in modern church history. 'It was not', he writes, 'through theological arguments or gifted oratory that these men moved vast numbers of people to God. It was through a revelation of the glory of God.'[3] Jonathan Edwards, who certainly did not lack theological argument, talks of a day walking in the woods in 1737 when he had a view that was extraordinary 'of the glory of the Son of God as Mediator between God and man, and his wonderful, great, full, pure and sweet grace and love.' Men as diverse as Howell Harris, Charles Finney and D. L. Moody all tell of similar experiences, 'I can only say,' wrote Moody, 'that God revealed Himself to me and I had to ask him to stay his hand.'[4] That such experiences have often been associated with the sealing or baptism in the Holy Spirit is not surprising since it is to the ministry of the Spirit which is with glory that we are called (2 Cor. 3.8). Such initiations into visions of glory make us susceptible thereafter to more frequent revelations and insight, which go on clarifying our call and ministry. What is happening here is that in revelation the call of God breaks the surface of our consciousness in a new way. By revealing himself to us God takes up the option on our lives his prior grace has given him. 'But when God, who set me apart from birth and called me by his grace, was pleased to reveal his Son in me so that I might preach him among the Gentiles . . .' (Gal. 1.15–16). Paul's own testimony burned into my heart as a very young man. Subsequent revelations of God to me by his Spirit have served only to illustrate the prior call of God on my life, making me secure in what I am doing and enlarging the vision of what I want to become.

From the bush burning with the glory of God yet unconsumed, Moses was given a revelation of God and his purposes for Israel that shaped the future of both leader and people.

Let us look first at the effect of revelation on Moses as the leader of God's people. (Exodus 3.1ff)

(i) Revelation solved his identity crisis

'Who am I?' is Moses' reaction to the revelation of God's plans for him in leadership (Exodus 3.11). The thought of confronting Pharaoh turned Moses' muscles to water. But it is as if God says to Moses; 'Moses, it's not what you are that counts but what I AM!' All God's men get the same answer. As young as Samuel was, as unworthy as Isaiah confessed to be, as timid as Jeremiah felt, as impossible a candidate as Saul of Tarsus was – all these men came to say 'here I am Lord, send me; I'm your man.'

(ii) Revelation solved his authority problem

'What right have I got to say this to the people or to lead them in this direction?' (cf. Exod. 3.13). 'Whose name shall I mention as authorising me to do what I am doing? Tell them 'I AM has sent you!' Again, no fancy embroidery of our authority is needed. We have met the living God, have seen a vision of what he wants his people to become and where he wants his people to arrive. What more do we need? Go in my name, as my representative.

(iii) Revelation bridges the credibility gap

' "What if they do not believe me" ' is Moses' next rejoinder! (Exod. 4.1) This is a regular defence mechanism in leaders baulking at a new challenge. This is the 'what-if' syndrome. 'What happens if nothing happens' is the haunting thought. What if we pray and no one is healed? What if the house group doesn't get off the ground? What if the ministry of the word doesn't take off? What if the children go off me when I discipline them? What if I witness to my neighbour and he rejects me . . . ?' This 'what if' will paralyse me if I let it. It will lead me to postpone new ventures to the never-never land of wishful thinking.

Only the 'I AM' bridges the credibility gap and prevents me being what A. W. Tozer called a 'pro-tem atheist.' It is the revelation of who God is that will bridge the gap between desires and effects, between needs and provision; between giving up and going on! Learning to live in the 'now' we start where we are, and committing what we do have (4.2) to the ring, we see signs following our faith.

(iv) Revelation answers the ability problem

'I can't do it, Lord' is the next refusal. Every leader at some time questions his ability to do the job. He may feel he lacks the necessary gifts, and is ill-equipped to handle the task. Moses goes over the top. Only naivety saves him from blasphemy. 'No way am I a speaker, Lord; I never have been, and I'm not one now; not even since meeting you Lord have I become one!' (cf. Exod. 4.10).

'Yes you are, Moses because I AM with you and will be your mouth!'

The leader who has met God will know that his 'I am nots' are no match for God's 'I AM's'.

(v) Revelation is the basis for a leader's security

When Aaron and Miriam become jealous of his leadership and accuse him of being elitist Moses is meek and lets God hear the criticism (Numb. 12.1–16). This meekness is a mark of a man who has seen a revelation of God and a vision of God's plans for his people. He does not react to criticism in a defensive way for God is his authority and vindication. When dissidents tell a leader that he has gone too far, he is not panicked into beating a hasty retreat. He stands his ground with God knowing that it is his opponents who have over-reached themselves (Numb. 17.1ff). A vision of God gives the courage to say unpalatable things. Isaiah said hard things because he saw his glory (John 12.41). Only a man who has seen what Isaiah has seen can say what he said. So Moses can stand his ground with Pharaoh because he has a revelation of the glory and will of God.

Moses had learnt this lesson dearly. As a well-educated man, powerful in word and deed, he had the brainwave of leading Israel out of Egypt (Acts 7.22 ff). Assuming that the people he wanted to lead would see him in the same favourable light, he attempted to assert himself to change the situation. Prompted by his own carnal thinking and strength, Moses made a terrible mistake that took him into a forty-year exile in the land of Midian. Not until the revelation of God in a burning bush consumed all his own ideas and natural self-confidence did Moses become the deliverer of Israel, the role to which deep down he knew God had called him.

Where There is Vision

The effect on a people of a leader with revelation is also clear from Moses' leadership of Israel which had the promised land in its sights (Exod. 3.8).

(i) A leader with a clear vision gives to his people a true sense of destiny

Lifted above their own pre-occupation with themselves, his followers rejoice in being part of God's larger plans and purposes in the earth. Leaders with vision bring to the people a true taste of God's glory. This glory becomes their chief end. No longer is it a kingdom of man with God to serve in it but a kingdom of God with men to serve in it. Not only do we rejoice that we have been taken out of our 'Egypt' but that 'Egypt' is being taken out of us. Without a revelation of God's glory and purpose we may rest in the knowledge that God is 'for us' but never venture on the fact that 'we exist for God'.

(ii) A visionary leader brings coherence *to his people*

This vision holds them together, unites their disparate energies and gifts, channels their diverse abilities into one common good. Without a prophetic vision from its leaders a company of people fragment, each person going off at his own tangent, following his own guidance. Lacking this unifying objective, people become 'unrestrained' or 'scattered' (Prov. 29.18). That 'every man did what was right in his own eyes' (Judges 21.25 NASB) in the days of the Judges could be traced directly to the fact that 'the word of God was rare in those days; there were not many visions' (1 Sam. 3.1). Eventually, in Delitsch's version, 'without a revelation the people become ungovernable.'

(iii) The vision that a leader brings to his people breeds endurance
in them
The Lord used a prophet to bring Israel up from Egypt and 'by
a prophet he cared for him' (Hosea 12.13). Like its leader,
Israel 'endured as seeing Him who is invisible'. The leader with
vision can keep his people going and keep them on course.
Without knowing at every phase exactly where we're going we
can know what we're heading for! This spares us from many
diversions and cul-de-sacs. A leader with a clear vision from
God of what God wants his people to become will be able to
prise them away from the merry-go-round of incessant activity
and turn them in God's direction. When I first entered the
Baptist ministry I was amazed to find how many organisations
were kept going long after losing any inspiration they might
once have had from God. No one ever questioned whether God
wanted us to run this organisation again the next year. 'As it
was in the beginning, now, and ever shall be', seemed to be
the motto. The 'anniversary' disease confirmed this cyclic view
of how things went. Every year the same special events turned
up with such monotonous regularity that the sense of pointless-
ness was reinforced in our minds. The leader with vision gets
the people out of this rut of going round and round the same
mountain and points them to the unknown future with its
promise of glory and fighting to be achieved.

(iv) A leader with vision provides continuity *for his people*
Because he is attracting them to his vision and not just to his
personality, he can make way for worthy successors to whom
he has transmitted the same dreams. Fired as Moses had been
with the vision of the promised land, Joshua did not head up a
'Threshold of Canaan Church' which settled where Moses had
stopped. He had the Spirit of Moses and so led the people on
into the land Moses had seen with the eyes of his heart right
from the beginning. Rather than stop where I stop I would
rather you started again from where I started.

The Price of the Vision

'Keep paying the price of the vision. Let God see that you are
willing to live up to the vision'.[5] To see what this can mean we
turn again to the life of Abraham.

(i) Vision makes me willing to live in 'tents' (Hebrews 11.9–10)
Because he was 'looking for a city' Abraham was willing to live
in a tent even *in* the promised land! In other words the price

that has to be paid for the vision is willingness to live in a transition. It is to preface every ministry with a 'towards'. This means accepting that we inhabit the interim, where every extra-biblical definition is preliminary, every prophecy is partial, every arrival a new starting-point. The cost of vision is felt in every seeming failure when what we experience falls short of what we envisage. The great 'not-yet' of a salvation that is to come wipes the smirk of satisfaction off the face of the complacent, the critical and the apathetic. Equally it wipes the smile of smugness off the face of a naive and false triumphalism. Only the sight of the city enables you to live in the tent without disillusionment. Those who refuse to pay the price of the vision become either idealists or cynical reactionaries.

(ii) Vision will cost me friendship

The vision that draws me to those whose hearts burn with the same glow, will cut me off from others whose blood runs cold at the thought of the unknown. Many who set out together in recent years in the adventure of the Spirit have parted company because where one was taken on the other was left, hugging his caution. In any great movement of God there are those swept along by the tide, who do not have the call of the sea in them; those who climb on to the bandwagon but do not have the tune ringing in their hearts. There are those for whom the revelations coming from the Holy Spirit today have become merely interesting topics for discussion rather than convictions they would die for.

So Abraham has to part company with Lot. Lot had come a long way with Abraham. But the vision of the city wasn't in his heart. He had glimpsed no glory and dreamed no dream. Stirred by the sense of adventure, feeling that anything was better than the boredom of life in Ur, he had gone along with the prophet of God. But he is willing to settle for short-term gains, unwilling to pay the price of the long-term objective. 'Charismatic' means for him a pepped-up denominational worship service, house groups grafted on to the same old structure, a few choruses borrowed from the pioneers squeezed into the morning meeting. Enjoying the spin-offs of what God is doing but not committed to its vision; this is the Lot-mentality.

Abraham eventually had to bear the pain of parting from Lot. 'He lived in tents, as did Isaac and Jacob, who were heirs with him of the same promise' (Heb. 11.9). Not all fellow-travellers are fellow-heirs. We learn this to our cost as we try to live up to the light we have received.

(iii) Vision will make me dissatisfied with anything man has built Abraham was 'looking forward to the city with foundations whose architect and builder is God' (Heb. 11.10). Nothing that is temporal, traditional or sectarian will do for the leader with God-given vision. He is willing to be non-conformist for the sake of it. He will make trouble for himself because he will try to administer in the church only those principles that are compatible with the final heading up of all things in Christ (cf. Eph. 1.10). He will be able to tear himself away from churches or work to which he has given long years of envisioning. He will do this for the sake of the vision that is bigger than anything he has been able to accomplish. Without owning an inch of the land, he rejoices in all of it as his inheritance! (Acts 7.5). 'Lift up now your eyes and look from the place where you are' (Gen. 13.14 NASB). And what do we see for ourselves? Nothing of the success we may have desired in our leadership. Yet everything of the land, the fulfilment of all our dreams and the ultimate glory is ours even as we look again. 'It is glorious,' said Campbell Morgan, 'to do without and still to have by sharing in the process that moves towards God's final victory'.[6]

Revelation and vision are then vital to leadership and their price is well worth paying. As leaders we consistently need the Spirit of wisdom and revelation which Paul sought for the Ephesians. The Spirit will reveal to us further dimensions and directions in the hope of our calling. 'I pray that your inner vision may be flooded with light, to enable you to see what hope the fact that he has called you gives you' (Eph. 1.18 Barclay).

8. No Plastic Prophets

Once upon a time someone, somewhere, poured a huge bucket of cold water over the emotional life of leaders. Cool, calm, and collected is the rigid image of a leader in many people's minds. Not long ago a Presidential candidate in the United States put himself out of the running by weeping in public. The church has not been immune from this. For a long time we took our leaders straight out of the deep freeze and wondered why our Christianity was so cold and uninspiring. The Holy Spirit is now showing us that it need not be, nor always has been, like this with God's leaders.

The story is told of an American tourist in the nineteenth century visiting Robert Murray M'Cheyne's church in Dundee. Standing in the pulpit at St. Peter's he asked an old janitor who remembered M'Cheyne to show him how the godly man preached. Advice was given. Holding the Bible in the way M'Cheyne had done, adopting his posture and stance, the tourist asked the janitor if there was anything else he needed to do. 'Yes, there is' replied the old man, 'now weep!' Without the tears the picture would have been incomplete.

The call of Moses to be the deliverer of Israel has already taken our attention. But it is important to see that behind the emergence of Moses lie the emotions of God himself. ' "I have indeed seen the misery of my people in Egypt. I have heard them crying out because of their slave drivers, and I am concerned about their suffering." ' (Exod. 3.7 cf. 2.23–25). God is not unmoved by his people's plight; he is feeling their hurt and sharing their pain. Because God is emotionally affected by the distress of his people he raises up a man to lead them out who will not only do what he says but who will feel what he feels. Centuries after Moses, Ezra shared the feelings of God over Israel's idolatry. 'When I heard this, I tore my tunic and cloak, pulled hair from my head and beard and sat down appalled' (Ezra 9.3). Clearly here is one leader not at this point cool, calm, and collected! Nehemiah's reaction is similar. Hearing of the distress of the remnant struggling to re-establish itself in the land, Nehemiah felt his heart breaking within him! 'When I heard this I sat down and wept. For some days I mourned. . . .' (Neh. 1.4). The man of God is not only filled with human sympathy for the people but is sharing the reproach and shame God feels at the disgrace of his people. For an Israel that has, for the moment, rejected her Messiah but is still the object of covenant-love, Paul feels in his heart 'great sorrow and unceasing anguish' (Romans 9.2). In every respect this is a far cry from stiff upper lip leadership!

Prophetic Emotions

Of all God's men it is *prophetic* leaders especially who are called to reflect God's feelings. Prophets are often called to grasp the twin terminals of man's sin and God's holiness and the shock to their system is usually acute. This should not excuse needlessly eccentric behaviour on the prophet's part but it does help to explain that certain mystery and strangeness which sometimes colours his ministry. *For the prophet is not just a bearer but an embodiment of the Word God gives him.* He is called therefore to convey not only the message but the feelings of God to his people. The great Jewish scholar, Abraham Heschel, roots the subjective side of the prophetic calling in what he calls *'pathos'*.[1] The prophet, he says, enters into an emotional communion with God's feelings as well as God's Word, for both are part of God's truth. This is illustrated by the ministry of Elisha. Foreseeing what the ruthless Hazael will do to Israel when he succeeds Ben-hadad as King of Syria, Elisha predicts the King's immediate recovery and subsequent death. The prophet fully realises the implications of his words. Burdened with this terrible knowledge he breaks down in front of Hazael. 'The man of God stood there like a man stunned until he could bear it no longer; then he wept' (2 Kings 8.11 NEB). This is not sentimentality but sympathy with God and is itself an expression of how God puts his heart into his Word. This is the Word burning like fire in Jeremiah; the Word that breaks his heart and intoxicates his whole being (Jer. 23. 9,29). *Without the Word pathos is just pathetic; but with the Word pathos is prophetic.*

Uniquely among the prophets it is Hosea who most embodies this. His own intensely personal domestic anguish becomes itself the moving parable of God's heart-ache over adulterous Israel. For Hosea it was not what he thought but what he suffered that made him a prophet. We are not called today to such terrible enactments of the Word for the Incarnation has upstaged all prophetic symbolism. But we are called as leaders to lay down our lives for God's word. The leader who has nothing to die for has little to live for. It is our calling to feel what God feels and to communicate something of this to the people of God. We are to do this even when it entails withstanding the emotions of the people, as Paul and Agabus did, that God's word might be fulfilled (Acts 21). Feeling what God feels, at least in measure, will affect how we speak for God. Our prophecies do not come through playback machines but through men. No one loathes more than I do the phony religious confidence or quavering voice that tries to bolster prophetic utterance. But our words for God should carry conviction and convey feelings. When God speaks he is not reading from the telephone directory!

In Richard Baxter's words, 'If you give the holy things of God the highest praises in words and yet do it coldly, you will seem in the manner to unsay what you said in the matter. The manner as well as the words must set them forth . . . that the people can *feel* us preach when they hear us.'[2] Because the prophet is as much an embodiment of the Word as a mere bearer of it, his sensitivities are opened to a wider range of experience than others. He is therefore more prone to fluctuations of feeling and mood than other men, more liable to hear discordant notes because his ears are tuned to grander harmonies. Enlarge his vision and he becomes more prone to impatience and disillusionment. Elijah is a case in point. In the inevitable psychological anti-climax that followed the spiritual 'Everest' of his encounter with the false prophets of Baal, the prophet is especially vulnerable. Nervously exhausted, Elijah is open to the spiritual attack and emotional manipulation of Jezebel. He lapses into self-pity and abject despair, feelings so at odds with his very recent faith and boldness on Mount Carmel. The Lord's first answer to this state of mind in his prophet is typically wise and gracious. The Lord gives Elijah just what he needs, which is not a refresher course in theology or an intense counselling session but a square meal and a sound sleep! Then to the slowly recovering but still fragile heart of his prophet the Lord speaks not with earthquake, wind, or fire – any of which might have blown Elijah's emotional fuses yet again – but with a quiet word in his ear. The dramatic natural phenomena may have reactivated Elijah's jaded awareness but at this point the Lord knew how to get through to his man in a winning way.

The prophet's temperament is to be taken into account here. He is to be tested by his character but not judged for his temperament. It is just this variety of temperament in God's spokesmen that helps him colour in his Word and shows us that his wisdom is a many-splendoured thing. Could a more self-confident man than Jeremiah have borne such universal rejection? When you think the worst of yourself what can man say of you that can hurt your feelings? Self-deprecation may have proved the deepest, if strangest, safeguard for a prophet called to a ministry of almost total unpopularity. Today, however, Jeremiah would more likely have been deemed a suitable case for treatment, been disqualified from ministry and made a candidate for inner healing. To attain emotional wholeness is a fine aim but we do well to set it just below a sight of God in all his glory as our chief ambition. For this Isaiah lost his well-integrated life – becoming ruined as he put it – but in doing so he gained his prophetic soul.

Stirring the People

All this is especially significant when we see that it is the role of prophetic leadership to stir up the people of God. Unresponsiveness in God's people is still the greatest barrier to the supernatural and miraculous breaking forth among us. Responsiveness is not merely, or chiefly, a matter of psychology, of course; the spirit and mind and will are essential in this. But emotional sluggishness is a bigger hindrance to spiritual advance than we often recognise. We lack emotional awareness and stamina, scarcely able to sustain a lengthy period of praise without sitting down and bowing out. The early Billy Graham crusades were often criticised for being too emotional. With hindsight we might well come to exactly the opposite conclusion that they were not emotional enough. If there were drop-outs from the conversion line, it was surely due to lack of emotional commitment not excess of it. Too many perhaps, when decision time came, at an artificially contrived moment, voted with their feet but not their hearts.

This emotional sluggishness is reinforced by the over-bombardment of our senses in an electronic age. Media exposure to tragedy for example has undoubtedly numbed our senses and dulled our reactions. Pictures of starving children no longer move us because we don't know what to do with the useless feelings they raise. The sight of so much tragedy far-removed from the sounds and smells of real events has devalued pain. In much the same way an over-diet of shoddy entertainment has trivialised pleasure. We are over-exposed to relentlessly unfunny comedy-shows and the synthetic heartiness of media personalities which, like the advertising that sponsors them, promise more than they deliver. Canned laughter is an apt symbol of our age. Why not canned crying? Emotionally anaesthetized, we know neither true joy nor true sorrow. All of this finds subtle reinforcement in our natural English horror of enthusiasm. Being English we prefer understatement to bold speech, oblique hints to direct talk. We rightly suspect exaggeration, ballyhoo and presumption. We recoil instinctively from the razzmatazz of the big American healers and evangelists. But in our reaction we may miss the point. Behind the bizarre, sometimes uncouth presentations which it is not difficult to dismiss as sensationalism and sentimentalism, lies a quite desperate attempt to gain a response from people, to rouse them from their spectator-sport to faith, action and involvement. This is not confusing grace and works; merely distinguishing between being passive and being receptive.

If we want to do better than this and avoid spurious or even dubious practices then we will need true prophetic men genuinely moved with holy wrath or pure compassion and able to stir the people to a true response. Then the sound of true sorrow and true joy may well be mixed (Ezra 3.12–13). Then the freshly-aroused leader will communicate new stirrings to the people. 'So the Lord stirred up the spirit of Zerubbabel . . . and the spirit of all the remnant of the people; and they came and worked on the house of the Lord of Hosts their God' (Haggai 1.14 NASB). This is not just keeping up morale by some technique of positive confession or positive thinking but a genuine warming of the hearts of the people by a fresh encounter with the living God, who through his prophet confirms that he is with them. Through the prophet we learn that the tragedy *of* the world is more grievous than the tragedy *in* the world. Through him we learn that the pleasures for evermore at God's right hand are there to be increasingly and unendingly appreciated by all who in redemption have rediscovered their reason for living in worshipping God and enjoying him for ever.

What is clear is that the prophet himself needs emotional refreshment if he is to lead God's people in this way. He has to stir himself and be stirred again and again. He can easily become bored with what is less than God's best. He has to stir himself constantly if he is not to become a critic or, worse, a cynic. To do this and to find fresh inspiration Elisha called for music and a minstrel (2 Kings 3.15), while David remonstrated with himself and roused his own soul (Psalm 42). The company of brothers is a great stimulus here. Paul is glad to acknowledge that other men had 'refreshed his spirit' (1 Cor. 16.18, cf. 2 Cor. 7.6,13) and that Onesiphorus had been like a cool breeze to him by the freshness of his fellowship.

To know this joy, leaders need unrestrained affections. Paul's affection for the elders at Ephesus and theirs for him make for one of the most moving passages in the New Testament (Acts 20). 'With humility and tears' Paul had served the Lord among them; 'with tears' he had spent three years in close pastoral admonition and love. No wonder these men loved him in return and were not ashamed to show it. Not a stiff-upper lip anywhere. Kneeling together in fervent prayer on the quayside, arms round each other, kisses everywhere, tears streaming down softened faces – these are New Testament leaders and this was a 'leaders' meeting'! And not a note-book or clip board in sight. Let brotherly love continue.

9. Man After God's Heart

More than anyone else in the Old Testament, the man who sets the standard for leadership is David. In Leon Wood's words 'He was the strongest king Israel ever had. He was the measure of others. To be a king like David came to be the highest accolade a successor could have.'[1] Subsequent kings were measured by him. For 'walking in the ways of David' Josiah was commended; for failing to do so Ahaz was condemned. Many centuries later, Israel's leaders in restoration, Ezra and Nehemiah, were still carefully following what had been 'prescribed by David, king of Israel' (Ezra 3.10, Neh. 12.24). It is David who is prophetically set forth as the model for Messiahship (Ezek. 34.20–24) fulfilled in his 'greater', in fact greatest, son. David's leadership was so symbolically and strategically important that it is surprising how little attention he is given in manuals of biblical leadership.

His leadership is wide-ranging in its lessons and far-reaching in its implications. David deserves the study of every leader of the people of God.

Generation Game

Before all this greatness intimidates us we can take heart from Paul's assessment of David's rule. Speaking to the synagogue congregation in Antioch Paul tells us that 'David served the purpose of God in his generation.' (Acts 13.36). This is all the more heartening to us for being so prosaic. However strategic David's leadership was to prove in God's plans in history it is merely said of him here that he did what he could for God in the time that he had. Although David's leadership, prophetically, had implications for the future which we in our day are enjoying, it is heartening to realise that he was content also to be a man of his time, serving eternal plans going far beyond the limits of his lifetime. Much of what he envisaged as God's work for him he did not in fact achieve. Another built his temple for him. A lesser man than David might have become frustrated or cynical so that his later energies drained away in disillusionment. David did not let this happen. Much of what was promised him, as he realised, was for a 'distant future' (2 Sam. 7.19). Being a man of faith, however, he did not become an idle dreamer, considering the affairs of the present to be beneath him, too mundane to be bothered with. Leaders, especially those with great vision, need to watch that they do not become so high-minded as to be of no earthly use.

Paul adds of David that 'he fell asleep' *after* having served God in his generation; not, we might add, *during* it as some leaders of the people do! As a leader David was wide awake to every opportunity to serve the living God. His repeated 'I will awake the dawn' is typical of a man who can't wait to maximise the moments of today with tomorrow in view. This is second nature to any farmer for whom there is no reaping tomorrow without sowing today and who is wise enough not to allow long-term aims to paralyse present activity.

The secret of this alertness as of every other aspect of David's leadership is that he was 'a man after God's own heart'. Looking on the heart not on the outward appearances which impress us so much, God picks the man to lead whose heart is set on doing his will (1 Sam. 13.14, 16.7, Acts 13.22). Two features especially of this 'heart set on God' are relevant for leaders.

(a) There is about David a *wholeness of heart*, a single-minded commitment to the will of God as he understands it. This whole-heartedness was meant to be emulated by his son, Solomon, but sadly wasn't. 'As Solomon grew old his heart was not fully devoted to the Lord as the heart of David his father had been' (1 Kings 11.4 cf. 1 Kings 9.4). Undoubtedly though it was this very quality in David which other men of leadership strength found compelling. Double-minded men gain few worthwhile followers. David, on the other hand, was able to ask others to make sacrifices for God because he would never himself offer to God anything which cost him nothing. 'No, I insist on paying the full price' he presses Aruanah when the latter offers to give him the threshing-floor for nothing as a site for the altar. Later when costly giving is required of the people, David as their leader has the moral authority to ask for it. 'Who is willing to consecrate himself today to the Lord?' First to step forward were David's fellow-leaders who gave lavishly towards the work of the temple. 'The people rejoiced at the willing response of their leaders, for they had given freely and wholeheartedly to the Lord.' (1 Chron. 21.24, 29.5–9).

(b) There is in David an *integrity of heart* we do well as leaders to prize. Asaph who was close enough to David to know otherwise testified to this feature of David's rule over Israel and praised God for it. 'And David shepherded them with integrity of heart; with skilful hands he led them' (Ps. 78.72). The skill was in safe hands because the heart was sound. Sinless, David certainly wasn't but he could claim to know the blessedness of being a guileless man. (Ps. 32). As a leader with his fair share of sin and mistakes he nevertheless kept short accounts with God and was honoured for it.

A clear conscience, as Paul so frequently reminds us, frees us from crippling self-analysis to do the work of God with clear intent, leaving judgement on ourselves to the Lord. This is a leader's best vindication. 'Our sole defence is a life of integrity' (2 Cor. 6.7 JBP).

In all this David was, as Stephen later described him, 'greatly favoured by the Lord.' Being a forgiven man David knew what it was to live under grace. The freedom he was given in leadership was unusual, a certain sign of God's favour. Almost uniquely, David at various times was enabled to be prophet, priest, and king. Where others had been condemned for usurping the restricted role of the priest, David was granted diplomatic immunity as a herald of the coming kingdom of Jesus (cf. Mk. 2.24). It was said of him that 'the Lord helped him wherever he went' so much was the grace of God on his leadership. Any leader with the favour and grace of God resting on his life can expect to be extended and enlarged in his sphere of ministry. Surprising skills and surprising scope are given to the leader who is moving in the fullness of God's blessing.

Last Words

For further light on the matter in hand we turn to David's swan-song recorded for us in the twenty-third chapter of the second book of Samuel. David's last words are not the last word on leadership but they are magnificently practical. From them we make a number of points.

(1) He is proud to be known as '*the son of Jesse*' (2 Sam. 23.1). The family had been David's first school of leadership. The

youngest of nine brothers, David learned not to let any false inhibition hinder him or big brother deter him. When David turns up to deal with the giant Goliath he is roughly handled by his eldest brother Eliab. 'What are you doing here anyway? You're supposed to be back there looking after the sheep. You cheeky brat! You just want to watch the battle!' (1 Sam. 17.28). Undaunted, David keeps asking how long they are prepared to let this pagan giant taunt the armies of the living God. Any leader who feels his family background is against him in any way can take heart from this. No childhood oppression or adolescent disadvantage can ultimately thwart God's call in a leader's life.

In the family too, David had learned the principle which Jesus later laid down so clearly as a rule for leaders in his kingdom. We shall have occasion to notice this again. Suffice it to say here that David learned his leadership by first being faithful in small and natural things. Faithful in caring for a flock of sheep, he is made shepherd of a nation. Faithful in tending what belonged to someone else, he is given responsibility for his own. Faithful in protecting the flock against lions and bears, he is given grace to protect the people of God against Goliath and deliver them from hostile nations.

(2) He never forgets that he has been *raised to eminence by God* (2 Sam. 23.1). Never forgetting his roots, knowing where he'd come from, he never ceases to marvel at having come so far and having attained so high a place. Never ceasing to wonder at this, he gives God all the credit. He knows himself to be a man 'exalted by God' who owes his rise to fame and leadership only to the Lord. David is no self-appointed leader. Not originally the people's choice but God's, he is never in danger of self-congratulation. 'Who am I and what is my house that you should treat me as a man of high standing?' is his attitude when talking to God (1 Chron. 17.17). And when talking to the people he reminds them that it was God's pleasure not theirs which had made him king (1 Chron. 28.4). He could sing from experience that God exalts the humble but abases the proud, that such decisions are in divine hands, and that it is God's condescension which makes a man great (Ps. 75.6, 18.35). David was a leader who never got above himself – except that is when he was in trouble; then he knew there was always one rock higher to climb to! (Ps. 61.2). Likewise any leader who is confident of God's choice of him can

have the same blend of boldness and humility, able to rise above even the 'contentions of the people' (2 Sam. 22.44). Such a leader knows his place in God's order because he has heeded the counsel 'not to think of himself more highly than he ought to think but to think of himself so as to have sound judgement' (Romans 12.3). Neither over- nor under-estimating himself he can fulfil his calling to lead with a sense of security and purpose.

(3) He knows himself to be the man '*anointed* by the God of Jacob' (23.1). David looks back across the years to his original anointing to be Israel's leader. 'So Samuel took the horn of oil and anointed him in the presence of his brothers and from that day on the Spirit of the Lord came upon David in power' (1 Sam. 16.13). Even before he had come to his own kingship he had felt by the Spirit an instinctive respect for the spiritual authority of the Lord's anointed, Saul. Saul's bad example did nothing to dull this sense in David of the vital importance of God's anointing on a leader's life. It was the one thing above all else that marked him out as having the right to rule. In this anointing David rejoiced continually. 'He shows unfailing kindness to his anointed' (Ps. 18.50). 'You anoint my head with oil; my cup overflows' (Ps. 23.5). He looks to this to iron out the inconsistencies in his life. 'May your good Spirit lead me on level ground' (Ps. 143.10). Always dependent on the anointing of the Holy Spirit David rejoices when it is freshly given: 'I have been anointed with fresh oil' (Ps. 92.10 NASB). Every leader of God's people, certainly in these days of spiritual renewal, knows his absolute reliance on the Holy Spirit to make his leadership valid. Apart from asking for forgiveness, there is no prayer I pray more often as a leader than David's own heart-cry – 'Do not take your Holy Spirit from me' (Ps. 51.11). Only the Holy Spirit can qualify us for leadership. Only he can make good the defects that sin exposes in us – the need for a cleaner heart, a more steadfast and willing spirit. (Ps. 51.10–12). In short, as we have seen in an earlier chapter, the Holy Spirit's anointing is essential for leadership. Astonished often by what we accomplish with this anointing of the Spirit, alarmed to the point of terror at the thought of losing it, we share David's feelings.

(4) He is a *worshipper*, the 'sweet psalmist' of Israel (23.1 NASB). David is the singer of songs for all seasons, songs of pain and pleasure wrung out of him by the intensity and

intimacy of his life with God. David is the psalmist who tugs at the heart-strings of every mood in the spiritual life. Singing, shouting, silent, wondering, clapping, dancing, David ransacks the whole repertoire of response to bless his God. To be a leader is to be first and foremost a worshipper. David shows us what Ezekiel later explained more fully, that the first privilege and first priority of God's leaders is their 'ministry unto the Lord' (Ezek. 44). Ministering to the Lord precedes ministry to his people. Every leader needs to know that ministering to the house of God in work for his people is no substitute for ministering to the heart of God in worship of him alone. The first leaders of the Early Church knew the secret, for it was 'while they were worshipping the Lord that the Holy Spirit said – 'Set apart for me, Saul and Barnabas'' (Acts. 13.2).

Nor was David the sort of leader who sits on platforms in public meetings in days of charismatic renewal with arms folded and face glum. He leads others in worship. 'Magnify the Lord with me, let us exalt his name together' is his exuberant invitation. We read in 1 Chronicles 15 of the care and creativity with which David set out his directions for it. Leaving the Mosaic tabernacle with its prescribed animal sacrifices at Gibeon, he built a tabernacle in Jerusalem solely for continuous praise and worship. It was an incredible trailer for the spiritual worship of the coming kingdom of Jesus. The praise the Holy Spirit is now drawing from so many today is no passing fad. It is modelled on the very worship David was prophetically given to offer as a foretaste of praise in the kingdom. His leadership here was therefore of immense prophetic significance. Nothing will make us more surely men after God's own heart in our own day than becoming leaders like David of the prophetic praise of the people of God.

(5) He recalls with relish that 'the Spirit of the Lord spoke through me' (23.2). Every leader called in some measure to be God's spokesman will savour the experience which David here describes. In his relationship to revelation, of course, David, as part of God's infallible word, stands apart from us. Knowing what forgiveness is at first hand, he can be the prophet of justification by faith. (Ps. 32, Romans 4.6f). Looking ahead down the centuries, as Peter later pictured him, David becomes the prophet of a rescue from death and ascension to glory which only the resurrection and exaltation of his greater son can fulfil (Acts 2.25–35).

While none of us can claim the Spirit's inspiration in such a way or for such a range, we all need to know, whether for public preaching or private counselling, that his word is on our tongues (2 Sam. 23.2). The leader who listens to God before he talks to his people is more likely to find them listening to him. The leader who is in any measure a man after God's heart will covet for himself David's retrospective confidence that 'the Spirit of the Lord spoke through me'. Today's leadership, as never before, knows that worn-out clichés heal no wounds. Apart from the gift of prophecy there have been no gifts I have more earnestly desired of the Holy Spirit than his words of wisdom and knowledge. Just occasionally I think I've been sensible enough not to lean on my own understanding entirely but to let him get his word in edgeways. To make David's claim my own all I need, in common with other leaders, is that what is occasional should become habitual. Then I too might be able to say as a servant of God, that 'the Lord God has given me the tongue of disciples, that I may know how to sustain the weary one with a word. He awakens me morning by morning. He awakens my ear to listen as a disciple.' (Is. 50.4 NASB). Only a warm bed stands between me and being a prophet!

The Lord has the Last Word

Not least among the benefits of hearing God speak is that of learning his views on leadership! In David's last words the last word on leadership is spoken by God. For all the benefit we derive from secular sources on management techniques, leadership training, the art of delegation and counselling and so on, this is not where we begin or end. The writing of this book has behind it the clear desire to let God define leadership for us.

A true leader is one who 'rules over men righteously, who *rules in the fear of God.*' (2 Sam. 23.3 ASB).

No man can be a leader among God's people whose leadership is not rooted in an encounter with the Holy One of Israel. 'The Lord confides in those who fear him' (Ps. 25.14). At the heart of Messiah's spiritual authority and of all who are his delegates is the 'Spirit of knowledge and of the fear of the Lord' (Is. 11.2). This fear will be a delight not a dread. It frees the man of the Spirit from superficial or partial judgements. He will make decisions not on the basis of the way things seem but on the way things are. (Is. 11.3–5). 'He shall draw breath in the fear of God' (George

Adam Smith). Throughout his reign David exemplifies this, making few moves, except the wrong ones, without entering the presence of the Lord for permission. 'David enquired of the Lord' (2 Sam. 2.1). 'David sought the face of the Lord' (2 Sam. 21.1). Because he was sensitive to God's wisdom David discovered the different stratagem needed on each occasion to bring him victory (2 Samuel 5).

Ruling in the fear of God enabled David to accept God's 'no' to his own plans and prevented resentment or negativism from taking root in his life. When things do not work out exactly in the way he has hoped or planned, the leader who lives in the fear of God will not react like a spoiled child. Forbidden by the prophetic word to build the temple he had set his heart on, David comes before the Lord in moving simplicity. 'He sat before the Lord' – a delightful image showing us that the fear of God is not a craven or cringing attitude but the relaxed and restful humility of a son before his Father. 'Who am I, O Sovereign Lord, and what is my family that you have brought me this far. And as if this were not enough in your sight, O Sovereign Lord you have also spoken about the future of the house of your servant' (2 Sam. 7.18–19). God's plans, as David found, are always bigger than ours; what is in his heart always much grander than what is in ours. Knowing this, a man who leads in the fear of God will not be peeved to learn the true scale of his own contribution to God's cause but only proud to feel he has a part to play at all in the grand scheme of things. The fear of the Lord gives both a healthy sense of proportion and a hopeful sense of significance to our best efforts.

Ruling in the fear of God also enables David to take responsibility for his sins and mistakes, for the lust that claims Bathsheba and the pride that numbers the people. Fearing God, David shows a readiness to confess and repent. 'I am the man, Nathan; you are right, I have sinned.' Fearing God with a trembling trust, David submits to God's wrath over the census of Israel, never doubting for a moment that he would sooner take judgement from God than take his chance with men (2 Sam. 24.10–25). In leadership, for sure, the fear of the Lord is the beginning of wisdom. It is this fear that makes us play to God as our audience and frees us from the self-consciousness encouraged by the criticism of others, especially of those closest to us. 'When David returned home to bless his household, Michal daughter of Saul came out to meet him and said, "How the king of Israel has distinguished himself today, disrobing in the sight of the slave girls of his servants as any vulgar fellow would." David said to Michal,

"It was before the Lord, who chose me rather than your father or anyone from this house when he appointed me ruler over the Lord's people Israel – I will celebrate before the Lord" ' (2 Sam. 6.20–21).

God's blessing on the leadership which fears him is poetically described. 'When he rules in the fear of God, he is like the light of morning at sunrise on a cloudless morning, like the brightness after rain that brings the grass from the earth,' (2 Sam. 23.4).

With this lovely description of its effect surely no one can doubt that leadership is a good thing!

I see from it that God-fearing leadership *brings fresh hope* to people. With the dawn of a new day people's hopes of a new start rise. Such a leader will bring a keenness to the air around him. Others will find his leadership and presence invigorating. Coming to a situation that has been locked up in despair or weary resignation an anointed leader can bring a fresh sense of well-being, making people feel again, in a way impossible to articulate, that it is good to be alive. Onesiphorus in this way was able to refresh Paul. 'Many times did that man put fresh heart into me' says the apostle. 'His visits revived me like a breath of fresh air' (2 Tim. 1.16 JBP and LB). God fearing leadership *brings cleanness to the atmosphere around him*. Unresolved issues that have become stale and mouldy are dealt with. Situations on which the door of fear has been shut so that they have become musty have fresh air let into them. The moral atmosphere seems suddenly cleaner and healthier, and the spiritual air sweeter and sounder. A leader ruling in the fear of the Lord will be a moral antiseptic to any community and one which lasts (cf. Ps. 19.9).

God-fearing leadership *brings a new clarity to life* like a rain-washed sky in the morning sun. It sharpens the thinking of God's people. Others begin to see things in a new light because the leader seeks to live in the light of God.

God-fearing leadership *brings a new impartation of energy*. As grass starts to grow in the sunshine that follows rain so things start to happen when a man takes charge who rules in the fear of the Lord. Things start moving again. People start to grow and develop and become fruitful under his leadership. When people become weary in well doing, such a leader can arouse them to new achievements, as Haggai did to the dispirited remnant rebuilding Jerusalem.

All these things David to some measure exemplifies. As a result his house is ordered and secure and prospering (2 Sam. 23.5). There is no place in it for the unsubmissive, for those who refuse to be taken in hand (23.6). Any leader willing to be taken in hand by the fear of God will however bring the dawning of a new day to the Church's life.

So David is a model for leadership not least because at the end of his rule he can still sing about it! The man after God's heart sets a high standard. But God has pledged his prophetic word to have more 'shepherds after my own heart' (Jer. 3.15). Being awed by God but not over-awed by David, we can take heart as leaders from Zechariah's promise that 'the feeblest among them will be like David'! (Zech. 12.8).

10. All The King's Men

One mark of a leader is his ability to attract other men who have leadership potential. With this ability will be a desire to draw out and develop the potential in them. By gathering such men together for this purpose the leader both establishes his own existing leadership and encourages emerging leadership. In my own experience the turning point for introducing change and renewal into a traditional church came when I called together the men of the church to identify with me, my vision and the direction in which I was leading the people. Without this I would have been able to lead the people nowhere. At the same time I began to discover those brothers who had instincts for leadership and over a period of time to delegate responsibility to them, knowing that we were working to the same ends. In this way the work of God advances more rapidly because the revelation given to one man by the Holy Spirit is being entrusted to other 'reliable men who will be qualified to teach others' (2 Tim. 2.2). From the start this has also been the aim of the Towards Leadership training programme in which I am involved. And it is not only strong natural leaders who have benefited from the stimulus this has given them. Unrealised assets lie hidden in many men in our churches for want of recognition and encouragement. For every impetuous Peter needing to be held back there are ten timid Timothys needing to be thrust forth. 'Stir well before using', is more than good advice on the label of a paint pot. Stirred well, in gift and spirit, many men, otherwise reticent, will take their rightful place in the Body and prove their usefulness to it.

To do all this is to fly in the face of current social attitudes. The image of the downtrodden and inadequate male has taken firm hold in our society. The TV critic of a leading national newspaper in Britain deplored the arrival of two new situation comedies as peddling the 'myth that the British male has become in our time a pitiable near-idiot, good for little more than a laugh'.[1] He drew attention to 'what appears to be an unrelenting campaign by TV comedy writers to deny or denigrate the manliness of the native Briton. I need not again detail the long parade of ripe dolts and dunderheads who have made their way across our screens, dropping plates, walking into walls, generally getting it wrong. I look forward', he says, 'to a comedy series which sees the British male as enterprising, masculine and alert'.

Although the robust image shown by the British soldier in the Falklands Campaign may temporarily have stemmed the tide, the trend is well-established in our culture. It is this which makes the success of the award winning British film 'Chariots of Fire' so surprising and so heartening. And no one in their right mind would ever accuse Eric Liddell of being unmanly.

Masculine Spirituality

If the church is to do the will of God then in face of this emasculating trend it will need to teach and demonstrate a new image of Christian manhood. Writing in the magazine Pastoral Renewal, Kevin Perotta has argued that contemporary Christianity lacks a 'clearly articulated understanding of men's relationship with God'.[2] What is needed, Perotta urges, is a revival of what might be called 'masculine spirituality'. The current emphasis in much charismatic thinking is on spiritual and emotional experiences, on an approach to weakness, need and vulnerability which is more psychological than theological. A truer spirituality would affirm our basic dependence on God, our unworthiness to stand before him apart from the atoning work of Jesus, and our absolute reliance on the indwelling power of the Holy Spirit. But on this basis a masculine spirituality would be built which would both challenge and attract men, and prove a viable spiritual framework for the emergence of leadership. In such a spirituality, as P. T. Forsyth once said of Jacob at Peniel, a man would 'cling to God with his strength as well as his weakness'.[3]

David's Mighty Men

This is God's call to men today. Such a spirituality is what is needed to strengthen existing leadership and stimulate emerging leadership. Biblically, no one was a more attractive leader than David and in the features of the men he gathered around him we can see the sketch-plan for a manliness that makes for leadership. From the Cave of Adullam onwards David had the gift of turning a disorganised rabble into a disciplined fighting force. Thirty men formed his outer circle, three men were in his inner more intimate circle. Men of some stature who were included in the thirty did not 'attain to the three' (1 Chron. 11.25). These three loved him enough to die for him. They risked their lives to bring him water from the well in Bethlehem and no one was more sensitive to their sacrifice than David. Now the men who were coming to David were no longer those in need of his patronage or dependent on his provision. With the taking of the Jebusite stronghold of Jerusalem, men of great stature and calibre were attracted to his cause; 'mighty men of valour, men trained for war, who could handle shield and spear, and whose faces were like the faces of lions, and swift as gazelles on the mountains' (1 Chron. 12.8 NASB). We can trace in them pointers to a masculine form of godliness, essential in emerging leaders.

These men gather to David to identify with God's man (1 Chron. 12.1). They *recognise spiritual authority* and rally to God's appointed leader, even while he is still 'restricted because of Saul'. As Israel was 'baptised into Moses' (1 Cor. 10.2) so men of God today are called to find and follow their spiritual fathers, prophets and shepherds and to do so even under the restriction of the old unrenewed structures of the church.

Moved by the Holy Spirit they submit to him, embrace his vision and embark on discipleship and training. (1 Chron. 12.18) 'Then the Spirit came upon Amasai, chief of the Thirty, and he said: 'We are yours, O David! We are with you, O son of Jesse! Success, success to you, and success to those who help you, for your God will help you.' So David received them and made them leaders of his raiding bands'.

So men become in Elton Trueblood's phrase, 'the company of the committed', repudiating the spectator mentality, willing for their lives to be shaped, responding to the prophetic spirit, and learning to be themselves 'leaders of the band'. These men come to *support the leadership, not passively to observe it.* 'Day after day men came to help David' (1 Chron. 12.22). 'Is there anything I can do to help you?' is music in a leader's ears. It marks out the man who can be trusted to lead because of his willingness to serve.

Their concern is with the *kingdom* – the transfer of its authority to the anointed leadership (1 Chron. 12.23). They are willing to bring all areas of life under God's word as they face the changes brought about by the demolition of institutions based on human will (Saul's kingdom) and the restoration of God's rule and choice among his people (David's kingdom).

They will include men of prophetic spirit, men like the sons of Issacher, who *understand the times and know what God's people should do.* (12.32). Not self-regarding in their spirituality, nor narrow-minded, they have an awareness of what God is doing in his world as well as in his church.

Such men are *equipped for battle* (12.24,33). For them life with the people of God is not a rest from their labours but the reason for their labours. For them godliness has to do not only with emotional and psychological needs but also with moral conquest and overcoming. They have a fighting spirit and the zeal of the Lord guarantees their enthusiasm for his work. For them the church is an army not only a refugee camp, a barracks as well as a hospital. The gifts of the Spirit they know are weapons not toys, and meant for real warfare at that, not a ceremonial march-past every Sunday morning! Loyalty counts for such men. They become of *one heart with their leader*, identifying with him without secret reservations (12.33). The colleague who is always trying to keep his options open is liable to find the door to leadership closed. My own experience is still painfully fresh in my mind. I tried to work with a man towards leadership for ten years, sharing our vision and ideas, excited often together by what God was doing and planning. But somehow we never made it together. Our hearts never became indissolubly one. Finally our relationship broke down. As I look back I realise that in the cold times we were never able to warm our hearts at the fire of each other's love. When the heat was on we were never able to rest easily in the shade of each other's trust.

A masculine spirituality will encourage men to *become friends and to share life together* (1 Chron. 12.38–40). Relationships between such men are never formal or institutional. Brotherliness not business is the basis for our being together. Our aim, in Kevin Perotta's words is to 'build a masculine environment in which men can speak openly of their love for God, can learn from one another about handling their responsibilities and difficulties as men, and can support one another as brothers.'(4)

One great benefit of this soon becomes apparent. *Their unanimity breeds unity among the whole of the people* (12.38). When brothers dwell together in unity, 'as many of us have proved, 'there God commands the blessing' of a happy and harmonious fellowship of God's people (Psalm 133).

David now has *men he can consult*, not just opinion-givers but those who can confirm the will of God for the people and themselves begin to take responsibility for implementing it. 'David conferred with each of his officers, the commanders of thousands and commanders of hundreds' (1 Chron. 13.1). The gift of discernment makes men consultants where the gift of suspicion would merely make them critics.

Now of one mind about the desire to let God have full control over them, and mindful of the past neglect of God's presence and power, they command and deserve the assent and confidence of the people in opening up the situation to God again (13.2–4). The people of God do not resent such leadership, feeling that their wishes have been over-ridden in a roughshod way. Rather, they respect united leadership which has a clear grasp of God's will and gladly submit to its direction as being 'right in the eyes of all the people' (13.4 cf. Acts 6).

Leaders of thousands, hundreds, in fact every leader has been drawn into the vision for God's glory and kingdom, and, fired by the initiative of David, is now committed to its outworking.

These pointers to a masculine spirituality clearly strengthen our hand in the reproduction of leaders and the restoration of the church. Then as now, in E. M. Bounds words, 'God wants better men not better methods'.[5]

11. Two Are Better Than One

Leadership should properly be listed as a collective noun. The apostles, let's not forget, went into the world as the animals went into the ark – two by two! As leaders we are not called to 'go solo' all the time. 'Plurality' is the rather ugly word that has recently attached itself to this principle but a rose by any other name is just as sweet and the concept of shared leadership is nowadays becoming more widely appreciated and applied. 'For in abundance of counsellors there is victory' (Prov. 24.6 NASB). The news that the ministry is no longer a 'one-man band' has come as a glorious relief to many, not least to those in the so-called 'full-time' ministry. My brothers have been a great joy to me as I have sought to fulfil my ministry. When I have needed genuine appreciation it has best come from other leaders on a peer-level whose recognition really counts because it is honest and objective. When I have needed support it has been there. When I have needed correction or adjustment it has usually come from the Lord through them. Proverbs deftly describes the way that admonition can get past our defences when given by a friend we trust – 'faithful are the wounds of a friend' (Prov. 27.6). The mental and spiritual stimulus of meeting with other leaders is one of the chief delights of shared ministry. 'As iron sharpens iron so one man sharpens another' (Prov. 27.17). One way to hone the cutting edge of one's own gift and ministry is to keep in honest and loving relationship with other men of equal calibre and calling. I have never found my own role inhibited by this but rather enlarged and enhanced. In fact I suspect that only in such a plurality do we begin to find out who and what we are in God. No one loses authority by shared leadership. Rather my own measure of God-given authority was re-inforced in the eyes of the people when they realised and later saw that behind me were other men of God whose backing they could trust. No longer did they feel that I was a maverick, riding my own particular hobby-horse of vision and strategy but a true representative among many others of what God was saying to his church. This threatened some of course and called their bluff. But for most it was a welcome reassurance and only served to increase my respect among the people.

These obvious gains from shared ministry and the fact that a leader loses nothing by opening his life and ministry to others, should not minimise the cost. 'Its obvious price', as Derek Kidner so aptly puts it, 'is a person's independence; henceforth he must consult another's interest and convenience, listen to another's reasoning, adjust to another's pace and style, keep faith with another's trust.'(1) Meetings with other leaders both within the local church and more widely in an area, now take top priority in my diary. These times together are not regarded as luxuries in my timetable, a welcome but non-essential break from the real work of ministry. On the contrary, we have come to see these as strategic and essential to the work of God in our day. For the same reason the personal enjoyment and strength gained from such relationships should not be taken to imply that they are optional, intended only for the weak in faith or poor in gift. What we are describing in fact is a provision and pattern for leadership which has strong biblical support.

The need for leadership to be shared is perhaps most vividly seen in the ministry of Moses. We view this need first *from the outside*, as it were, looking in – and then, from the inside as we feel the pressure Moses is under. Exodus 18 views the need in Moses' life from the outside through the eyes of Jethro, his father-in-law. Jethro is heard remonstrating with Moses. 'What do you think you are? a one man band? Look at yourself, you're exhausted and I'm not a bit surprised! Have you seen how long those queues are outside the counselling tent? All day some of them have been there; they weren't too pleased when we put the 'closed' sign up tonight. Some of them are still out there waiting for us to open up in the morning. But, Moses, there are a lot of frustrated people out there. There's a lot of hassle nowadays. I'm telling you, it's not good, Moses. What are you up to? Is this a DIY-counselling service or something? Listen to me, Moses! Why are you trying to do it on your own? You'll kill yourself, I'm telling you that! It's not good; it's not good for them and it's not good for you. You'll wear yourself out and you'll wear them out! Don't you see, you can't handle this on your own? Take a piece of advice from your old father-in-law, son . . .' And thankfully, Moses did take Jethro's advice.

What Jethro said was a word in season, in a situation near to getting out of hand. He told Moses three things.

(1) Talk more to God about the people than to the people about their problems (Exod. 18.21). Your wisdom would be worth more if you did, and some problems would disappear immediately.

(2) Teach the people more clearly to walk in God's ways. Many of them will stop being parasitic on your wisdom and good nature and will begin to stand on their own two feet, mature enough to discern for themselves between good and evil (Exod. 18.20, cf. Heb. 5.14).

– and, above all –

(3) Delegate responsibility to others and share the burden of pastoral leadership with them (Exod. 18.21).

The word of the Lord through Jethro even spelt out the kind of men Moses was to select to stand with him in leadership. They were to be able men, capable of ruling over and caring for the people; God-fearing men whose godliness matched their gifts; men of truth keen to bring matters into the light of God's word; unbribable men who could not be corrupted; humble men willing to serve at different levels of responsibility without envy or competitiveness.

In turn these men were not to be left without the covering of Moses but in disputes which demanded too much of them could have recourse to 'higher authority' by bringing the issue to him. Such 'plurality' works! Moses can now endure pressure, his nervous breakdown avoided; the people can now enjoy peace, their rebellious breakout averted! All in all a recipe for righteousness and rest for leader and people.

The Priesthood of Other Believers

For a view of a similar situation *from the inside* we turn to Numbers 11. Here we see that behind the cheerful bedside manner lurks a smouldering irritation not to say resentment. The door bell rings as the family sits down to dinner. 'Hope it's not an inconvenient time to call?'. 'Not at all, come right in; how can I help?' As far as Moses is concerned it's one time too many! Later with the gritted teeth relaxed, he lets God have it. 'Why pick on me, Lord? What did I do to get landed with this lot? Whose children are they anyway? Am I their father? Surely I don't have to spoon-feed them all the time? Do I have to carry them personally into Canaan? Sorry, Lord, it's just not on; I can't cope with it all. It's killing me; I'll be dead and buried before I'm a hundred at this rate. It's not fair; it's an impossible situation.'

Let's face it, we've all been there haven't we? What's more to the point is that the pressure on Moses reflects a pressure on the people. Over this the 'anger of the Lord was kindled' (Numbers 11.10). Sensing this divine concern, Moses reacts defensively and lets his self-pity boil over.

Once again God's answer is *delegated responsibility*. Seventy men are given a measure of the Spirit which rests on Moses for rule and leadership. Because Moses is also a prophet they receive the Spirit of prophecy as a bonus (Num. 11.25). Moses now has Spirit-filled men who can share the weight of leadership with him. Any doubts Moses had felt at his inability to meet the needs of so large a company of people are subdued by this dynamic move of God to meet his own need for help. Because his own load has been lightened, and being a prophet, Moses is given to see in prophetic yearning a yet future company of God's people in whom the prophethood and priesthood is opened to all believers. What it is to lead among such a people Moses was not to know but we do. As leaders in the Body of Christ and as leaders together a microcosm of it, we know the relief of being able to 'bear one another's burdens' for this is the law and the Spirit of Christ to us (Gal. 6.1f). Without this one is left to conclude that 'Every labour which is done is the result of rivalry between a man and his neighbour.' (Eccl. 4.4 NASB). This competitive spirit can be overcome only in a community where men are willing to serve one another for a common end. The loner is in danger not only of being competitive but also of being compulsive. This is the man who never stops to ask himself awkward questions about what he is doing. 'There was a certain man without a dependent, having neither a son nor a brother, yet there was no end to all his labour. Indeed his eyes were not satisfied with riches and he never asked, 'And for whom am I labouring and depriving myself of pleasure'' (Eccl. 4.8 NASB). For him work has become an obsession. The reason for this is that he has no one who is dependent on him. Lacking relationships he has lost the point of what he is doing. But when a man is willing to accept his share of corporate responsibilities his work immediately becomes meaningful. So shared leadership covers a multitude of sins. Above all it is more efficient. D. L. Moody once said 'I would rather set ten men to work than do the work of ten men!'

The effects of shared leadership then are relished by every leader experiencing them. Solomon was right. 'Two are better than one, because they have a good return for their work; if one falls down, his friend can help him up. Also if two lie down together they will keep warm. But how can one keep warm alone? Though one be over-powered, two can defend themselves. A cord of three strands is not quickly broken' (Eccl. 4.9–12). Here in shared life is shared success, help, comfort, protection and strength.

(1) Here is 'a good return for labour', an increased measure of success for those who share leadership. So Moses needs Aaron as his mouthpiece and, with Hur, as the upholder of his praying arms for Israel to prevail. Ezra is matched by Nehemiah and both need the prophets if the work is not to be left half-finished. Zechariah is the visionary ('I saw flying scrolls'); Haggai the practical prophet ('Go and chop wood'); each perfectly complements the other in a way that makes their joint success greater than the sum of what each could have achieved on his own.

(2) Here is mutual support for 'if one falls down his friend can lift him up.' 'At my first defence no one supported me but all deserted me' confesses Paul, regretting the lack of what he was normally used to. Elsewhere he greets Priscilla and Aquila as a leadership couple and fellow-workers who risked their necks for him (Rom. 16.3).

(3) Here is the warmth of love and fellow-feeling for 'how can one keep warm on his own?' The devil has done his utmost in our generation to debase genuine love between men but he has not succeeded. Even in the media he let one or two items slip through his net. The success of the American TV series 'Starsky and Hutch' was fascinating for this reason at least. It clearly showed a close, manly friendship and brotherliness between two New York cops, two buddies unashamed to show physical affection or their evident concern for each other – and all without a trace of innuendo as to the propriety of the relationship. The biblical precedent is even more clear and satisfying. 'The soul of Jonathan was knit to the soul of David' (1 Sam. 18.1 NASB). In this deep bond of manly love, sealed in covenant, they find tremendous support and mutual delight. His life threatened by Saul, David constantly looks to his friend for help and rescue. When out in the cold it is to Jonathan he looks for warmth and welcome. 'And Jonathan went to David and encouraged him in God' (1 Sam. 23.16 NASB). No wonder David mourned for Jonathan, and for losing the comfort of a love which surpassed the love of women. Any leader who scorns this or is a stranger to it is the poorer for it. Paul for his part longs to see Timothy for without him his joy is halved (2 Tim. 1.4). Stephanas, Fortunatus, and Achaicus

have refreshed Paul's spirit (1 Cor. 16.18). And as for Titus what could be more moving and revealing of the true humanity the Holy Spirit creates among leaders than this: 'I still had no peace of mind because I did not find my brother Titus there', but later 'God who comforts the downcast, comforted us by the coming of Titus' (2 Cor. 2.13, 7.6).

(4) Here is safety and defence for 'two can defend themselves'. Leaders find safety in an 'abundance of counsellors'. 'Many advisors make victory sure' and plans succeed with many advisors (Prov. 11.14, 15.22). This is the wisdom from above which is 'open to reason and willing to yield' (James 3.17). Here a leader can test his plans and dreams on the sounding board of his brothers' discernment. After much debate and hard-thinking James announced that it 'seemed good to us and to the Holy Spirit.' So one or two prophets may judge the revelation purporting to be from God. In this way the leadership is saved from individual arrogance and error and the Body of Christ protected from the tyranny of the self-willed leader's private interpretation of what God is saying. For 'no prophecy of Scripture is a matter of one's own interpretation' (2 Peter 1.20). So the gathered prophets and teachers confirm the call of God in Paul and Barnabas (Acts. 13.1f), while the elders in concert confirm the gift for leadership becoming apparent in the young man Timothy (1 Tim. 4.16) by laying on of hands and prophetic utterance. In this submitting of our ideas and judgements to other leaders we find safeguards against deception and confidence for action. By submitting our intuitions to one another, we let in the fear of God which is the beginning of wisdom.

(5) Here finally is the secret of surprising strength for 'a threefold cord cannot easily be broken'. Sharing our leadership in the way we have described is not just a useful stratagem, a convenient tactic for making the church run more smoothly. In it there is a mysterious working of supernatural strength. 'Where two or three come together in my name there am I with them.' And this is just the gathering of strength. For 'if two of you on earth agree about anything you ask for, it will be done for you by my Father who is in heaven' (Matt. 18.19–20). Even in his unique agreement with the Father, Jesus admits to a reliance upon the same divine principle. 'I am the one who testifies for myself; my other witness is the one who sent me – the Father' for 'it is written that the testimony of two men is valid' (John

8.17). Jesus and the apostles had presumably walked past the lame man at the gate of the Temple many times until one day Peter and John felt within them and in the strength of their relationshisp, a mysterious agreement. 'Look at us' they said, and out of the mouths of these two apostles, in a unity of faith, is established the truth that the name of Jesus brings healing and salvation as no other name can do! Leaders in heart agreement form a partnership for power that we have scarcely begun to exploit.

Not Another Committee

So far so good. There is room only for a few cautions on the outworking of plurality amongst leaders. One is that we may rush into it too quickly, running the risk of being 'hasty in the laying on of hands' (1 Tim. 5.22). Eager to grasp the principle, find the relief, and enter into the power of shared leadership, a man of God may act impetuously. To draw in too many men too soon simply in order to achieve a numerical 'plurality' is self-defeating. Most of your time will be cut out solving problems among your hastily assembled leadership group. Too many leaders in this case spoil the broth. Their lack of gift may well make them unacceptable to the people; their lack of grace unworkable with as fellow-leaders. Either way the desired effect is forestalled. The priesthood of all believers does not mean the leadership of anyone, any more as we saw than it means the leadership of no one! Charismatic worship for example fails when there are too many ostensible 'leaders' all 'having a go' with the result that the people feel nagged rather than exhorted and become insecure, not knowing really who their shepherd is. Rush into a recognition of plurality and you risk denying the gifts and calling of God without which no man can be leader.

A second caution is one Charles Blair expresses out of an experience of losing the safety in numbers which plurality should bring. 'Are your co-workers a completion of yourself? Or simply an extension. If I am called to leadership and find helpers who are simply echoes of myself, I double my strengths but I also double my weaknesses.'[2] Leaders who 'measure themselves by themselves . . . are not wise' (2 Cor. 10.12). Comparisons within our own circle are rarely odious and this is good but they need to be honest. As Rehoboam discovered, the views of some men you consult are not worth having because they merely echo your own immaturity (1 Kings 12.1ff). Plurality needs to be a true meeting of ministries that are genuinely complementary to one another, not carbon copies of each other. This forges a relationship which is strong enough to allow a Paul to withstand a Peter to his face and not lose friendship.

Lastly, we must not let plurality blur the clarity that anointed leadership brings to a church. In an effort to be humble and submissive we may falsely try to play down our distinctive abilities and ministry. Like it or not though all leaders are equal, some are more equal than others! It would be ironic to avoid the pitfalls of democratic church government only to fall into the trap of leadership by committee. And we all know what happened to the horse designed by a committee!

None of this should deter us from walking down the road of plural leadership for the gains are too precious to miss. Concealed in this simple strategy for leadership is the very life of God himself. In his trinity of love and power there is surrender of individualism without loss of identity, and subordination of will without inferiority of status. Since Bethlehem it can never be 'beneath me' to 'come under' someone else. This is the greatest incentive we need to enter into the joy of shared leadership and – if we are already enjoying it – the greatest incentive to keep it. Maintain this subtle unity and God has a blessing commanded for us. It's something worth guarding at any cost. After all, Gilbert and Sullivan fell out over a carpet and never spoke to one another again!

12.   Without Fear or Favour

On my first trip to Israel I was privileged to visit the splendid Museum of the Diaspora in Tel Aviv. On the wall of a section devoted to the Jewish community's government of its affairs I found inscribed this word of wisdom, attributed to Rabbi Israel Salanter. 'A rabbi whose community does not disagree with him is not really a rabbi; and a rabbi who fears his community is not really a man.'

The relationship between a leader and those he leads is rarely very simple. Its complexities cannot easily be analysed. But one thing is clear. This relationship makes great demands upon a leader's emotional and psychological resources. He is called to a variety of responses as befits the needs of his people and the immediate pressure of God. Paul's emotional agility is a gift from God. 'To the Jews I became a Jew, to those without the law as without law . . . to the weak I became weak'. Timothy was urged to be equally sensitive in his relationships, for the tone and stance appropriate to one person is inappropriate to another (1 Tim. 5.1). This flexibility in response takes time and maturity to achieve if we ever do. Too often this healthy emotional growth is stifled at the outset of one's leadership.

My experience as a minister in a main-line non-conformist denomination confirmed this. I would like to think this only happens to men in churches where congregational-type forms of church government are in operation, though having observed leaders from other traditions I doubt it. On entering the pastorate of such churches the new leader finds himself without choice enmeshed in a whole web of expectations of what he should and should not be doing. His attitudes are in part programmed in advance by the concept of ministry he is working under. It is assumed that he will act as a figurehead to whatever organisations he has inherited, irrespective of their value. It is expected of him without question that he will play certain well-defined traditional roles in the ecclesiastical game. His independence of action and reaction is severely curtailed and his range of possible responses narrowed down by a quickly acquired sense of the people's assent or disapproval. He rapidly becomes *typecast* and often stilted and stereotyped in his humanity.

All this is subtly reinforced by his dependence on the people for his stipend and house. To notice this is not sour grapes, nor is it to question the sincerity of those who operate the system. Still less does it imply that all pastors are cowards. Yet even raising these kind of issues in ministers' fraternals has brought wrath down on my head. Much of this is an understandable defensive reaction. But the question of where a leader derives his emotional security from is one that needs to be faced. If a leader is voted in, he can be voted out not always for godly reasons. Hired on flimsy evidence he can be fired for even less. Not that being popular is proof against the process I am describing. We all like to be liked. When all men speak well of us is maybe just the time when we need to examine the basis of our emotional security. For the situation I have outlined is a recipe for caution and conserving the status quo. Only men of a strong prophetic spirit and a certain emotional detachment avoid succumbing to it. It is heartening to realise that Jesus faced both popularity and hostility and treated those two imposters just the same. 'They got up, drove him out of the town, and took him to the brow of the hill on which the town was built, in order to throw him down the cliff. But he walked right through the crowd and went on his way' (Luke 4.29). 'After the people saw the miraculous sign that Jesus did they began to say 'Surely this is the Prophet who is to come into the world'. Jesus, knowing that they intended to come and make him king by force, withdrew again into the hills by himself' (John 6.14–15). No one is suggesting a fate or a temptation anything like as grand for us as for him. Our crosses and our carrots are altogether on a much more minor scale. But then our resistance is so much lower than his that we need to keep him in our sights. Secure in his Father's love and calling, satisfied with nothing less than the Father's joy and reward, he cut through the web of other people's enforced expectations. They had not paid him to be the Piper and so could not call his tune. There was no threat that could deter him and no inducement divert him from his Father's will. At this point it is good to ask a question or two about my emotional well-being as a leader of God's people.

Am I Motivated to Lead by my own Emotional Insecurity?

The danger here is that leadership meets too great a psychological need in my life than is good for my integrity in ministry. A survey by a clinical psychologist of over 50 of America's top comedians found that most of them were sad and depressed men. Their comedy performances were an outlet for their rage and anxiety. What kept them going psychologically was the love and laughter of the audience. Similar pitfalls face any frontman even in spiritual ministry, as A. W. Tozer has pointed out. 'The free man has never been a religious tyrant, nor has he lorded it over God's heritage. It is fear and lack of self-assurance that has led men to try to crush others under their feet.'[(1)] Every one of us has emotional deficiencies of some kind, but it is probably wise not to appoint as leaders those who have serious psychological problems. This may be one reason for Paul's warning about appointing recent converts to positions of responsibility within the church. The overseer 'must not be a recent convert, or he may become conceited . . .' (1 Tim. 3.6). Every one of us was a newcomer to leadership at some time or another and we must make allowances if budding leaders are to develop. But in the current trend among charismatic churches towards greater freedom and naturalness in public ministry and meetings I have noticed a constant fault among emerging leaders. In an effort to be relaxed and natural with the people, they have become slovenly in style and expression. They often behave in a 'jokey' and self-conscious way that makes others embarrassed. But no one should impose his immaturity on others under the guise of greater informality.

Scrambled Ego

Even those of us who are neither neurotic nor novices end up in a tangle of emotional reactions from time to time. When, for example, I am afraid to disagree or am annoyed at being disagreed with, the warning signs are there. My zeal to call down fire on those I think my enemies may on reflection turn out like James' and John's outburst to be merely natural hot-headedness (Luke 9.54). My excessive caution when adventurous moves are suggested and my proneness to raise every conceivable obstacle to committing myself to some new initiative may appear to be the height of wisdom and maturity. In fact, like the leader in the parable, I may be burying my talent, venturing nothing because I do not know God well enough to make mistakes, fearing his wrath when I should be trusting his grace (Luke 19.21).

To attempt to 'un-mix' our motives is as futile as trying to unscramble an egg. Paul didn't attempt such self-analysis: 'I do not even judge myself. My conscience is clear but that does not make me innocent. It is the Lord who judges me.' (1 Cor. 4.4).

Unscrambling our mixed-up egos is the Lord's work for when he comes 'he will bring to light what is hidden in darkness and will expose the motives of men's hearts.' So the answer to all this is not an obsessive introspection. What I need to do is to repent and to gain God's sense of proportion. I need to get things into perspective again and to renew that purity of heart which seeks God's glory above all else.

Am I Governed by Fear in Attempts to be a Leader?

Newcomers are especially vulnerable here. Joshua feels it when faced with the task of succeeding Moses in the leadership of Israel. Timothy feels it when given responsibility by Paul, his 'spiritual father'. 'Be strong and very courageous' Joshua is urged. 'Fear not' seems a recurring exhortation in God's instruction manual for leaders. Isaiah is called not to fear what the people fear (Is. 8.12). Jeremiah was commanded: 'Do not be afraid of them for I am with you and will rescue you' (1.8). To fear men here would only plunge the prophet into deeper doubt. 'Do not be terrified by them or I will terrify you before them' is what the prophet hears and it cuts off his escape route immediately. The Lord is quick to add by way of reassurance: 'Today I have made you a fortified city . . . they will fight against you but will not overcome you' (Jer. 1.18–19). 'Do not be afraid of them or their word' is the encouragement Ezekiel receives (Ezek. 2.6). In a vision Paul is told: 'Do not be afraid, keep on speaking, do not be silent' as he faces the daunting task of evangelising pagan Corinth (Acts 18.9).

Inferiority and inadequacy can make us emotional cripples.

'I'm not young enough' (Abraham).
'I'm not eloquent enough' (Moses).
'I'm not old enough' (Jeremiah).

These can be our first reactions when faced with God's call to lead. Abraham is told not to limit the possibilities open to God, Moses is given a partner to be his spokesman. Timothy is told to let no man 'despise his youth', nor to bury his talent in the field of defeatism and inferiority but to dig it up and use it! 'For God did not give us a spirit of timidity but a spirit of power, love and self-discipline' (2 Tim. 1.7).

The task of restoring order and truth to the church of God is hard enough in our day for us to be able to identify with Nehemiah. Faced with fierce antagonism and opposition to the work of reconstruction to which he is called, he sees clearly what is happening. 'For all of them were trying to frighten us, "Their hands will not get too weak for the work and it will not be completed". But I prayed, "Now strengthen my hands"' (Neh. 6.9).

I recall an incident some years ago when the church of which I was pastor was at a crucial and early stage of renewal. Not everything I was teaching or seeking to do was proving acceptable to everyone. Hostility to me as the leader was increasing. One lady wrote me a very bitter and accusing letter. My father was staying with us at the time and he knew what to do. 'Let's bring this to the Lord, son'; and we did, spreading the letter out on the bed as we knelt beside it. We prayed that the Lord would strengthen my hands so that I might not be deterred by fear from going through with the changes the Holy Spirit was calling us to. Later I realised there was good scriptural precedent for this in the life of Hezekiah. Receiving a hostile and accusing letter from Rabshakah, I read, 'Hezekiah spread it out before the Lord' asking the Lord to deal with it and the opposition it expressed (Is. 37.14). What the Lord did for Hezekiah he did in fact do for me if less dramatically. The lady left for a new postal district! Out of this experience and others like it later I was able to encourage another Pastor who was also being used of God to bring change to the church. He too was being unjustly and bitterly misrepresented and resisted by some members of his church. I gave him a slip of paper. Written on it were two lines of a hymn by Charles Wesley which I had recently taken to heart.

'Shall I for fear of feeble men
The Spirit's course in me restrain?'

If nothing else it gave me, as I hope it did him, a wholesome sense of perspective and helped me laugh at myself and my fears.

As the wise man saw, 'the fear of man brings a snare' (Prov. 29.25). The escape for the leader here as elsewhere is that 'fear of the Lord which is the beginning of wisdom' and the start of an emotional stability in his relationship with the people he is called to lead. The fear of the Lord frees me as a leader from the anxious need to defend or vindicate myself. The love of the Father frees me to challenge people's assumptions and to break the mould even at the risk of their misunderstanding. The leader who grows towards this end will stay genuine and avoid the typecasting that can destroy his integrity.

13. Alarm Bells for Leaders

Every leader has his weak spot! Graffiti scrawled on a wall in Canterbury during Dr. Coggan's reign as Archbishop and Primate of all England, accused: 'Dr. Coggan cheats at Scrabble.' Were this all we had to worry us as leaders we could rest easy but unfortunately it isn't. Leaders are in the frontline of the spiritual battle. Often they are among its first victims. Leaders are exposed to pressures and temptations beyond the usual run of testing. Pitfalls face the unwary and traps abound even for the experienced. 'We all stumble in many ways' as the apostle James observed. For this reason the apostolic advice is clear: 'Not many of you should presume to be teachers, my brothers, because you know that we who teach will be judged more strictly' (James 3.1).

Charles Blair's story is a salutary one. Pastor of one of the biggest churches in America, his drive and ambition led him and his people into debt and litigation. Found guilty of the fraudulent sale of securities, Dr. Blair faced total humiliation. His realism, and honesty in accepting responsibility and his subsequent restoration make for moving reading. 'Alarm bells should have rung', he admits, 'when they called me the "man who could do no wrong" '.[1]

'Take heed to yourself and your ministry' was more than once Paul's word of warning. 'Watch your life closely, keep a grip on your life's purpose, concentrate on your ministry' – these bring out the flavour of his apostolic injunctions (Acts 20.28), 1 Tim. 4.16). The misgivings about leadership that have been hinted at so far in this book have now huddled together in this chapter and we need to look at them in order to be on our guard against them. Mistakes can be avoided if a leader will only ask himself the right questions.

1. Am I over-concerned with image building?

Am I more ready to believe what people say about me than what I know God says about me? Am I becoming less able to cope with their appreciation, turning their praise into flattery which feeds my vanity? Paul needed a deliverance from the people before he could safely minister to them! (Acts. 26.17). Professionalism is the greatest danger here, forming a protective shield behind which a man may cherish all kinds of inflated ideas of his own importance. Have I become adept at deflecting just criticism by pulling rank or manipulating the situation to put myself in a good light? To have no guile here is to be really blessed. Overexposure to spiritual things can breed unreality unless we are living in the good of them. Fenelon once pointed out that reading about extraordinary matters can stimulate our imagination to the point where self-love flatters itself that it has attained the attitudes it admires in the books.

2. Am I a member of the Body of Christ?

'For the first time', I once heard Graham Pulkingham say, 'the clergy are joining the church!' This is good news, for the very men most concerned about the 'fringers' have often been one of them. When I was a student it was received ministerial wisdom for the pastor not to have any close friends in the church. Doubtless many still believe it as they eke out their lives in loneliness. Leaders who can't be ministered to by the people they are serving lose, as Peter was in danger of doing, a large and personal share of Jesus in his body (John 13.8). Having overcome the fear of being taken advantage of, my wife and I enjoyed and depended on the prayers, support and friendship of the saints in the church of which I was pastor for 13 years.

3. Do I have a growing awareness of the extent of my gift and ministry?

Am I moving easily within what God has called me to be? Every leader needs to know his limitation, his measure, and his sphere.

(a) He needs to know the *limitation of his gift*. When Peter said 'not the cross, Lord' he was falling into the trap of knowing better than the Lord, of presuming to dictate to him what should and should not happen. But to do this is to fail to recognise the limits of one's gift and is to forget that each of us has a God-given responsibility to bear which need not burden us.

(b) He needs to know his *measure of faith*. Peter failed here in becoming over-confident, in thinking that his loyalty was beyond question. This is precisely where we need to take heed to ourselves as leaders. With each gift comes 'a measure of faith' (Romans 12.3f). It may be enlarged but is sufficient for the task in hand. To go beyond it involves us in dangerous presumption; to stay within it brings joy to us and benefit to the body of Christ.

(c) He needs to know *his sphere of service*. Peter in his enthusiasm was tempted to assume responsibility which God was not giving him. But he was told that it was none of his business what another man was given to do. Paul wanted to re-assure the Corinthians about himself and his team that 'we will not boast beyond our measure but within the measure of the sphere which God apportioned to us . . .' (2 Cor. 10.12–18 NASB). In fact our authority has greater weight, Paul says, because 'we are not over-extending ourselves'. Pressed to undertake commitments on every side, today's leaders would do well to take this to heart. Knowing our limitations is a saving grace. When Thomas Buckley ran for the post of auditor of Massachusetts in 1941, his speech is said to have consisted of just seven words: 'I am an auditor, not an orator!' He won. It may never be as cut-and-dried as this for men of the Spirit growing into an always expanding ministry. But Paul at least did not seem abashed at regularly defining who and what he was.

Character and Charisma

4. Have I a healthy determination to maintain integrity?

Many of the great 'healers' of the 1950's in America came to a sad end. Some died young, others took to drink or drugs, others still took early retirement and live out their lives in obscurity. With such immense gifts amidst a supernatural outpouring it is tempting to ask what went wrong. Before we judge such men too harshly we need to appreciate the tremendous pressures such a ministry put them under. Clearly in too many cases these men over-loaded their systems, living beyond their emotional, spiritual and moral resources. Their charisma outstripped their characters. Character weaknesses were overlooked in the glamour and pressure of the ministry of the miraculous. The fact that God in his infinite mercy did not withhold his power or his anointing led many to the wrong conclusion that miracles justified immorality. In Judson Cornwall's words, 'Pride in their success, attitudes of superiority over other ministers, resentment toward people for the pressures they exerted on them, and an inflated self-evaluation of their own personal worth took its toll'.[2] Deception was not far away. It was not long before many of these greatly gifted servants of God felt themselves to be above normal standards and criteria, operating to a different law of righteousness from everyone else, not answerable or accountable as others were for their inconsistencies and lack of integrity. The way to avoid this slippery slope is by an honest facing and confessing of our weaknesses and mistakes, consistent willingness to 'judge ourselves that we be not judged', and a commitment to 'seek first the kingdom of God and his righteousness'.

Asking 'Why?'

5. Am I prepared to ask awkward questions of my own leadership?

Comparison with the temptations of the Lord Jesus will help to underline this need to scrutinise our motives closely. Jesus was first tempted to *prove* his sonship by performing miracles. Like him we do not need to prove ourselves to Father in this way. But insecurity at this point will cause us to strive too hard for success. Like the compulsive worker described by Solomon, we may succumb to activism, never asking 'And for whom am I labouring?' (Eccl. 4.8). Zeal without knowledge was a feature of the worst kind of Pharisaism. The problem in this is a failure to ask 'Why?'; why am I doing this? why am I going there? Asking the question will at least keep us on our toes, help to cleanse us of egotism and revive in us an exclusive concern for God and his glory.

Asking 'How?'

Jesus was next tempted to *presume* on his sonship to do a startling but needless act. The danger of presumption is ever-present, especially for men called to an adventurous ministry of faith. Moses strikes the rock to produce water on one occasion and then presumes quite wrongly that this is to be God's method on a later occasion. Once before he had confused carnal zeal with spiritual boldness when he fell into the trap of '*supposing* that his brethren understood that God was granting them deliverance through him' (Acts 7.25 NASB). This is to mistake self-will for God's will. It is to have a God-given idea but to make wrong assumptions about the methods God wants to employ. The question to ask is the one Mary asked; '*how*, Lord?' Having the vision as Charles Blair found is only half the story. 'The second half is discovering his means for bringing it about.'[3] God's ends do not justify our means. We need to ask him how he wants us to act or to approach a matter, as David was wise enough to do (2 Samuel 5).

Asking 'When?'

Jesus was also tempted to *pre-empt* the gains of the cross by accepting the kingdoms of this world from the hands of the devil. Abraham tried to speed up the fulfilment of God's promise and got Ishmael for his pains. 'Impatience', says Charles Blair, 'was my biggest problem.'[4] We want a short-term success at the expense of God's long-term will. We over-ride scruples and mis-givings in an attempt to be men of faith. We put our faith in faith, claim more than we can honestly provide evidence for, exaggerate the effects of our work – all in a desire to accelerate the hand of God. This is sheer presumption. It shows a consistent unwilling-ness to ask the crucial question '*When?*'. To seek to know God's timing is especially the need of men with prophetic vision who otherwise might seek to hasten and thus distort God's programme (1 Peter 1.10, cf. 1 Tim. 5.22).

Asking '*why?, how?*' and '*when?*' then is the kind of self-scru-tiny that will help us avoid many pitfalls. Of the others, two are perhaps quite obvious but worth mentioning for that reason.

6. Am I becoming authoritarian?

One sign of this in a leader is that he becomes over defensive in the face of criticism. He finds it difficult to hear any criticism of his work without becoming resentful. And what of his attitudes to those in his care? A pastoral leader can sometimes degenerate into a mere 'busy-body' anxious to put other people right. At worst, like Rehoboam who forsook the wisdom of his father Solomon, a leader can become over-bearing and harsh. Ignoring the advice of the more experienced elders who assured the new king that he would win the hearts of the people if he was willing to serve them, Rehoboam listened instead to the counsel of hot-headed younger men who urged him to assert his authority and make the yoke of the people heavier not lighter (1 Kings 12.1–11). This domineering spirit is one we need to guard against. We are called to shepherd the flock of God 'not lording it over' those

entrusted to us (1 Peter 5.3). There is one final question that
needs asking.

7. Am I serving the Lord or his house?

The distinction is made by the prophet Ezekiel who tells us that
the sons of Zadok were rewarded for their faithfulness by being
called to minister directly to the Lord while others merely served
the sanctuary (Ezekiel 44.15f). Neglecting our personal ministry
to the Lord is a perennial danger for leaders. It was partly to
offset this that the apostles involved others in the work of administration so that they could devote their full attention to the ministry
of the word and prayer. Jesus told a pertinent parable about this.
After a long hard day in the fields, a servant arrives home to be
told by his master: 'Prepare my supper, get yourself ready and
wait on me' (Luke 17.8). Beyond all the tiring and necessary work
demanded of us in his service, we are also called to minister to
the master's own personal satisfaction. To worship him, to love
him, to wait upon him, is a leader's greatest safeguard as well as
his greatest refreshment. The question, the Chief Shepherd most
wants his under-shepherds to answer is not 'Do you know more
than these?' or 'do more than these?'. It is 'do you love me more
than these?'. Keeping this in mind, the self-questioning leader will
not hear the alarm bells toll for him. Before we leave the subject
and to do justice to the Apostle Peter, we take note of F. F.
Bruce's verdict on him. 'Peter had it in him to be a stone of
stumbling or a foundation stone. Thanks to the intercession which
his master had made for him in a critical hour, he strengthened
his brethren and became a rock of stability and a focus of unity'.[5]

14. Watergate in the Church

One of Britain's most-respected preachers admitted to me ruefully when talking of two fellowships with which he was involved, that 'one had no leadership, the other had wrong leadership'. Apart from having no leadership at all, the next worse thing that can befall any community of God's people is to have bad leadership. Ever since Nadab and Abihu, there have been those only too ready to offer strange fire on the altar of God's service by taking matters into their own hands. Ever since Uzzah steadied the Ark, men have tried to balance things up as if they knew better than God. Some have been simply misguided, a few openly cynical, but phonies, charlatans, and hirelings have climbed over the wall of God's fold all too often.

According to the prophet Isaiah, one way in which God exercises judgement on his people is by removing their established leaders altogether (Isaiah 3.1–12). The ensuing vacuum is quickly filled by opportunists, by the inexperienced and immature, by capricious and incompetent youths, by women acting as men or, worse, by men acting as women! 'Israel's kings will be like babies, ruling childishly' (3.4 LB). 'O my people!' grieves the Lord, through his prophet, 'can't you see what fools your rulers are? Weak as women! – Foolish as little children playing king. True leaders? No, misleaders!' (3.12 LB). The results of this are tragic (3.6–7). Leadership goes begging, standards fall, desperation sets in until 'anybody will do'. The reluctant are press-ganged into leadership and arm-twisting replaces the call of God.

This is serious if for no other reason than that a people's prosperity is measured by its priests, its level of life by its standard of leadership. The prophets plainly laid the responsibility for Israel's declension at the door of its official leaders. Prophets who prophesy falsely, priests who lack knowledge, kings who rule unjustly, shepherds who pull the wool over everyone's eyes – all feel the impact of the prophetic indictment (Jeremiah 2.8, Ezekiel 22.6). Where renewal is needed it starts with repentant leaders (Joel 2.17).

The current resurgence of interest in spiritual leadership as vital for the Church's welfare and progress has not come a moment too soon. It is very clearly the need of the hour. In Britain at least, the church has suffered from a generation of false leaders who have sold out to the theological bankruptcy of liberalism.[1] Having repudiated the supernatural in favour of philosophy, having torn-up an infallible Bible, these 'shepherds' have scattered the flock and destroyed its faith. Now God is raising up a new generation of leaders at every level of the church's life to be the leaven in the lump.

But so important is it to guard the flock of God from its hireling shepherds, that we must note the marks of false leadership. Jeremiah 8 is a prophetic place to start.

False leaders have an unquestioning trust in accepted tradition. Complacently going by the book, they may fail to realise how badly they are confusing God's will with men's wisdom (8.8–9). They are the 'blind leading the blind' which, with an appropriate religious veneer, becomes the 'bland leading the bland'. 'Shadow boxing' Paul called it; 'going through the motions' might be his description now. Every leader must fear the onset of this disease. Constant contact with the living God is the only safeguard against it.

False leaders are mere professionals. If few are in it for the money – so poorly paid has the church's traditional ministry been – the temptation still confronts men in various forms (8.10). When the role outstrips the emotional security we have, then keeping our status may become subtly but surely too important to us. This is to feed ourselves rather than the sheep and is to run the gauntlet of Ezekiel's protest (Ezek. 34.2,8). Clifford Hill has said 'I often speak to ministers who admit they have no faith and don't know what they really believe, but who are caught in the trap of the ministry . . .'[2]

One recurrent feature of leaders who lack integrity and truth is that *they pander to the people.* Speaking to please the people, telling their hearers what they want to hear, false prophets bring superficial healing to the church's deep wounds. Afraid to be unpopular, such leaders lull their followers into a false sense of complacency before God (8.11). Ezekiel calls this 'smearing whitewash'. Speaking 'pleasant things' and 'illusions' is how Isaiah describes it (Is. 30.10). Paul warned Timothy of the time coming when men, tiring of 'sound doctrine' and 'to suit their own desires', will 'gather around them a great number of teachers to say what their ears want to hear' (2 Tim. 4.3). The true prophet of God will not be misled by receiving appreciation for his style at the expense of adherence to his word (Ezek. 33.30–33). And the true son of the prophets among the messengers of Jesus will be uneasy when too many speak too well of him (Luke 6.26) 'for in the same way their fathers used to treat the false prophets'.

This sensitivity to God and his truth is lacking in the false leaders. According to Jeremiah he is *shameless in his contribution to the scandal he is part of*. He does not 'even know how to blush' (Jer. 8.12). He feels no pain at the reproach God's people bear. He is impervious to the embarrassment God feels at his people's disgrace. But the true leader is grieved that God's advertisement in the world is so poor a representation of him. 'Let the Lord's ministers weep and let them say: "Spare Thy people, O Lord, and do not make thine inheritance a reproach, a byword among the nations" ' (Joel 2.17 NASB). And they do this not because denominational statistics are in a nose-dive but because the world has stopped even asking 'where is your God?'

The false leader to be sure may not lack enthusiasm for his task. He is often *keen to try out his own theories* on an unsuspecting people. But his own theories are exactly what they are and God's revealed will what they are not. 'I have not sent them nor appointed them' is God's dismissive judgement on such men (Jer. 14.14). 'They are prophesying to you a false vision, futility, and the deception of their own mind' (v14 NASB). Such an assessment runs the risk of being toned down in our indulgent and over-tolerant age, marked down as 'a fascinating point of view' or 'a controversial contribution to the debate'. So old heresies have tried to make a comeback in new disguises, usually clerical ones. Theology, the queen of sciences once, is almost thoroughly discredited as an academic discipline as unbelieving scholars dissect the minutiae of each other's increasingly far-fetched theories. 'I am against the prophets who steal from one another words supposedly from me' (Jer. 23.30) – almost a reconvening of Ezekiel's 'conspiracy in our midst' (Ezek. 22.25 NASB).

Nor are we evangelicals and charismatics immune. Although we are not liable to fall for the latest 'myth of God incarnate' heresy, we are liable to hook the complete red-herring. Bryn Jones, a widely recognised prophetic leader in Britain, was moved to write a warning letter some years ago. At a time of energy crisis, some believers claimed to be receiving prophecies directing them to stockpile food and resources against the evil day. As Bryn pointed out this was a wrong and unbiblical reaction made out of fear not faith. What made it more insidious was the fact that its spokesmen were respected figures. As Bryn pointed out, prophets who prophesy falsely are even more dangerous than false prophets. 'False prophets,' he wrote, 'bear no relation to Christ, whereas the prophets who prophesy falsely will be, at heart, good men of standing and reputation in their spheres of influence and consequently with their being deceived will speak out of their own minds and hearts and not out of the mouth of God.'

'The false prophet', in John Oman's classic definition, 'is a shell gathering up and echoing the temper of the age; the true prophet is no echo of the moods and passions of the age but a living voice declaring what is its true lesson'.[3]

To the men in ministry with whom I regularly meet this true word of prophecy was given.

'I do not want you to be men who collect things from other men like Aaron.

I want you to go up the mountain yourselves.

I want you to be men of *the first phase not the second phase*.

You are to be men of integrity even above human friendship and to press on with me.

You are to come down and be angry if need be with the people, not popular; otherwise you will produce a copy of something seen long ago.

I will lead my people through men who have been in my presence.

I will speak and engrave it in your hearts.

You will see things. Be impatient for this, to see things.

Be discontented, not satisfied with a collection of gold from other men.

For what I say and do will be eternal.'

As a prophecy it was just for us: but as a prayer I share it with you. Pray it with me and keep strange fire off God's altars.

15.   Checkpoint

It's time for a check-up to see if the story so far is our story.

1. Am I using the *ability* God has given me?
    In fact, what is my basic gift? What other gifts do I desire
    in order to serve the Lord better? Do I need to stir up the
    gifts I have to fulfil my potential?

2. What is my *ambition* as a servant of God?
    Are my aspirations godly desires or private fantasies? Am I
    'seeking great things' for myself or am I wanting to do more
    with a view to glorifying God?

3. Have I an *anointing* for what I am doing?
    Do I need the Holy Spirit to do it or not? Am I relying on
    the resources and energies of the Spirit or getting by on my
    own? Am I eking out my strength in Christian ministry or
    am I 'always abounding in the work of the Lord'?

4. Is my ministry by divine *appointment*?
    Am I pushy or an opportunist or do I have a genuine calling
    in God? Have I the deep unrest that comes from attempting
    to be a self-made ministry or do I have the peace which
    comes from working within the scope of my calling?

5. Who gave me *authority* to do what I am doing?
    Do I submit to the authority of the Word of God by being
    a doer of it as well as a hearer of it? What is the impact of
    my life (what I am), my calling (what my role is) and my
    function (what I can do)? Am I under the authority of any
    other man or men of God?

6. Does my ministry find its *authentication* in my life?
    Do my actions speak differently to my words? Does my
    character match my charisma? By my fruits am I known as

a credible representative of Jesus? Do I have moral authority as well as spiritual authority?

7. Do I enjoy the *approval* of God in what I am doing?
Is there an ease and a grace about what I am doing? Am I serving the Lord with a sense of freedom that promotes faith and a sense of mastery that produces confidence in others? Am I always struggling to do the job or do I relish tackling the tasks my calling brings?

8. Have I the *assurance* which enables me to serve without striving?
Am I manipulating people or events to put myself in a good light or to make myself needed? Am I aware of a competitive spirit that jostles for position or status? Am I beginning to need praise and appreciation out of emotional insecurity? Do I enjoy the praise which comes from integrity and the immunity from fear which a good conscience provides?

9. Do I accept the principle of *accountability*?
To whom am I responsible for my ministry? Am I willing to answer for my results? Is there anyone I can go to for help and honest advice? Is there one other person I can trust to know the worst about me who will love me just the same?

10. Can others count on my *availability*?
In replying to tributes made to him on the occasion of his eightieth birthday, Karl Barth reminded his friends that a donkey once had the privilege of being allowed to carry Jesus to Jerusalem. 'If I have done anything in my life', he went on, 'I have done it as a relative of the donkey that went its way carrying an important burden. The disciples had said to its owner 'The Lord has need of it'. And so it seems to have pleased God to have used me at this time, just as I was, in spite of all the things, the disagreeable things, that quite rightly are and will be said about me. Thus I was used. That is how I happened to be present and that was my work. *I just happened to be on the spot*'.[1]

Part Three
Follow My Leader

16. Jesus: His Clash with Leadership

In the United Kingdom, unlike the United States, a change of government does not bring a change in the Civil Service. The permanent staff who keep the machinery of government going can stay at their posts even when an election puts another political party in office. This makes for great stability. Unfortunately, it is also a major barrier to change. Friction between the permanent officials and ministers of the incoming government is frequent, especially when more radical political parties assume office.

When Jesus appeared with the radical impact of the government of God, he threatened the ruling establishment of his day. Between him and the religious civil servants he met there was inevitable conflict. He clashed with the guardians of the legislature who had obscured God's pure law with the small print of man-made regulations and by-laws. The trustees of tradition and the custodians of the Temple and its treasury both found him too prophetic to accommodate. Hawkish Pharisees, liberal Sadducees, middle-of-the-road scribes, extremist Zealots with their 'extra-parliamentary' methods – all found him too different to fit into their category or group. To them all he was a provocation. Small wonder he so consistently predicted that his death would be at the hands of the 'chief priests, and scribes and Pharisees'. This was no accident but part of God's plan to remove a decadent leadership and to raise up a new leadership for the people of God.

Matthew, our 'civil servant' evangelist, shows us that the clash started at the earliest possible stage. When the magi asked Herod 'where is he who has been born king of the Jews?', he was 'disturbed and all Jerusalem with him' (Matt. 2.3). Herod's 'think tank' then correctly identified his birthplace as Bethlehem by tracing the source of this threat to their kingdom to the prophecy of Micah. 'And you Bethlehem, land of Judah are by no means least among the leaders of Judah; for out of you shall come forth a *Ruler* who will *shepherd* my people Israel' (Micah 5.2). Herod's

brutal and indiscriminate massacre of the innocents in the Bethlehem area shows just how afraid he was that this shepherd-ruler
might materialise to destroy his already crumbling power-base.
What was prophetically certain is that it would. Campbell Morgan,
very significantly, analyses the message of Micah into two main
sections: the 'unmasking of false authority' and the 'unveiling of
true authority'.[1] The shepherd-ruler would be a breaker of the
old and a maker of the new. 'I will bring them together like sheep
in a pen, like a flock in its pasture; the place will throng with
people. One who *breaks open the way* will go up before them'
(Micah 2.12–13).

Lords of misrule

In Matthew 23 there is an unmasking by Jesus of the false
authority he confronted. He does not advocate a coup d'état to
overthrow the teaching of the Pharisees but shows up the sham
in their behaviour. He exposes them as leaders who fail to practice
what they preach (v. 3), who offload responsibility on to others
less able to bear it (v. 4), who are publicity conscious and blatantly
concerned for their professional image (v. 5), who are status
seekers and status keepers (v. 6–7).

Such leaders close down rather than open up the kingdom to
men (v. 13). They exploit the vulnerable and perpetuate their
own errors in the converts they make (v. 14–15). They are legalists
who have lost all sense of perspective, unable now to see the
wood for the trees (v. 23–24). They turn truth inside out and
upside down while pretending to be its defenders (v. 25–28). They
show a phony reverence for the past, claiming to be the heirs of
the very men their forefathers murdered! (v. 29ff).

Jesus, for his part, is training a new leadership for God's people.
On to this scene of misrule he plans to send his own representatives and delegated authorities: 'Therefore, behold, I am sending
you prophets and wise men and teachers' (Matt. 23.34). Their
brutal rejection by the existing leaders of Israel will be the indictment and the undoing of all the false leaders of God's people.
The calling of the twelve by Jesus was more than a mere pragmatic
action reinforcing our earlier lessons on plurality among leaders.
It was a key strategic decision. By choosing twelve men Jesus was
serving notice of his intention to raise up a messianic ministry and
leadership among God's people. In John Yoder's words, 'New
teachings are no threat, as long as the teacher stands alone: a
movement, extending his personality in both time and space,
presenting an alternative to the structures that were there before,

challenges the system as no mere words ever could.'[2] It is a simplistic error to say that the church has replaced Israel just as it is a literalistic error to say that Israel and the church are to remain for ever two separate entities. Better to say that through the death and resurrection of her Messiah, Israel is being *reconstituted* as the called-out people of God in a church which includes Jew and Gentile on equal terms. Over this final 'one flock' there will be one Shepherd with his twelve appointed undershepherds as co-leaders with him. 'You who have followed me, in the regeneration when the Son of Man will sit on his glorious throne, you also shall sit upon twelve thrones, judging the twelve tribes of Israel' (Matt. 19.28). Meanwhile as we saw at the outset of this book, the style of his leadership is in sharp contrast to the corrupt leadership it supplants. 'Do not be called Rabbi; for one is your Teacher. . . . Do not call anyone on earth your father for one is your Father . . . do not be called leaders for one is your leader, even Christ' (Matt. 23.8–10). His 'lords' are all brothers, his shepherds are also sheep, his teachers are themselves disciples, his leaders are followers, his rulers servants.

In Matthew 15 and 16 the contrast and the clash between true and false authority is clearly drawn. Here Jesus accuses the religious leaders of his day of exalting their tradition over the express commands of God. For the sake of this tradition they have, he says, 'invalidated the word of God' (Matt. 15.6). Emptiness in worship and hollowness in praise are to be traced to a slavish adherence to the precepts of men (15.8–9). Leaders need always to give sound reasons to people for their obedience. Unless we tell them 'why' they are to do certain things, we are breeding another tradition. Doing it merely because the leaders say so is the beginning of institutionalism (cf. Isaiah 29.13). These leaders which Father has not planted will be uprooted; these blind men vainly seeking to lead a blind people will bring about their own downfall.

Rock Against The Drift

In the midst of this crumbling foundation Jesus will place a rock and on it build his church (Matt. 16.18). The era of messianic leadership is being inaugurated when 'a king will reign righteously and princes will rule justly' (Isaiah 32.1f). In desert conditions sand storms are the enemy of life. The wind whips up the sand never allowing it to settle for life to develop. Barrenness prevails. The rain brings fertility to the unlikeliest places and plants begin to spring up. But it doesn't last. Blasted by the wind, the sand drifts and the fragile vegetation is swept away. But a rock makes all the difference. After rain, in the lee of such a rock, shoots begin to show. Sheltered from the drift, plants have a chance to root and grow. Messiah's leaders are like this. 'Each will be like a refuge from the wind, and a shelter from the storm; like streams of water in a dry country, like the shade of a huge rock in a parched land' (Isaiah 32.2). This is Peter's calling initially. He is not the dogged defender of the traditions of men but the bold proclaimer of the mysteries of heaven. Entrusted with the Father's revelation of his Son Jesus, he will be anchor man for the early church. Like the leading bird in the V-formation of the flock he will bear the brunt of the headwinds. In his apostolic succession every anointed leader stands. As a refuge from the wind he will protect the fatherless and widows. As a rock against the drift he will shelter the church from error and heresy and every force of anti-Christ. As gullies in the foot of the rock retain the precious water where elsewhere it has evaporated he will be a source of life and faith and hope to the people he leads. As a shade from the sun he will take the pressure off the weak and vulnerable, and give them a chance to grow and develop. Jesus is pledged to base his church on such men. These are the leaders he is raising up.

Leaders with the keys of the kingdom implement heaven's will on earth and move in righteousness and peace. Replacing leaders who have taken away the key of knowledge, they bring God's people into clarity and truth. Such leaders create the conditions for growth. The blind now see because they are led by men of vision; the wayward receive clear direction; the confused understand as if for the first time; the incoherent speak clearly and with one voice. Fools have their day of reckoning and true spiritual judgement and discernment restore right values to the church. Foolish talk is stopped, ungodly attitudes are rooted out, and manipulative scheming is eradicated. No longer are their fifty-seven varieties of opinion plaguing the church because there is now a 'noble man' making 'noble plans' in which all the people are secure (Isaiah 32.3–8). Such leaders create the conditions for great growth.

'I will build my church' is a prophecy of what he will do after his resurrection. But already Jesus is laying the foundation for it by training the twelve. Extending his base of ministry through these men, with a view to expanding the work, Jesus is the originator of 'the pyramid principle' of church growth.[3]

Workers for the Harvest

'When he saw the crowds, he had compassion on them, because they were harassed and helpless, like sheep without a shepherd' (Matt. 9.36). Jesus felt the misrule keenly because he saw the devastating effects of it in people's lives. The ultimate argument for good leadership is neither pragmatic nor even strategic but pastoral. Suffering people need sensitive shepherds. The Lord Jesus out of his great compassion aims to provide them.

Calling twelve men he delegates to them his own authority to cast out demons and to heal the sick (Matt. 10.1f). Travelling light, they are to preach what he preached and do what he did! Their coming would prove crucial for every community they visited (10.11f). Shepherds though they may be, they are made of the same stuff as their sheep and suffer accordingly (10.16). In their very vulnerability they will prove the presence and power of the Holy Spirit (10.18ff). To receive them is to receive Christ himself (10.40ff), so closely does he identify himself with him. Going first to the lost sheep of the house of Israel, they are to have the many sheep not of this fold in view. He was training leaders with the multitudes in mind. The false shepherds have fed themselves rather than the sheep. The scribes and Pharisees have failed to strengthen the weak, or bind up the broken. They have not sought the lost but have dominated the people, ruling with force and severity (Ezekiel 34.1–4). His leaders, by contrast, will 'tend the lambs and feed the sheep' not because they have to but because they want to, 'not greedy for money but eager to serve, not lording it over those entrusted to you, but being examples to the flock ' (1 Peter 5.2–3).

To them the appearance of the Chief Shepherd will not be a threat but a reward.

Matthew pinpoints the crucial events which see the final unmasking of false authority and the unveiling of true authority. 'Then Jesus said to them, 'You will all fall away because of me this night, for it is written: "I will strike down the shepherd and the sheep of the flock will be scattered." But after I have been raised, I will *go before you* to Galilee' (Matt. 26.31–32). The clash of leadership has come to a head. Even the trainee leaders of the Shepherd-Ruler have to go through the crucible of failure. The intended rock crumbles like soft sand; Peter denies his Lord (26.34ff). But the Great Shepherd of the sheep through the blood of everlasting covenant is the one who 'breaks open the way' (Micah 2.13). He breaks through his enemies, the lords of misrule and the unseen evil powers behind the scene; he breaks through sin and death and going before them into Galilee, he regroups his scattered flock and trainee under-shepherds. The resurrection which raises the Stone rejected by the experts to the head of the house, reinstates the shaky disciple to be the rock on which he will build his church. Through men like this he will gather the lost and bind up the broken, especially reaching out to all those who have been cynically disregarded by the professional leaders of God's people. In this resurrection reunion the wraps are off. As Micah foresaw, 'their king will pass through before them, the Lord at their head' (Micah 2.13). All authority is now safely back in his hands; the ecclesiastical establishment has been deposed, the religious civil servants have been over-ruled and made redundant. Every position of responsibility among God's people is a 'situation now vacant'. All appointments to leadership are exclusively in his gift and patronage. 'And he gave some to be apostles, some to be prophets. . . .'

17. Jesus: His Model for Leadership

It is as a son apprenticed to his father's trade that Jesus becomes a model of leadership for us. He is confessing success not failure when he says 'I can do nothing on my own initiative' (John 5.30 NASB). If we are to follow him in this we shall have to recognise, in F. B. Meyer's words, that 'most of us are too strong for him to use; we are too full of our own schemes, and plans, and ways of doing things'.[1] If we are to be like him in doing only what we see the Father doing, we shall need to listen more attentively to the Father's voice and be more aware of where the creative Spirit is doing new things. To be a leader like Jesus, God's starting-points must be my starting-points. Doing only what we see Father doing will demand a break with the pattern of expectations put upon us as leaders by our particular brand of churchmanship, or even by our supposedly charismatic spontaneity. Following Father like this will certainly free us from rigid preconceived ideas of ministry. Because it was so purposeful his life was unprogrammed. He did not have a five-year diary! Responsive to his Father's will he was flexible enough to withstand even popular demand in order to move on to the next appointed place. 'The people . . . tried to keep him from leaving them. But he said, "I must preach the good news of the kingdom to the other towns also, because that is why I was sent" ' (Luke 4.42–3). As well as creativity and flexibility, this gave him great objectivity too. 'By myself I can do nothing; I judge only as I hear' (John 5.30). Prisoner of no one's prejudices, in the patronage of no sectarian school, he spoke the truth firsthand from his Father. Any leader who follows his master in this will be radical and prophetic in his thrust and will inevitably disrupt the polite diplomacy and cautious consensus that passes for wisdom in most church circles. Above all, a realisation of sonship brings an immense sense of security. It was out of such a sense of deep security that Jesus felt so free to serve as the lowest slave in washing the feet of his disciples. The thirteenth chapter of John spells out for us the style of leadership on which our own is to be based.

He Stoops to Conquer

Jesus is secure in knowing who he is and this frees him to serve. 'Jesus knew that the Father had put all things under his power' (v.3) – and knowing what he had received from his Father, he knew what he had to give to men. 'Jesus knew . . . that he had come from God' (v.3) – and knowing where he had come from, he knew what his calling was. 'Jesus knew that . . . he was returning to God' (v.3) – and knowing where he was going, he knew what his aims and objectives were. 'Jesus knew that the time had come for him to leave the world' (v.1) – and knowing the timing of God he knew when to make significant moves in his ministry. Uninhibited by self-consciousness, or by fear of losing face or reputation, he is free to stoop to wash the feet of uncomprehending followers. Secure in being a Son of God, he is able to risk their misunderstanding and to do for them prophetically what only later will they come to thank him for. He is our example of leadership. Secure in our sonship we will not need to strive for position in order to prove who we are. We will not use our leadership opportunities to find emotional wholeness but to express it. In this security we will be able to lay down our reputation as leaders in order to fulfil our calling. We will be freed to act prophetically at the risk of being misunderstood. We will have no need to waste emotional energy on vindicating ourselves. 'For we do not preach ourselves, but Jesus Christ as Lord, and ourselves as your servants for Jesus' sake' (2 Cor. 4.5).

Servant of God

The role of the servant is most clearly drawn out biblically in the so-called 'servant songs' of Isaiah's prophecy in Chapters 42, 49, 50 and 53. These songs provide a corrective to a rather slipshod and inaccurate concept of servanthood that has become current in the church. Today this concept seems often to be used, in Douglas Webster's words, 'to suggest a multi-service agency, responding to every request, rather like a continuing bob-a-job week but, of course, without the bob.'[2] This is to have too manward and social a view of servanthood. Isaiah's picture is very different. He portrays the servant not as a general factotum but as fulfilling specific tasks and embarked upon a special mission. Furthermore, he is God's servant before he is man's helper. It is

God who sets him these tasks and equips him for them. The world neither writes the agenda for the Church nor the work-schedules for the church's leaders.

The first servant song makes this clear. *The servant-leader is God's man first and foremost.* God chooses him, upholds him, delights in him. As we have seen before it is only God who can adequately equip him. 'I will put my Spirit on him and he will bring forth justice to the nations' (Isaiah 42.1). Endorsed by God he is sent out to do God's work and implement his will in the world. A feature of the servant-leader is his remarkable reticence, his distinctive modesty, which means that he does not 'shout or cry out or make his voice heard in the streets' (Isaiah 42.2). He keeps a provocatively low-profile. He does not draw needless attention to himself. One wonders how much at home he would be in that brash side of evangelicalism which is almost a branch of show business. By the same token he might well disdain the over-bearing manner that passes for confidence in some charismatic circles.

The servant-leader is marked by a gentleness which makes him great. 'A bruised reed he will not break and a smouldering wick he will not snuff out' (Isaiah 42.3). He is keen to encourage the weak and bolster the confidence of the timid. He will seek to impart faith and hope to the dispirited and to fan into flame potential gifts and abilities in others. Not allowing his own spirit to be broken or his own light to be snuffed out, he maintains an unquenchable optimism and an uncrushable determination. Miraculously, 'he will not falter or be discouraged' (Isaiah 42.4).

The key to the servant's success is a secret life with God. The second servant song speaks of this. As a sword stays bright in its scabbard and an arrow sharp in its quiver, so the servant maintains his public effectiveness by continuous fellowship with God. In Robert Murray M'Cheyne's now famous words 'do not forget the culture of the inner man – I mean of the heart. How diligently the cavalry officer keeps his sabre clean and sharp; every stain he rubs off with the greatest care. Remember you are God's sword. A holy minister is an aweful weapon in the hand of God'.[3] Even when he feels he has 'laboured to no purpose' (49.4ff) he refreshes himself in God and soon finds himself with a renewed and even enlarged mission.

He is a servant also of the word of God. What he hears in secret he speaks in public. 'The Sovereign Lord has given me an instructed tongue, to know the word that sustains the weary. He wakens me morning by morning, wakens my ear to listen like one being taught' (Isaiah 50.4f). This freshness and immediacy of the word makes him a source of counsel and makes his words 'spirit and life' (John 6.63). Nourished by the living word himself he provides daily bread for others. He is able to speak different things to different people according to their needs. Freed from secondhand clichés and stock-in-trade answers, he gives words of wisdom and knowledge appropriate to the occasion. This daily responsiveness to the will of God inevitably brings him to a Gethsemane crisis in which he looks to God for his vindication. The servant-leader, face set like flint, remains nonetheless strangely vulnerable.

To say all this is, of course, only to hint at the riches of truth in these prophetic songs of the Servant. Jesus who is our model for leadership fulfils them all. Matthew knew at once that he was watching a life he had read about before when he watched the servant-Lord at work (cf. Matt.12.15–21), combining sensitivity and strength to bring hope and healing. Further than this we cannot go. Into the fourth servant song in chapter 53 of Isaiah we cannot follow. More than serving, he must suffer. And there is too much in this which is unique to Christ for us to venture far. Except perhaps to say one thing: actions speak louder than words. Redemptively his mission is accomplished but every leader in some measure is called to fill up in his flesh 'what is still lacking in regard to Christ's afflictions, for the sake of his body, which is the church' (Col. 1.24). We can at least, in our leadership, imitate Paul as he imitates Christ.

The Good Shepherd

Of all the pictures of Jesus given in the gospels, the one which shows him as the Shepherd has a particular appeal and special relevance to leadership.[4] It is perhaps difficult for us in an urban and industrial society to realise how widely this concept was once used to depict leadership. Outside the scriptures, in the ancient world, the shepherd imagery was frequently used to describe secular rulers. In the Old Testament it is a clear and consistent motif. As the history of the flock of God is unfolded so the story of its faithful or unfaithful under-shepherds is recorded. Moses lists the essential functions of such men when he asks God for a new leader to succeed him. 'May the Lord, the God of the spirits of all mankind, appoint a man over this community, to go out and come in before them, one who will lead them out and bring them in, so that the Lord's people will not be like sheep without a shepherd' (Numbers 27.16–17). When the leaders failed in this duty, the prophets revealed the pain and anger in the heart of

God, the Lord of the flock. Ezekiel accused the leaders of his day
of being false shepherds. In feeding themselves they were guilty
of exploiting the sheep. In failing to care for the weak and sick
and scattered sheep they were guilty of criminal neglect. In every
way they had been domineering in their leadership. It was against
such a background that Jeremiah in a Messianic prophecy
promised the coming of a true shepherd. (See Ezekiel 34 and
Jeremiah 23). This true shepherd, Isaiah heralded as the one who
would rule, feed, gather, carry and lead God's people (Isaiah 40.
10–11). 'I am that shepherd' said Jesus. As the *good* shepherd he
lays down his life in a unique redemptive sacrifice. As the *great*
shepherd he rises up in resurrection to confirm the covenant.
(Heb. 13.20). As the *chief* shepherd he returns to reward the
faithful under-shepherds (1 Peter 5.4). He is the model for the
pastoral ministry, a ministry as much in need of renewal as any
of the others. In the tenth chapter of John we have the secrets of
a good shepherd.

1. He goes through the same door as the sheep. 'The man
   who enters by the gate is the shepherd of the sheep' (John
   10.1). Every leader is first a disciple himself, every shepherd
   is also a sheep and the true pastor enters into the reality of
   the Church's life in Christ in the same way as every other
   sheep. He is not a thief or a robber. Expecting nothing of
   them which he does not expect of himself, he takes charge
   of them because he has a moral right to do so.
2. He calls his own sheep by name (John 10.3). He knows
   them personally, knows their name and history, their hopes
   and dreams. He could well write to them as Paul did to the
   Romans and picture them all before him (cf. Romans 16).
   He knows when to carry them and when to prod them. He
   'knows his own' (John 10.14). Every pastor would have
   more prophetic courage and be unafraid to lose people if
   he realised that not every one who is on the church roll is
   his sheep.
3. He brings them out of the fold (John 10.4). He knows they
   cannot remain in the cloistered cosiness of the fold but must
   emerge into the wide world. So the true pastor seeks to
   break the ghetto mentality of his people. He will lead them
   out of their introspection into new adventures for God.
   This will not always be to their liking. The Greek word for
   'bring out' is 'ekballo' so that verse 4 is better translated
   'he puts forth his own' (John 10.4 NASB). With the rod of
   spiritual authority and the staff of the Word he may well

have to overcome their objections, quell their fears, or stir their lethargy by strong teaching and admonition to get them to move.

4. He leads from the front. 'When he has brought out all his own, he goes on ahead of them' (John 10.4). The true pastor is not playing a waiting game, taking his cue from the sheep. Nor is he a sheepdog constantly snapping at their heels. He is a man who asks people to do only what he is prepared to do. He is willing to stand in front of them, not hide behind them. He may prod them out of apathy or laziness but he will not drive the sheep. Instead he 'walks on before them and the sheep follow him' (John 10.4 AMP). He exercises positive pastoring, so that he does not simply respond to need or react to crises but creates initiatives for his people to move.

5. He is trusted for his voice. 'The sheep follow him because they know his voice' (John 10.4). Spiritual sheep instinctively know when the voice of the under-shepherd is the voice of God. By the fruits of his mouth they know him. Strange accents and foreign tones they do not respond to. Once more we see that the authority of a shepherd lies in bringing to those he leads the authentic word of the living God.

6. He guards the entrance to the fold. There is a sense in which every true pastor can say 'I am the gate for the sheep' (John 10.7). Savage wolves, many of them in sheep's clothing, will attempt to enter the fold and must be watched for. Such men will not always declare open war but will infiltrate the flock seeking to gain control and dominate others by psychological manipulation. 'Guard the flock of God of which the Holy Spirit has made you overseers', is Paul's parting charge to the Ephesian elders. 'Be shepherds of the church of God which he bought with his own blood. I know,' Paul warns, 'that after I leave savage wolves will come in among you and will not spare the flock' (Acts 20.28–9).

7. He is not afraid of confrontation. Unlike the hireling or mere professional, he does not shrink from face-to-face encounter with the enemies of the flock. 'The hired hand is not the shepherd who owns the sheep. So when he sees the wolf coming, he abandons the sheep and runs away. Then the wolf attacks the flock and scatters it. The man runs away because he is a hired hand and cares nothing for

the sheep' (John 10.12–13). The true pastor will always fight for his flock.

8. He feeds the sheep. Under his careful leadership the sheep 'come in and go out and find pasture' (John 10.9). Not going over the old ground of well-worn Bible studies, he feeds them with fresh revelation and nourishes them with the whole counsel of God. This brings them into abundant life but this life is not an end in itself. Since most of the flocks around Jerusalem in the time of Jesus were destined for sacrifice, the true shepherd will have a clear aim in feeding his sheep. The pastoral ministry will not be tickling ears to please the people or merely keep them happy. He will be fattening them for the offering of themselves as living sacrifices unto God (cf. Romans 12.1f).

9. He cares for the sheep at cost to himself. 'The good shepherd risks his own life for the sheep' (John 10.11 AMP). 'Laying down his life for the sheep' is much more modest for the average pastor than it was for Jesus. But it is still costly. It is the laying down of his privacy, his time, his emotional energy. It means being bothered and burdened by the incessant demands of the flock. This can only be done by love. Peter's threefold commission to tend his sheep and feed the lambs was built upon a threefold re-affirmation of his love for the great shepherd. This love sets the tone of all pastoral ministry. 'Be shepherds of God's flock that is under your care, serving as overseers – not because you must but because you are willing as God wants you to be; not greedy for money but eager to serve; not lording it over those entrusted to you, but being examples to the flock' (1 Peter 5.2–3).

10. He is interested in the whole of God's flock. 'I have other sheep that are not of this sheep pen. I must bring them also. They too will listen to my voice and there shall be one flock and one shepherd' (John 10.16). Envisaging the coming in of the Gentiles and the restoration of Israel to whom he was at first exclusively sent, the Good Shepherd prophetically declares the ultimate unity of God's flock. We take our cue from him. Far from being protective or in any way sectarian, true shepherding looks for the re-gathering of all God's people. The true pastor has a sense of history and an eye for prophecy. He is not out to create a cosy pastoral idyll, sheltered from the realities of life. He is seeking not to contain but to expand and enlarge the flock. Not content at seeing the pastoral ministry decline into the

sheer triviality of routine visiting with polite cups of tea, today's man with the shepherd heart will want big things for his flock. 'I will bring them together like sheep in a pen, like a flock in its pasture; the place will throng with people. One who breaks open the way will go up before them; they will break through the gate and go out. Their king will pass through before them, the Lord at their head' (Micah 2.12–13)

This was the prophetic spirit of the Great Shepherd who, knowing that the shepherd was about to be struck down and the sheep scattered, promised to go before them into Galilee after he had been raised from the dead. The 'breaker-through' and 'breaker-out' is a more dynamic role for a shepherd than we have made room for in our traditional understanding of the pastoral ministry. But since it was his spirit who is our chief shepherd we would do well to follow him in it.

18. Jesus: His Lessons on Leadership

The training of the twelve was for Jesus a major priority of his work. In his great High Priestly prayer he speaks as if this was 'the principal part of his earthly ministry'.[1] To accept his strategy is to accept that training leaders is the first step to evangelising the world. This is the justification for every leadership training programme and indeed for any contribution this book can make. At a time when long-overdue changes are taking place in the Church's patterns of ministry and when there is a widespread unease at our traditional methods of leadership training, the strategy of Jesus is again receiving close attention and study. This is not before time. It is vital in this changing scene to examine closely what he taught his potential leaders and how he trained them.

1. He picked the men he personally wanted. Mark tells us that 'he called to him those he wanted' (Mark 3.13). The fact that he did this after prayer only strengthened his confidence in those he selected. For their part as potential leaders, the twelve disciples knew, from the start, that they were part of his heart as well as part of his plans. They were to become his friends not just his pupils. Three of them were to be especially close to Jesus and the nearest any one came to sharing in his Gethsemane ordeal.
2. He called them to share his life. 'He appointed twelve that they might be with him' (Mark 3.14). Being with him was to be the basis of doing things for him. Jesus lived with his trainee leaders. He gave *himself* to them and not merely his principles. 'He actually spent more time with his disciples than with everybody else in the world put together'.[2] He laid down his life for them in countless ways in the years before Calvary, letting them invade his precious privacy by their eagerness to be with him, letting them try his patience

by their slowness in learning from him. He allowed them to
see him tired, hungry and homeless, schooling them in rejection and preparing them for their future as the 'offscourings
of the earth' (cf. 1 Cor. 4.11–13). Leadership in his church,
by implication, would be no sinecure.

3. He showed them how to live. His was true on-the-job training. He demonstrated before he explained. He showed
these potential leaders what to do and – what is much hard
– how to do it. Seeing him at prayer with his Father, they
ask him 'teach us to pray' with the implication, 'like you
pray'. Having stooped to wash their feet, he reinforces the
lesson by saying: "Do you understand what I have done for
you? You call me 'Teacher' and 'Lord' and rightly so, for
that is what I am. Now that I, your Lord and Teacher, have
washed your feet, you also should wash one another's feet"
(John 13.12–14). As Lord he clearly tells them what to do;
as Teacher he equally clearly shows them how to do it.

4. He involved them in ministry. From distributing bread and
baptising converts, his trainee leaders graduated to mission
work on their own (cf. Matt. 10.1ff; Luke 10.1ff). In releasing them for this he knew that he had to let them make
their own mistakes if they were to grow and mature. He was
prepared to accept their failures, using the occasion to teach
them something more (e.g. Matt. 17.14–21).

5. He sent them out in pairs. 'He sent them out two by two'
(Mark 6.7). From the start each disciple knew he was not
on his own. From the start each trainee leader knew he did
not have all the gifts necessary for ministry but needed to
be complemented by another. Each apostolic twosome was
a microcosm of the body of Christ and of this Jesus was
sowing seeds in their minds. As two men walked together
they learned the power which comes from deep spiritual
agreement between men (cf. Matt. 18.19). Together they
discovered the true interdependence which safeguards all
kingdom work.

6. He delegated to them his authority. 'He . . . gave them
authority over evil spirits' (Mark 6.8). This was a risk for
Jesus but he took it for their sake. Any leader is heading for
frustration and failure who is given a task to perform but
not the authority to carry it out. Jesus never exposes his
representatives to that danger.

7. He checked on their progress. 'The apostles gathered round
Jesus and reported to him all they had done and taught'
(Mark 6.30). He did not leave them in a vacuum but made

room for constant feedback on their experience. They questioned him closely about the reasons for their successes or failures. He answered them, not always directly, but in ways that egged them on to discover more and to ask more searchingly. They learned to face varied reactions to their word and witness and he explained to them how to respond. He was schooling them in the need to be accountable to him rather than answerable to the world.

The Secret of the Lord

But what did Jesus want his potential leaders to know? Without attempting to cover the whole scope of the teaching of Jesus, we focus on two special learning occasions for the disciples. At one key point in his ministry the Lord Jesus called his men aside for a time of retreat at Caesarea Philippi. Here he let them into his deepest secrets.

1. He taught them to understand his own person. There was no one they needed to be more sure of than himself! He drew from them their own estimate of who he was. 'Who do you say I am? (Matt. 16.15). They learned he was the Christ, though he counselled them to keep quiet about it. What he was telling them in the dark, they would, in due course, be able to speak in the daylight; what was being whispered in their ears they would one day soon be free and bold to proclaim from the rooftops. Meanwhile, the secret of the Lord is with them that fear him. Wherever afterwards their leadership took them, for them there would be no other name given among men worth naming to the world. And three of them would never forget being 'eyewitnesses of his majesty' (2 Peter 1.16).

2. He taught them to live by revelation. The importance of this has been emphasised in earlier chapters. But here again, in the strategy of Jesus, we see a vital stress on listening to Father for divine revelation. 'Blessed are you Simon son of Jonah, for this was not revealed to you by man but by my Father in heaven' (Matt. 16.17). As A. W. Tozer points out, others 'listen to the man who listens to God'. The secret is not given secondhand and each leader must hear it and confess it for himself.

3. He taught them the significance of the Church in his plans. 'I will build my Church' (Matt. 16.18). It is to be his building not man's. His leaders would serve him by serving his Church

and by making his aims for it their aims. He sowed seeds in their minds of the Church as a powerful agency of his kingdom, vested with authority. From the outset his intent was clear that 'through the Church, the manifold wisdom of God should be made known to the rulers and authorities in the heavenly realms' (Eph. 3.10). Protestantism, which has often lacked an adequate doctrine on the Church is now rediscovering the Body of Christ. To be a leader in such a Church was and still is the greatest possible honour.

4. He taught them the centrality of his death and resurrection. Overcoming their resistance to the idea, when they began to worry about the possibility of his death, he told them it was inevitable. Jesus impressed upon these trainee leaders how necessary was his death in the fulfilling of his mission. 'From that time on Jesus began to explain to his disciples that he must go to Jerusalem and suffer many things at the hands of the elders, chief priests and teachers of the law, and that he must be killed and on the third day be raised to life' (Matt. 16.21).

5. He taught them the cost of discipleship. He spelt out to them what becoming a leader in his Church would involve. Unable to carry his unique cross, every potential leader must take up his own and learn to follow on a self-denying road. Never, as their ministry for him took them across the Ancient World to their appointed martyrdoms or lonely Patmoses, would they ever be able to say he had disguised the cost. But in the light of the price he paid, which of us will argue with David Livingstone when he said 'I never made a sacrifice'. Every leader knows from first grade that 'a student is not above his teacher, nor a servant above his master'. (Matt. 10.24). If the retreat at Caesarea Philippi was one focal point for seeing what Jesus wanted his potential leaders to know, then the Upper Room was the other. In John's account of the 'farewell discourses' as they have been rather prosaically termed, there is an abundance of riches. But I want to pick out just three further points which are significant for understanding how Jesus prepared his men for ministry. This ministry, it had now dawned upon the disciples, was to be embarked upon without his physical presence and support.

6. He taught them to trust his words and promises. 'I am telling you now before it happens, so that when it does happen you will believe I am he' (John 13.19; cf. 14.29). He laid his credibility on the line that he meant what he said.

Often, 'after he was raised from the dead, his disciples recalled what he had said. Then they believed the Scriptures and the words that Jesus had spoken' (John 2.22).

7. He taught them to trust his Father. Here in the Upper Room he merely recapped the long education in faith he had given them. Rebuking their little faith or misplaced faith, he had long been schooling them in the assurance that 'Father knows'. Sending them out without money or luggage, with nothing but the clothes they stood up in, he had been training them to live by faith and prayer. Now he was sealing this lesson in their hearts. 'In that day you will no longer ask me anything. I tell you the truth, my Father will give you whatever you ask in my name. For the Father himself loves you' (John 16.23,27).

8. He taught them to trust the Holy Spirit. 'Do not worry', he had said to them on an earlier occasion, 'about how you will defend yourselves or what you will say, for the Holy Spirit will teach you at that time what you should say' (Luke 12.12). Now in the shadow of the cross, he reassures them about the advantages to be gained from his going and the Spirit's coming (John 16.7). There is no greater lesson or comfort than this for anyone called to leadership in His Church. The Holy Spirit will lead the leaders into all truth. Apostles will not only recall his mighty works and recount them with wonder but, by faith and through the Spirit, will themselves do even greater works than he did! Prophets will expect the Spirit to disclose to them what is to come. Teachers will rely on the Counsellor to teach them all things and to remind them of everything Jesus said. With relief evangelists will realise it is not their burden to convict the world of its sin; the Holy Spirit will do this through their word and witness. Unable at one stage to bear the weight of many revelations, they will trust the Holy Spirit to show them what they need to know as and when they need to know it. In short, to his potential leaders, the Lord Jesus promised that charisma, that 'Spirit of wisdom and revelation in the knowledge of him', which, as we saw earlier, is our indispensable requirement and his inimitable gift.

Good Stewards

Having seen how Jesus trained his leaders and what he wanted them to know, we turn finally to lessons on leadership to be gleaned from other areas of his teaching, especially from the parables. His teaching here will once again not only serve as a measure of our own existing leadership but will set out principles which will help us in the raising up of other leaders.

The concept of 'stewardship' was one Jesus frequently employed which has special lessons for leaders in his Church. A 'steward' was an estate manager given the task of administering the affairs of his overlord. In a controversial and debatable story, Jesus urged that the affairs of his kingdom should be administered no less shrewdly or adeptly than the affairs of commerce (Luke 16.1–9).[3] Jesus then goes on to show that the point of comparison is not the dishonesty of the steward but his logic. The lesson to be drawn is the inherent connection between our handling of earthly things and our handling of heavenly things. The sons of light need to know this if they are to prepare for the future and exercise leadership in the light of it. Three principles of leadership are clearly stated.

1. The man who is faithful in small things can be expected to handle big things. 'Whoever can be trusted with very little can also be trusted with much and whoever is dishonest with very little will also be dishonest with much' (Luke 16.10). A man who can rule himself is better fitted to rule others than the man who lacks self-control. 'Like a city whose walls are broken down is a man who lacks self-control' (Prov. 25.28). It is for this reason that a leader in the Church must be 'self-controlled . . . not given to much wine . . . not violent . . . not quarrelsome' (1 Tim. 3.2–3). On the same basis a man who can manage on the scale of his own household is qualified to be a leader in the larger household of God (1 Tim. 3.4). David could be trusted with his father's flock before he became the shepherd of God's flock. He had won victories over the lion and bear before he tackled Goliath, not in Saul's untried armour but with weapons that he had used successfully on lesser enemies. Faithful in small things he became ruler of Israel.

2. A man who is faithful in handling material things can be trusted to handle spiritual things. A man's attitude to money is a key to his suitability as a leader. For 'if you have not been trustworthy in handling worldly wealth, who will trust you with true riches?' (Luke 16.11). This was the test Ananias and Sapphira failed. It was awareness of this principle that made Paul so keen to be self-supporting as far as possible. 'I have not coveted anyone's silver or gold or clothing. You yourselves need to know that these hands of mine supplied my own needs and the needs of my com-

panions' (Acts 20.33–34). For those leaders who are financially supported by the churches there is the consolation of being in the Lord's will. For 'the Lord has commanded that those who preach the gospel should receive their living from the gospel' (1 Cor. 9.14.) But the principle applies. 'I have learned the secret of being content in any and every situation, whether well fed or hungry, whether living in plenty or in want' (Phil. 4.12). So a man who is 'not pursuing dishonest gain', who is 'not greedy for money but eager to serve' is proving himself faithful in material things, and qualifies himself to be a leader in the church (cf. 1 Tim. 3.8, 1 Peter 5.2).

3. A man who is faithful in what belongs to someone else can be trusted with his own. 'And if you have not been trustworthy with someone else's property who will give you property of your own?' (Luke 16.12). When a Christian applies for secular employment he usually goes to his pastor for a reference to take to his prospective employer. In Christian leadership the reverse procedure might well apply. Before recognising a man as leader in the church we might do well to ask his employer for a reference to give to us! A prospective leader after all, 'must have a good reputation with outsiders, so that he will not fall into disgrace and into the devil's trap' (1 Tim. 3.7). It is interesting to see how well this principle of Jesus is borne out by scriptural example. Joshua for example, 'had been Moses' assistant since youth' before succeeding him as leader of Israel (Number 11.28). Samuel first served Eli, becoming used to his every beck and call, before he heard the voice of God calling him to be a prophet and judge (1 Sam. 3.5). David, as we mentioned earlier, faithfully served his father Jesse by tending his flock before God entrusted him with leading his people (1 Sam. 17. 17–19, cf. Psalm 78.70–72). Elisha was Elijah's valet before eclipsing him as a prophet. He was willing to become Elijah's 'attendant' and to be afterwards known as the one who 'used to pour water on the hands of Elijah' as his personal servant (1 Kings 19.21, 2 Kings 3.11). Because Timothy proved himself by assisting Paul in his ministry he was entrusted with missions of his own (Phil. 2.22). All these are instances of good stewardship; men who in faithfully discharging their responsibilities to others, qualified to receive ministries of their own.

Each of the three principles we have looked at are facets of a basic law that applies in many areas of truth. It is that 'the spiritual did not come first, but the natural, and after that the spiritual' (1 Cor. 15.46). It is the devil, not the Lord that finds work for idle hands to do. The Lord looks for his leaders to men at work, calling them like Amos, from their ploughing to be his prophets; taking hard-working if not always successful fishermen and making them into successful fishers of men.[4] This is another way of saying that duty precedes love, that even charity begins at home, that paying your bills may be the first step on the road to preaching the gospel.

One heartening feature of this teaching of Jesus is that it assumes advancement in his kingdom. These principles of promotion in the work of God are sharply summed up in the parables of Jesus, especially the so-called parables of the Talents and the Pounds.

Both these parables in their context are addressed to leaders, and to leaders who had failed. Both are told against the expectation of the master's absence and eventual return and so contain principles of leadership that apply for all time to Christian leaders 'until he comes'. From Matthew's account of the story of the talents, we can sum up all we have said about stewardship.

1. A steward is a man on *trust*. Calling his servants to him, 'he entrusted his property to them' (Matt. 25.14). Leadership implies a trust placed in us. 'Now it is required that those who have been given a trust must prove faithful' (1 Cor. 4.2). Paul sees himself as 'simply discharging the trust' committed to him (1 Cor. 9.17). It is in the mercy of God that so often for us, as for Paul, he foresees our faithfulness and puts us into his service (cf. 1 Tim. 1.12). This gives confidence to any leader to know he is trusted. In releasing other leaders, we, too, will look for faithful men and trust them to do a work we might well at some stage feel better able to do ourselves.

2. A steward is given *ability*. 'According to his ability' tasks and talents are distributed to him. Freely we have received, freely we give. The gifts and callings of leadership convey their own sense of ability which gives confidence to a Christian leader that he does not approach people empty-handed.

3. A steward is given *responsibility*. Because his master has gone on a journey, the steward is left in charge. He has a responsibility to fulfil until the master returns. He accepts his leadership not as a sideline or hobby but as a serious duty. 'Choose seven men,' said the apostles, 'and we will

turn this responsibility over to them' (Acts 6.3). This responsibility is often for other servants of the master (Luke 12.42), to be in charge of them or over them in the Lord (1 Thess. 5.12). A steward acts best if given clear and explicit instructions on what to do. Leaders act best and most responsibly when their roles are clearly defined. Above all he needs to act upon his responsibility. The gravest indictment laid against a steward is that he failed to utilise what he had been given. 'Put this money to work until I come back' is the master's chief concern. It is irresponsible to ignore it. Use it or lose it is a leader's choice. 'For whoever does not have, even what he has will be taken from him' (Matt. 25.29).

4. A steward is *accountable*. He knows by the very terms of his engagement that 'from everyone who has been given much, much will be demanded; and from the one who has been entrusted with much, much more will be asked' (Luke 12.42). Every steward lives with the knowledge that the end of the story is that 'after a long time, the master of those servants returned and settled accounts with them' (Matt. 25.19). Jesus had schooled his trainee leaders in this (cf. Luke 9.10, 10.17ff) and they were only too ready to be accountable to him. Accountability gives a leader a sense of security in that he knows there is someone willing to oversee him and make the best use even of his mistakes. It also gives a man a sense that his work matters and the quality of it is of some concern. Far from inhibiting initiative, accountability positively encourages it. The cautious, do-nothing-for-fear-of-the-consequences attitude is precisely the one attitude that the master finds utterly distasteful in his steward (Matt. 25.24ff). Leaders who expect submission do so out of the humbling sense of having to 'give an account' for each soul in their care! (Hebrews 13.17). Presumption in seeking elevated ministry is discouraged by the principle of accountability. 'Not many of you', writes James, 'should presume to be teachers, my brothers, because you know that we who teach will be judged more strictly (James 3.1). A faithful steward however is glad to be accountable because he is out to bring satisfaction not to himself but to his master. The reward the steward looks for is not the fruit of self-interest but that promotion which will enable him to enter even further into the joy of his master (cf. Matt. 25.21). This is all part of the fact that to 'aspire to leadership is a noble ambition'. 'And when the Chief Shepherd appears, you will receive the crown of glory that will never fade away ' (1 Peter 5.4).

Unsealed Orders

In his final words to his men Jesus reiterated both what he expected of his under-managers and what they could expect of him.

1. He assured them he was to be as alive in his absence as in his presence by giving to them many convincing proofs that he was alive (Acts 1.3).
2. He left them with clear orders and instructions as to what to do (Acts 1.2).
3. He made sure they understood the principles of his government and administration (Acts 1.3).
4. He told them not to be tied down in too rigid programmes and timescales but to do their work in season and out of season (Acts 1.6–7).
5. He reassured them that they would have power to do the job (Acts 1.8).
6. He confirmed their authority to act as his representatives (Acts 1.8).
7. He arranged for special messengers to reassure them immediately he had departed that his promise to return would one day be made good (Acts 1.11).

It was because he knew that good leaders were so vital that the Lord Jesus invested so much in them. As Robert Coleman has put it, 'if we get the right quality of leadership, the rest will follow; if we do not get it, the rest will have nothing worth following'.[5]

19. Jesus: Legacy of Leadership

Jesus, then, had his own way of making leaders. He told them he loved them. He treated them as his friends, taking them into his confidence, opening his heart to them, risking even their rebuke. He teased them with parables, raising in their minds more questions that he was immediately prepared to answer. He taught them how to pray. He told them about his cross, again and again impressing upon them how necessary it was. He taught them the mysteries of his Father's kingdom. He trusted them to do what he could have done better himself. He tested them in experience, schooling them in a 'seminary in the streets' rather than sending them to the Qumran Bible College![1] He interceded for them, not always shielding them from failures but praying them through it so that they emerged stronger and better able to help others. He told them to wait for the Spirit's power before going anywhere. Then, having given them his Spirit, he gave them to the world.

Of all his legacies – his peace, his joy, his meal – none was more significant than the leaders he left to his church.

'As the Father has sent me, I am sending you' (John 20.21). These words put ex-fishermen and tax-collectors in line with the mission of the Son of God. It is an enormous privilege for any leader to be caught up in the same movement of divine grace that brought the Son of God into the world. Consecration to leadership and ministry takes its rise from the truth of his consecration in the blood of the cross: 'As you sent me into the world, I have sent them into the world. For them I sanctify myself, that they too may be sanctified' (John 17.19). By implication, those he sends are to be as dependent on, and obedient to, the Father as he was. In doing this they will provoke the same reactions as he did. 'Remember the words I spoke to you: "No servant is greater than his master". If they persecuted me, they will persecute you also. If they obey my teaching, they will obey yours also ' (John 15.20). Sent as he was sent, his leaders will face the same two-fold response he did; some will reject the word; some will receive it. Truly 'apostolic' leadership will always share in this ambiguity and will always have the paradoxes of the incarnation stamped upon it. His servants commend themselves by this ambivalence, 'through glory and dishonour, bad report and good report; genuine, yet regarded as imposters; known, yet unknown; dying and yet we live on; sorrowful, yet always rejoicing; poor, yet making many rich; having nothing yet, yet possessing all things' (2 Cor. 6.8–10).

Elsewhere it is argued (chapter 20) that his gift of the Twelve did not exhaust his gift of apostleship to the church. This is equally true of all the other ministries needed by the church. No passage of scripture is more important in establishing this or more relevant to today's Church, than the fourth chapter of Paul's letter to the Ephesians.

Ephesians 4

The verses which are especially important for our discussion are verses 7 – 13. 'But to each one of us grace has been given as Christ apportioned it. This is why it says: 'When he ascended on high, he led captives in his train and gave gifts to men'. (What does 'he ascended' mean except that he also descended to the lower, earthly regions? He who descended is the very one who ascended higher than all the heavens, in order to fill the whole universe.) It was he who gave some to be apostles, some to be prophets, some to be evangelists, and some to be pastors and teachers, to prepare God's people for works of service, so that the body of Christ may be built up until we all reach unity in the faith and in the knowledge of the Son of God and become mature, attaining to the whole measure of the fulness of Christ' (Eph. 4. 7–13).

From this passage we learn a number of vital things about the ministries set in the Church.

1. They are the Gifts of the Ascended Christ who is Lord of the Church

Paul here is quoting and reflecting upon Psalm 68. Having commented upon the 'he ascended' of Psalm 68.18 Paul goes on to comment on the 'he gave' found in the same verse. As 'he ascended' means that Christ has returned in triumph to the glory of his Father, so 'he gave' means that in his ascension victory he shares the spoils with his church. Because 'he gave' is picked up from the quotation from Psalm 68 the past tense does not imply that it happened only once, but that 'the Ascended One is the giver of gifts'.[2] This he continues to be.

Nor does the change Paul makes from the 'he received gifts' of
Psalm 68 to the 'he gave gifts' in his version of it alter the
picture. For in order to give gifts you first have to receive
them. The obvious parallel here which has more than verbal
significance is the gift of the Holy Spirit. Of Jesus it was said
that 'exalted to the right hand of God, he has *received* from the
Father the promised Holy Spirit and has *poured out* what you
now see and hear' (Acts 2.33). So the Lord Jesus takes captured
rebels and gives them back to his Church as its leaders and
ministers. In G. G. Findlay's words, 'he gives what he receives.
Yet he gives not *as* he receives. Everything laid in his hands is
changed by their touch.' In this way chief prosecutors become
chief apostles and Christ's fiercest opponents become his finest
protagonists. Here is the irony that makes God smile, of 'gifts
and succour coming to the Church from unlooked-for quarters
and reinforcements from the ranks of the enemy'.[3]

2. These Ministries Represent the Head of the Church who is Christ

Apostles, prophets, evangelists, pastors and teachers receive
their commission directly from the Ascended Lord himself. Like
Paul their prototype, they are not made by men. They do not
receive their authority from men. They represent the headship
of Christ as the charismata express his Body. 'The New Testament ministry is an antitype of Christ the head'.[4] They do not
take orders from the Body but convey authority to it. They are
agents of the spiritual authority and rule of Christ in his
headship of the Church. As the nervous system extends the
brain to the body so they bring to the Church the necessary
control, vitality, direction and co-ordination it needs to function. In doing so they are called also to show some of the same
selfless, sacrificial love and care which the head shows to his
Church (cf. Eph. 5.23ff).

3. They Express Together the Fulness of Jesus

No one man or ministry can adequately represent Jesus. But
together the five-fold ministries can bring the Church to an
experience of the 'fulness of Christ' (Eph. 4.13). Each of the
ministries is needed to do this because Jesus was every one of
them and each of them is a measure of the gift of himself (cf.
Eph. 4.7). Jesus was *the* Apostle (Heb. 3.1), the 'sent one' of
the Father (cf. John 8.42). Jesus was 'a prophet, powerful in
word and deed' (Luke 24.19, cf. John 4.9, 6.14), in fact, *the*
Prophet, like Moses, who would arise in the last days (Acts

3.22ff). Jesus was the great evangelist, the preacher of the good news of the kingdom with signs that follow (Mark 1.15f, Matthew 4.23ff).

Jesus was, as we have seen, the good shepherd through death, the great shepherd through resurrection, the chief of all under-shepherds who pastor his flock (John 10.14, Hebrews 13.20, 1 Peter 5.4). Jesus too was the teacher who spoke with unprece-dented authority and power under the anointing of the Holy Spirit (Matt 4.29, 7.28, Acts 1.1–2). So, 'when those with varying ministry gifts are together they will collectively', Trevor Martin has written, 'manifest the singular ministry of Jesus'.(5) Through these five ministries Jesus gives himself again to his Church. We will begin to experience his fulness only when we have them.

4. They Complement One Another and Produce Variety

The apostles, the appointed messengers of Christ to his churches, have a fatherly ministry, laying a foundation of life, obedience and doctrine in each place. The prophets, the seers and spokesmen of Christ to his Church, bring vision to believ-ers, giving them a sense of purpose and direction through the living word. Evangelists proclaim the good news of the kingdom, heal the sick and cast out demons. Pastors rule and care for the sheep, feeding and fattening them for God. Teachers expound in detail the revelation brought by apostles and prophets, applying the whole counsel of God to the lives of believers and making disciples in the process.

Traditionally, the concept of ministry has been narrowed to that of the pastor-teacher with evangelists forced to work outside the church and apostles and prophets relegated to the limbo-land of yesteryear. But all the ministries are needed in the Church if for no other reason than to produce that essential variety which is a mark of God's handiwork. When a church is monopolised by the ministry of a teacher then the people form an audience and tend to become passive. Often, when the teacher leaves, his listeners leave too. Similarly, where an evan-gelist works alone without the other ministries, a large number of spiritual babies will be produced with no one to help them grow up and mature. If a prophet is the only ministry operating within the body then more often than not he will end up on some mountain top with a tiny handful of élite followers staun-chly believing they have received more revelation than anyone else. Unbalanced by any other ministry the pastor too, on his own, produces distortion. The sheep become merely fat and

woolly, over cosy and over fed, content to graze and glad to
have their ears tickled, but lacking any clear sense of direction.
But the Ascended Christ gives all five ministry-gifts in order to
provide his Church with that richness and variety which can
more nearly reflect his own.

5. *They are Ministries for the Whole Church.*

If, as we shall see, elders and overseers and deacons are ministries of the local church, then apostles, prophets, evangelists,
pastors and teachers are ministries for the whole Church. They
are, in today's jargon, 'trans-local' ministries. Their writ runs
throughout the many congregations that make up Christ's body.
They cut clean across denominational allegiances. They break
the mould of the independence of the local church. This is what
makes their presence, or even the threat of their presence, such
a contentious issue today. For it is the restoration of these gifts
to the Church that undermines our ecclesiastical structures as
nothing else does. Traditions which can absorb or attempt to
absorb the baptism and gifts of the Holy Spirit and which can
accommodate certain changes in styles of worship, cannot
contain such a diversity of ministry and remain the same. The
roles of apostles and prophets are, of course, the most disputed.
But it is the trans-local nature of these ministries that makes
them such a challenge to existing arrangements. Even the
'pastor' in Ephesians 4.11 is, I believe, to be seen as a shepherd
to the wider Church, rather than as the caring elder of the local
church.[6] Timothy was sent to perform this role of the pastor-
teacher as an apostolic delegate in many of the churches Paul
founded.

6. *These Ministries Bring Wholeness to the Church*

The Ascended Christ gives the church such leaders to do four
things:–
(a)   to 'equip' or 'prepare' believers for service.
(b)   to cause the Church to 'be built up' and grow numerically.
(c)   to bring believers to maturity both individually and
      corporately.
(d)   to unite the Church.
The Church will be what its ministers are. The Church does not
make such men. It would be truer to say that such ministries
make the Church. Certainly they bring to it a measure of wholeness. No longer are believers childish, spoon-fed and self-willed;
they are responsible and caring and supportive of each other.
No longer are believers tossed 'back and forth by the waves' of

mood or emotion, lacking assurance and stability; they are calm and consistent and joyful. No longer are they 'blown here and there by every wind of teaching'; instead they are continuing steadfastly in the apostles' doctrine. No longer are believers at the mercy of the 'cunning and craftiness of men', the victims of manipulation or church politics; they are enjoying open and honest relationships with their leaders and with one another. No longer are they stuck; they are growing up into Christ in every way. No longer are they fragmented; they are 'joined and held together' in a harmony where each knows his place and gift.

Is this picture of wholeness idealistic? If it is then we have grown unduly pessimistic, failing to grasp just what a restoration of *all* the ministry gifts of the Ascended Lord might do for us. At a great international conference I attended in Jerusalem there was a renewed heart-cry for the unity of the Church. But is it any use praying for unity without beginning to embrace the ministries which Jesus gives to us in order to bring this about? Since Christ gives them who are we to refuse them? If we accept these five ministries as given today we need to do three things with them.

(a) Recognise them. The Church needs a new boldness in breaking the mould of its own tradition and in beginning to name names and recognise functions. Don't make sainthood posthumous. Call a man a pastor and no one minds. But call a man an evangelist and no one quite knows what to do with him. Usually for lack of recognition he moves off to start his own organisation. Call a man 'apostle' or 'prophet' and we are even more discomfited until the results overtake our reticence.

(b) Release them. Antioch was a model church in its ability to see what the Holy Spirit was doing and to respond to his direction. It was willing to see the break up of its ministry team of prophets and teachers in order to free two of their number for apostolic work. Drastic changes in patterns of ministry and a great release of finances will be required to bring us into the good of the gifts Jesus has for his Church.

(c) Receive them. To receive his servants is to receive Christ himself. If we receive a preacher because he is a preacher we get a good sermon. But if we receive him as a prophet we receive a prophet's reward (Matthew 10.40). 'Even though my illness was a trial to you,' Paul tells the Galatians, 'you did not treat me with contempt or scorn. Instead

you welcomed me as if I were an angel of God, as if I were
Christ Jesus himself' (Gal. 4.14).

'It is my conviction', writes Arthur Wallis, 'that recognising apostles and prophets and letting them function, will yet prove to be
the most important restoration break-through of our time.'[7]

'Function' is a vital word here. Walking round Wisley Gardens,
the home of the Royal Horticultural Society, a colleague and I
admired a bush with luxuriant foliage and flowers. We tried to
identify it but it had grown so much that it had obscured its label!
When Jesus gives his men to the Church, what they do is in the
end more important than what they are called. It is to the varied
functions of the minstries the Ascended Christ gives that we now
turn. We do this in the hope that as these five-fold ministries are
given room to work in the Church, the growth they produce will
obscure their labels!

Part Four
Leadership Today

20. Father

Our experience of fatherhood can make or break our leadership. We have all been sons if we are not all fathers. Whenever my colleague, Derek Brown, has spoken to leaders on this theme of fatherhood the response has been dramatic. Invariably he has opened up their hearts. Some men have wept unashamedly in confessing how inadequate has been the relationship between them and their natural fathers. Others have sought forgiveness for not honouring their fathers in a biblical way. Others still have found healing from the deep hurts caused by the abuse of a father's powers. Many have subsequently praised God for his fatherly love, so lavishly poured into them to make good their lack.

My own experience of being a son is good. To my mother I owe more than I know. Like Hannah, she gave me back to God soon after I was born, praying that one day I might become useful in his service. As for my father, I treasure his friendship and value his favour. And it is my father of whom I am first conscious as a definite influence on my life. When his work took him away from home for a fairly long time I missed him greatly. I still remember how the smell of his old overcoat spread over my bed for added warmth comforted me in his absence. Carrying me on his shoulders at football matches, model-making at the large kitchen table, reading to me from his precious books, sharing with me his history with God, firing me with aspirations for spiritual things, he shaped my life in his own special way. His advice was sound and would have made me a better man if I had heeded it more often. His admonitions went to my heart not least because he never gave them, anymore than he did anything, unfeelingly.

But many are less fortunate. The effect of two World Wars has been to rob many men in two generations of a true experience of fatherhood. The fatherless and the orphan have been with us in great numbers. This has caused a psychological deprivation that a matriarchal society has been unable to make good. This sense of lost fatherhood has been aggravated by more recent social attitudes which have demeaned the whole concept of fatherhood.

Where Have all the Fathers Gone?

Timothy is one biblical character who owed almost everything to the women in his life. From childhood he had known the sacred scriptures and if, as is generally supposed, his father was a pagan, then it was from his mother and grandmother that he had learned them. 'For I am mindful of the sincere faith within you which first dwelt in your grandmother Lois, and your mother Eunice, and I am sure that it is in you as well (2 Tim. 1.5, 3.15). Despite this, Timothy's faith seemed to need constant exhortation and strengthening. He seems to have been weak and vulnerable as well as warm and sensitive. For all the good qualities formed in him by predominantly feminine influence, Timothy seems to lack that manly confidence which a strong and loving father might have given him. Was it the lack of a close formative relationship with his natural father which accounted for his natural timidity and nervous disposition?

What is certain is that the apostle Paul became a surrogate father to Timothy, acting 'in loco parentis' both emotionally and spiritually. There is much to suggest that Paul was instrumental in Timothy's conversion for the apostle writes to him as his 'true child in the faith' (1 Tim. 1.2). What we do know is that on his second visit to Lystra Paul was impressed by the young disciple's progress. Having circumcised him, Paul with the elders in Lystra, laid hands on the young man, spoke prophetically into his life, and took him with him as a travelling companion and trainee apostle (Acts 16.1ff). It was the start of a close and lovely friendship. To Paul, Timothy was a 'beloved son' (2 Tim. 1.2). In Paul's eyes there was no one like Timothy in his lack of self-interest and eagerness to serve. With no one else did Paul have such a spiritual rapport as with Timothy. 'For I have no one else of kindred spirit who will genuinely be concerned for your welfare', he assures the Philippians,' but you know of his proven worth that he served with me in the furtherance of the gospel like a child serving his father' (Phil. 2.21,23). As fathers and sons do, these two men walked together, worshipped together and worked together. Living so closely to the apostle, Timothy was able to observe at first hand how Paul acted and reacted. It was a true, travelling apprenticeship in being an apostle. Timothy had begun watching Paul closely from the very beginning, even before joining him in active work. 'But you followed my teaching, conduct, purpose, faith, patience, love, perseverance, persecutions, sufferings, such as happened to me at Antioch, at Iconium, and at Lystra; what persecutions I endured and out of them all the Lord delivered me' (2 Tim. 3.10–11). What an education in faith this must have been for a young man with leadership in view.

In every respect this father-son relationship which Paul and Timothy enjoyed is a model of how brothers should love one another and of how an experienced leader can develop and train a potential leader. When men of God 'father' others in the ways of God we are on the safe road to the next generation of leadership. By this method, if it can be called that, we will transmit life and vision not merely theories and ideas. The church desperately needs more fathers with this stature. There are plenty of old 'pros' around ready to tell their cynical tale of yesteryear but few with sufficient grace and vitality to give themselves to forming another's life and ministry. 'My Father, my Father' cries Elisha to the prophet Elijah, the man from whom he wanted a double portion of his spirit (2 Kings 2.12). Later when Elisha gave his own leadership seminars to the next generation of student prophets, Elijah-like miracles were part of the curriculum! (2 Kings 6.1f).

Out of this relationship the 'son in the faith' is able to avoid distorting his 'spiritual father's' vision as so many disciples are prone to do. Instead he can be trusted as his reliable representative. 'I have sent to you Timothy, who is my beloved and faithful child in the Lord, and he will remind you of my ways which are in Christ, just as I teach everywhere in every church' (1 Cor. 4.17).

Who Cares About Leaders?

The shepherding of shepherds is a perennial problem in the church. Too many leaders are still neither accountable to any one nor cared for by any one. More apostolic fathers are now emerging to meet this need especially felt by younger men in ministry. Like the proverbial father, Paul did not under-rate the importance of his fatherly counsel. 'My son, if you will receive my sayings, and treasure my commandments within you . . . you will discern the fear of the Lord and discover the knowledge of God' (Prov. 2.1–5). Taking this seriously, Paul did not 'venture suggestions' but re-iterated 'faithful sayings', proven principles, reliable truths worthy of the widest acceptance (1 Timothy 1.5, 3.1, 4.9, 2 Timothy 2.11–13). 'I solemnly charge you' stressed the import of his words (1 Tim. 5.21, 6.13, 2 Tim. 4.1). In this way Paul's fatherly counsel became the Word of God to us and especially to youthful leaders.

Paul faithfully admonishes, encourages and warns his son in the faith, reminding Timothy of the prophecies made about him (1 Tim. 1.8). Don't be deterred, Timothy is told; don't give way to your natural fears and timidity; be strong in the grace that is in Christ Jesus (1 Tim. 1.18, 2 Tim. 2.1). Discipline yourself, take yourself in hand; 'Have nothing to do with godless myths and old wives' tales; rather, train yourself to be godly' (1 Tim. 4.7). Don't be disregarded for your youth but especially because you are young set an example to the other believers (1 Tim. 4.12). Don't neglect your spiritual gift but stir it up again (1 Tim. 4.14, 2 Tim. 1.6). Don't succumb to an easy-come-easy-go attitude but take pains with these things, be absorbed in them, pay close attention to what you are and what you're teaching (1 Tim. 4.15–16). Don't throw your weight around insensitively: have respect for the subtleties of human relationships. 'Do not rebuke an older man harshly, but exhort him as if he were your father. Treat younger men as brothers, older women as mothers, and younger women as sisters, with absolute purity' (1 Tim. 5.1–2). Be unbiased and impartial, the prisoner of no section or vested interest (1 Tim. 5.21), nor impulsive in judgements of people's character (1 Tim. 5.22). Look after your health, keep fit, take a holiday, but don't overstretch the bow! (1 Tim. 5.23). Steer clear of the temptations, usually in the areas of sex and money, which young men are especially prone to (1 Tim. 6.11, 2 Tim. 2.22); and pursue the righteousness which godly men are made of. Fight the good fight of faith, be obedient and above reproach, and keep short accounts with God (1 Tim. 6.12–14). Guard what you have been entrusted with and raise new leaders (1 Tim. 6.20, 2 Tim. 1.14) by committing it to other equally faithful men. Handle the Word of God accurately, trust the Scriptures to make you a man of God, equipped for every good work (2 Tim. 2.15; 3.14–17, cf. 1 Tim. 4.6). Assert your authority but don't become quarrelsome; concentrate on the certainties; don't be drawn into unprofitable speculation and divisive arguments (2 Tim. 2.23–24). Correct error where it arises; don't be afraid of being thought negative for doing so, but do it with gentleness not with a partisan spirit, not with a view to winning a point but with a view to arriving at the truth (2 Tim. 2.25). Be serious-minded, avoiding the flippancy to which young men are prone (2 Tim. 4.5).

All this and more Timothy is urged to do. So Timothy is encouraged and strengthened to do all the work of ministry; to command, to preach, to teach, to exhort, to rebuke, to correct, to refute.

'Make every effort to come to me soon' reveals Paul's heart and reminds us that this is not a clinical handbook of pastoral practice but an apostolic father writing to his 'son' in the faith.

Paul's apostolic fathering extended of course to the churches under his care. 'I write,' he tells the Corinthians, 'to admonish you as my beloved children. For if you were to have countless tutors in Christ, yet you would not have many fathers; for in Christ Jesus I became your father through the gospel.' (1 Cor. 4.14–15). This is a vital apostolic function which has an effect even where the apostolic ministry has not actually founded the church. To such churches Paul as a father-figure is a model of faith and practice. 'I exhort you therefore be imitators of me' (1 Cor. 4.16). Paul reminds the Thessalonians of how he has exhorted and encouraged and implored them, just as a father would his children (1 Thess. 2.11). Far from being remote and managerial the apostolic ministry was concerned with individuals ('each one of you') as well as the Body as a whole. As Juan Carlos Ortiz says: 'In order to form lives, we must stop being speakers and start being fathers. Speakers have only hearers. Fathers have children. Learning doesn't come by hearing but by obeying'.[1] In the present development of our ministries, men of apostolic gift and measure are delegating more and more areas of shepherding to emerging leaders under them. This is right. And yet we are conscious of the need to nurture new converts and to bring them into the full reality of life in God. In our fellowship we are finding that these fragile young lives are frequently by-passing house group leaders and other under-shepherds in order to be with members of the ministry team. We could react to this by insisting they conform to our structure of shepherding and receive help from others. Or we could recognise that it is part of the original call of apostles to make disciples, immersing them in the full trinity life of Father, Son and Holy Spirit. Rather than hoping from a distance that commitment classes are meeting such needs, apostolic fathers may well have to 'travail in person for such people, until Christ is formed' in them. After all, Peter was told to feed the lambs!

Writing again to the Corinthians, Paul speaks with the protective jealousy of a father for his virgin daughter in danger of being spoiled and corrupted (2 Cor. 11.2). Bringing people through spiritual adolescence while preserving their priceless simplicity in Christ is the aim here. We are living in a time of newly emerging churches, many of which have young men at their head to whom God has given special grace to be 'elders'. At no other time could we have needed more this fatherly ministry of truly apostolic men.

21. Masterbuilder

'Remember always', wrote Jim Eliot in his journal, 'that God has taught you the importance of a *building* ministry.'

To bless is one thing; to build quite another – is how my colleague often puts it. There's no doubt which is harder. To bless people needs charisma and a fast car! It usually results in much appreciation, large love-gifts and return bookings. All of this is good and necessary but it is not enough. Jesus is not blessing the crowds but building his church. To build with him is hard work.

A ground plan is first required. The masterdesigner is not haphazard. Leaders with desire to build will need insight into the strategy of God for his church. In close collaboration with their prophetic team-mates such men will seek to build 'according to the pattern' shown to them on the mountain of revelation. Unfortunately, in today's church we cannot guarantee clear ground to work on. As in Nehemiah's day there is 'much rubbish' to remove before building can commence. Some churches have tried to graft the new structure of praise, body-life, cell groups onto the old without changing anything. So the old pattern of meetings, events and organisations competes with the new order of things. The result is chaos and exhausted and confused labourers. Clearing away the accumulated clutter is the only answer. Hand-picking the workers may then be the only way to start. Nehemiah found that not everyone who seemed outwardly keen on joining the reconstruction work was after what he was after (Ezra 4.2–3). There are some people we can well do without if we want to see God's house built. So-called experts in the building business have been wrong before after all!

Foundation-laying

To secure the base for building is then the first objective. 'According to the grace of God given me', writes Paul, 'as a wise master builder, I laid a foundation' (1 Cor. 3.10). A New Testament apostle is an 'architekton'. This means far more than the English word 'architect' implies. It conveys the idea of a superintendent of the building process, who oversees its erection. This apostolic function is the necessary basis for every local church which forms part of the household of God 'built upon the foundation of apostles and prophets' (Eph. 2.20). What does an apostle do in laying a foundation?

1. He lays a foundation of life in Christ. 'For no man can lay a foundation other than the one which is laid which is Christ Jesus' (1 Cor. 3.11). This is how he fathers the church as we have seen previously. The apostle is a life-source to the church. He is a channel of faith becoming like Abraham a 'father of the faithful'. To bring people to birth in Christ and to see them established causes him travail and pain until Christ is formed in them (Gal. 4.19).

2. He lays a foundation of obedience to Christ. An apostle stresses clearly from the beginning the Lordship of Jesus Christ for whom he is pledged to make disciples. He aims to bring about the 'obedience of faith' and looks for that obedience to be complete (Romans 1.5, 2 Cor. 10.6). It becomes harder to get away with the minimum when an apostle is involved with your life. He aims to help each individual in the church to build his house upon the only sure foundation of obedience to the commands of Jesus (Matt. 28.18f, 7.24f).

3. He lays a foundation of doctrine. Before the church can go onto maturity the foundational doctrine must have been clearly laid. This is apostolic building work. It is to ensure that every member of the church is clear on repentance and faith, on baptism in water and in the Holy Spirit, on eternal judgement and the resurrection of the dead (Hebrews 6.1ff). The apostle establishes believers on the sure foundation of their death and resurrection with Christ (Colossians 2.6ff). He confirms them in the dynamic of what it means to be united with Christ (Romans 6.1ff). He contends with every error and distortion that would detract from the fulness of Jesus and would diminish the believer's full experience of him. Legalism, antinomianism, mysticism, asceticism, pseudo-spirituality – all alike are refuted and corrected (e.g. Galatians, Colossians). For the apostle, the truth is the best basis for building.

Fit for Divine Habitation

According to the second book of Maccabees, the 'master builder is responsible for the whole construction'. He supervises the entire work, and is especially concerned for the fitting out of the building for its intended purpose. The brochure I collected from the estate agents when house-hunting stressed the selling points of the property I was interested in:–

> 'integral garage' . . .
> 'central heating' . . .
> 'fitted wardrobes . . . fully equipped kitchen'.

All this suggested it was ready for occupation! An apostolic leader is similarly concerned for the house of God. He is concerned for its internal integrity, that nothing in it is superfluous or unrelated to the stated purpose of the building. He wants the central heating of love to be working well so that the building is attractively warm and welcoming. He sees to it that the parts of the building are fitted and equipped to serve their function. All this is so that the church may once more be a dwelling place of God in the Spirit (Eph. 2.20–22).

During construction he will measure the house against the plumbline of Jesus (Revelation 1 – 3) who as cornerstone determines the shape of the building. 'Unfit for human habitation' used once to be scrawled on the walls of slums awaiting demolition. 'Fit for divine habitation' is now being written once more on the walls of the church undergoing restoration. For this the ministry of apostles under the Holy Spirit is largely responsible.

What is an Apostle?

The verb behind the noun 'apostle' means 'to send forth'. It implies that the person sent forth has received a commission to represent the authority which sends him. There is much uncertainty as to how deeply New Testament concepts were influenced by contemporary Jewish practice. The 'shaliach' were the legal delegates of the Sanhedrin and although not missionaries did travel with letters of authorisation. Saul of Tarsus was a typical case (Acts 9.2, 26.10). There is a rabbinic saying to the effect that 'the one sent by a man is as the man himself'. We are on surer ground if we seek a precedent for apostleship in the Lord Jesus himself. Not only is he The Sent-One of his Father (John 8.42) but he is in turn the Sender of others (Luke 11.49, John 20.21

'As the Father has sent me, I also send you'). He identifies himself totally with those he sends so that 'he who receives you receives me' (Matt. 10.40).

Apostles are the gift of Christ to his church. Here we must distinguish carefully between two different kinds of apostles. The distinction that needs to be made is between what might be called 'apostles of the Resurrection' and 'apostles of the Ascension'. The original Twelve, minus Judas, are those recommissioned by the Risen Christ. They receive the inbreathing of resurrection life directly from Jesus as the first fruits of his new creation. From him they receive proof of his being alive and the principles of the kingdom at firsthand. He gives them their orders through the Holy Spirit. Reinforced by Mathias, they receive the promised Holy Spirit at Pentecost. These are the 'apostles of the Lamb' with a special place in God's plan (Revelation 21.14, Matt. 19.28). To them Paul must be added as the one who completes the group of 'Resurrection apostles'. 'Last of all, as it were to one untimely born, He appeared also to me' (1 Cor. 15.8).

The testimony of this exclusive group of men forms the definitive standard of teaching and doctrine for us. We believe Jesus through their word (John 17.20). Strictly speaking, their only true successor is the New Testament itself which preserves the record of their inspired testimony (cf. John 16.12–14). All subsequent apostolic ministry must submit to and accurately reflect this normative apostolic testimony. Their word is primary and is Scripture; any other apostolic word is derivative and Scriptural.

Paul, however, is unique and pivotal. For not only is he the last of a series of apostles who have seen the Risen Christ: he is the *first* of a new series of what might be called 'Ascension apostles'. Not an original member of the Twelve, Paul accepts his call from Jesus without personally referring to them. In describing himself as 'untimely born' Paul may well be reflecting this conviction that he was a bridge between the original apostles and their successors. What is clear from Paul's case, is that the apostolic office was not limited to the Twelve. J. B. Lightfoot was surely right in stating that 'neither the canonical Scriptures nor the early Christian writings afford sufficient ground for any such limitation of the apostolate'.[1] Barnabas, James, the Lord's brother, Julias and Andronicus, Timothy and Silas, are others given an apostolic role. No longer do apostles have to come down from Jerusalem. Antioch is the new starting-point for those commissioned by the Ascended Christ through the Holy Spirit. As Paul makes clear to the Ephesians, it is 'he who ascended far above all the heavens that he might fill all things' who gives 'some to be apostles'. He is building his church still. To that end his ascension gifts of ministry have no more ceased than his ascension gift of the Holy Spirit. Today's church needs both.

What kind of men are apostles? How do we recognise them? In writing to the Thessalonians, Paul gives us the marks of an apostle.

1. He likes to work as part of a team. 'Paul and Silvanus and Timothy' write to the church at Thessalonica. Over 20 men were at one time or another associated with Paul in his apostolic travels. True apostles are not charismatic lone-rangers who lack or even despise the checks and balances of plurality. Rather they relish the tension and joys of peer-level relationships. That is why they can lead others. Keen to move with other men of God, they attract other ministries to them in a complementary team. For the same reason they love to bring on younger men in their calling in God (1 Thess. 1.1). Building together is great wisdom.

2. He moves in a measure of gift and anointing. 'For our gospel did not come to you in word only but in power and in the Holy Spirit and with full conviction' (1 Thess. 1.5). They have spiritual power not ecclesiastical status. Enjoying the charisma of the Holy Spirit they may not be 'officially ordained' in today's church.

   In this respect those who are beginning to move out in apostolic calling are the first to admit that what they are is embryonic. All of them that I know covet the 'wonders and miracles' which are one of the true signs of an apostle (2 Cor. 12.12). Builders in a spiritual house, they are men of the Spirit.

3. He has proven character. 'You know what kind of men we proved to be among you' (1 Thess. 1.5b). They are men of integrity, who have the mastery over wrong motives. They are not out to deceive or flatter or make money from those they minister to (1 Thess. 2.2–6). They are men worth imitating in order to draw nearer to Jesus (1.6).

4. He is a man of patience and gentleness. 'Even though as apostles of Christ we might have asserted our authority, we proved to be gentle among you . . .' (1 Thess. 2.6–7). Because he is a man of faith an apostle can afford to wait. Being a man of love he does not throw his weight about. Building with living bricks takes time and trouble. Paul describes himself as 'imploring each one of you as a father would his own children' (1 Thess. 2.11). We have looked at

this in the previous chapter. It is worth adding here that such fathers to the church have a concern for 'each one' in the family. True apostles are not remote office managers presiding over some new charismatic empire which they lay claim to 'covering'. True apostles are prepared to spend time with individuals and not just leaders at that. They are 'on-site' superintendants of the work.

5. He is a bearer of the word of God. 'You received from us the word of God's message' (1 Thess. 2.13). Paul describes himself proudly as 'a preacher and an apostle and a teacher of the gentiles in faith and truth' (1 Tim. 2.7). No man can ultimately be recognised as an apostle who does not have a proven ministry as a preacher or teacher of the Word of God. For it is God's Word which is his root of authority. It is God's Word in him which is his source of life and makes his ministry effective (1 Thess. 2.13).

6. He stands or falls by the church. 'You became imitators of us . . . so that you became an example to all the believers in Macedonia and Achaia. (1 Thess. 1.6–7, 2.19 – NASB).
(a) Like Peter, an apostle should be a fellow-elder in a local body. There he can be tested and checked as he learns like the rest of us what it means to 'submit to one another in the fear of the Lord'. As a fellow-elder he knows the responsibility of rule and pastoral care which leaders in the church have and as an apostle will be able to speak into other churches with greater sensitivity (1 Peter 5.1f). He will not want the 'last word' in a legalistic manner, preferring to find the authority of Christ in agreement with the local eldership.
(b) Because he is sent out by the church to which he belongs, an apostle carries credibility with him. Those who receive him can expect that he will have worked out at home whatever he is laying on them as counsel (Acts 13.1–3).
(c) And because they are sent out by the church of which they are part, true apostles are eager to return to give their report. 'From Attalia they sailed back to Antioch, where they had been committed to the grace of God for the work they had now completed. On arriving there, they gathered the church together and reported all that God had done through them and how he had opened the door of faith to the Gentiles' (Acts 14.26–27). True apostles appreciate being accountable. This gives them a sense of security, saves them from the wrong kind of independence, and reminds them that they exist to serve the body and not themselves. So they want the best for the church not least because their reput-

ation is at stake! 'For what is our hope, our joy, or the crown in which we will glory in the presence of our Lord Jesus Christ when he comes? Is it not you?' (1 Thess. 2.19). They take care how they build so that God's house may be fit for Him to live in.

Apostles Today

The more we see what apostles do and are the more we realise how indispensable their ministry is. The Acts of the Apostles is a book without an ending. It records that what 'Jesus began to do and to teach' he continued to do and say through his apostles. The Acts of the Apostles has proved such a consistent source of inspiration to reforming hearts in every generation of the Church because it records the beginning not the end of her story. The teaching of the apostles is as basic as their acts. 'They were continually devoting themselves to the apostles' teaching' (Acts 2.42). This teaching needs to be restated in every age as the foundational doctrine of the church (cf. Heb. 6.1f). It must be re-applied in every fellowship as the pattern of truth to which each disciple is committed for the shaping of his character (Romans 6.17). Apostolic words and deeds are vital to us. The foundation-laying ministry of apostles is essential if churches undergoing radical change are to come onto clear ground and those wholly new groupings of God's people are to come onto a secure and biblical basis. Apostolic men with ability to father the church, its pastors and people, are a real blessing from God. It goes without saying that we need such men today.

This is, of course, fiercely disputed. Some, for sincere biblical reasons, rule out the possibility of apostles today. Others scarcely seem able to conceive of any pattern of ministry other than that which history has left us as its confused legacy. In his otherwise helpful little book 'Ministers of God', the evangelical Anglican scholar, Dr. Leon Morris, reviews the three main forms of church government current in the institutional church: Episcopalianism (bishops), Presbyterianism (eldership), and Congregationalism (the church meeting). Each is a partial reflection of the New Testament, Dr. Morris suggests; and each is therefore defective. Furthermore, as attempts at unity have shown, each is a barrier to the other. Dr. Morris's conclusion is that with larger doses of humility and forbearance we shall learn to live with the muddle! One suspects that behind many fine words too much is at stake for anyone to admit we might all have been wrong. There is an alternative. It is not an innovation. We assert as our starting point what the other three viewpoints deny: that the apostolic role is as valid and vital today as ever before. This is to agree with the German charismatic theologian, Arnold Bittlinger, when he says that 'the New Testament nowhere suggests that the apostolic ministry was intended only for first-century Christians'.[2] Dr. Morris argues that the early church had a flexible approach to its patterns of ministry. But it is precisely its flexibility that makes the new wineskin of apostleship so necessary and desirable.

Is the building finished? Is the Bride ready? Is the Body full-grown or the saints completely equipped? Has the church attained its ordained unity and maturity? Only if the answer to these questions is 'yes' can we dispense with apostolic ministry. But as long as the church is still growing up into Christ who is its head, this ministry is needed. 'If the Church of Jesus Christ is to grow faster than the twentieth-century population explosion, which I assume to be God's intention, then we will need to produce, recognise and use Pauline apostles.'[3]

22. Eye-opener

In Richard Adam's classic story 'Watership Down' we share the adventures of a small band of rabbits as they leave their threatened field in search of a new and safer warren. We are introduced to Hazel, the courageous leader, to Bigwig, the brave warrior, to Strawberry, Buckthorn and the rest. And then there is Fiver, perhaps the most interesting character of them all. Fiver is different. More sensitive than the other rabbits, he seems to be on almost constant alert. His body tense, his whiskers trembling, his ears pricked, his eyes staring, his nose sniffing the air, he seems perpetually on watch. It is Fiver who sees what the others don't see, who senses danger and warns others of it. He smells the breath of hope wafted from afar. He exhorts and cajoles his fellow rabbits in order to stir them to action. In short, Fiver is the prophet of the group. He convinces the other rabbits that change is not merely as good as a rest but is necessary for survival. He forces them to make decisions they ordinarily would not want to make. He opens up to them possibilities they cannot at first envisage. Acting on intuition, he frees them from the paralysis of well-tried habit. By following his counsel they are saved.

Prophets have invariably proved to be the 'salvation' of the Church. Their importance is not to be measured by the number of times the word 'prophets' is used in the New Testament. In fact, only one man, called Agabus, is featured as a prophet in the Acts of the Apostles though others, including Paul, are named in this category. But Agabus certainly turned up at a crucial time especially for the Jerusalem Church. He appears as a trans-local ministry, fired with the Holy Spirit, with a strongly predictive message from God. Forecasting a severe famine, Agabus stirs up the disciples in Antioch to give money to help the brothers back in Judea (Acts 11.27ff). Prophecy is as practical as famine relief!

Agabus appears once more in the record of the Early Church in a way which throws further light on the New Testament understanding of prophecy. In apostolic teaching there is a clear distinction made between the gift and the ministry of prophecy. Though all can prophesy by virtue of their baptism in the Holy Spirit, not all are prophets. Though all can 'manifest' the gift of prophecy, only some are 'appointed' to the ministry of a prophet (cf. 1 Cor. 12.7, 28–29, 14.29ff). So Agabus arrives at Caesarea to meet Paul who is staying with Philip the evangelist and his four daughters. Although these four girls have the 'gift of prophecy', Agabus has the ministry of 'a prophet'. And it is Agabus not one of the four girls who is entrusted with a major directive prophecy for Paul (Acts 21.9ff).

But in discovering what a prophet is and does we are not restricted to the brief references to Agabus however great a man of God he was. Evidence of prophetic activity is far more wide-spread in the New Testament than a concordance might suggest. For the prophet 'receives an *insight into the mysteries of God*'. [1] In fact, wherever the words 'revelation' or 'mystery' occur we are in touch with prophetic activity (cf. Rev. 1.1–3, 10.7). Much of what the Apostle Paul and the Apostle John saw comes into this category.

The 'mystery' which a prophet deals in, is a major New Testament concept. By 'mystery' is meant not a hidden truth but a truth inaccessible to man's knowledge which is now revealed by the Holy Spirit. It becomes an 'open secret', a manifestation of those plans and dispensations of God which are hidden from human reason and hence must be revealed to those for whom they are intended.[2]

At the heart of this 'mystery of the kingdom' is the person of Jesus Christ himself, in whom the kingdom has come in advance of its final manifestation (cf. Mark 4.11).[3] This is why Jesus is central to the prophet's theme. For both Old Testament and New Testament prophets it is the 'testimony of Jesus which is the spirit of prophecy' (Rev. 19.10, cf. 1 Peter 1.10–11).

The 'mystery' has several important dimensions.

1. It can be seen as the total purpose of God in redemption made known in the revelation of Jesus Christ (Romans 16.25–26) who is the embodiment of all wisdom and knowledge (Col. 2.2).
2. It can be seen in the indwelling of Christ in Gentile believers (Col. 1.29) and his intimate union with his Church (Eph. 5.29), which ultimately includes Jewish and Gentile believers in one body as one New Man (Eph. 3.3–6).
3. It can be seen in the present rejection of Israel being to the benefit of the Gentiles in such a way that must still lead

to the recovery of Israel to faith in her Messiah (Romans 11.25–26).
4. It can be seen in its final form in the restoration of all things and their summing up in the Lordship of Jesus Christ (Eph. 1.9–10) which will involve believers in putting on resurrection bodies like Jesus' own (1 Cor. 15.50–51).

All this is the burden of the prophet. He is concerned to open our eyes to these dimensions of the 'mystery' and to spell out their implications for us. The prophet will therefore always want us to see four things.

1. He will want to show us *what God is up to in history*. He will open our eyes to the overall plan of salvation. He will not allow us to become locked in to any one culture or epoch. He will insist that God's strategy is bigger than any exclusive national expression and more far-reaching than any temporary phase. To use an old cliché, he stops the church marrying the spirit of the age because he knows she will be widowed in the next. The prophet does all in his power to prevent the Church becoming bogged down in details or preoccupied with non-essentials. He forces us to stand back and take the larger view. When he senses we have lost our way he seeks to get us back on course; if we become stuck he urges us to move again. Like his biblical predecessors a prophet vigorously 'explains the meaning and progress of the divine redemptive activity'.[4] All the time he will give our puny efforts significance by relating them to the total purpose and victory of God in Christ.

2. The prophet will want to show us *what the Church is really meant to be*. He is concerned for the shape of the Church, for the form it takes in the world. The prophet's yardstick for the Church is Jesus and he can be quite ruthless in applying it (cf. Rev. 1.1–3). Anything in the Church which obscures Jesus from needy men, comes under his scrutiny. Inevitably, he challenges accepted ideas and hallowed habits with a view to making Jesus more visible in his body. He aims to uproot unrighteousness from the church and to bring judgement to the household of God. He gives the Church purpose and sets goals to be achieved. He brings much needed order to the Body of Christ and gives it clear direction. The Church, he insists, exists for God and the world, not for itself. Its worship, its fellowship life, its shepherding should all have a clear prophetic root. He strives to break

any ghetto mentality and to implement God's 'intent that now, through the Church, the manifold wisdom of God should be made known to the rulers and authorities in the heavenly realms' (Eph. 3.10). Always he keeps before the eyes of the Church the vision of the One New Man.

Prophecy involves dramatic action and the prophet motivates the people of God to be doers of the Word and not hearers only. The symbolic actions of the Old Testament prophets were isolated and sometimes eccentric acts of individual men of God. Today the prophet will do his utmost to ensure that the whole Church has a prophetic lifestyle – a lifestyle of simplicity, of sacrificial love and truthful speech which will give credibility to its message. The prophet works to produce sacramental men and women who once truly immersed in the dying and rising of Jesus will become broken bread and poured out wine for one another and for the world. Through anointed prophets the Church will become, like her Lord, 'mighty in word and deed'.

3. The prophet will want to show us *what is going on in the world*. He will be aware of world events though not preoccupied with them. He will keep reminding the Church that it does not merely exist to preserve certain timeless truths. Rather he will show the Church that it is part of a historical movement, with roots in history and by its own faith and response able to shape history. He will not date-fix because he does not know the date or the hour. But he will have an acute sense of the seasons in God's dealings with me. He is aware of the undercurrents of evil in the world not just of its more blatant manifestations. So he saves the Church from moralistic reactions and makes it truly prophetic in its judgements. Like a true son of Issachar he understands the times and knows what God's people should do. Above all he is quick to detect movements of God's Spirit and to stir the Church to respond.

4. The prophet, finally, will want to show *what is coming from the future*. I put it this way so as to avoid the impression that a prophet predicts the future in a detached or analytical way. For he presents a future fashioned by the grace of God, and in this prospect there is nothing rigid or deterministic. The fixed points are promises of personal appearances and personal resurrection. The certain fact of judgement to come makes moral decisions crucial now. The prophet brings the future into today and exhorts the church to live in the light of it. He brings true hope by eliminating wishful thinking.

He is the enemy of fatalism and the friend of faith. He opposes panic but resists passivity just as strongly. His view of the future is attractive enough to drive men to their knees in prayer and sure enough to keep them on their toes in eager anticipation. For the prophet the 'End' is not so much a distant date in a diary as the 'final state of affairs'. In this sense it is always at hand, pressing in on the Church to shape its thinking and action. By the Spirit the prophet shows us the things that are to come as and when we need to know them. He detects the cloud no bigger than a man's hand which will break with blessing on our heads. He shows us what the future can become, that it is not all fixed and settled but awaits our response and engagement. So the prophet argues for flexibility in the Church, with nothing permanent that isn't scriptural, with everything possible that is initiated by the Spirit.

So the Church is enabled to glimpse things which eye cannot see in any other way than by the prophet. Seeing this, the Church is challenged to change and to do nothing that is incompatible with the glorious end now staring it in the face. So the prophet will prove an uncomfortable man. He will object when things seem to be running too smoothly or along well-established lines. When everything is weighed up in advance, when predictability threatens to stifle faith, the prophet will be moved to protest and to plead with the Church to make room for the surprises of the Holy Spirit.

Doors of Perception

Unlike his biblical predecessors, the prophet today, of course, is not the original source of definitive and normative doctrine. They were part of the unique and inspired revelation of Scripture. He is a part of the necessary but secondary process of unveiling this previous revelation to his own generation. This needs to be said to guard against any misunderstanding of the position I am adopting. Sadly, the 'faith once delivered to the saints' has often been distorted or totally obscured by extra-biblical revelation purporting to come from God through a self-appointed visionary or prophet. To acknowledge this is not to go back on our conviction that the prophet is a valid ministry today but merely to emphasise the proper limits under which it operates. Only that prophetic ministry is valid which ratifies, clarifies or confirms the written word of God, the Bible. Having said that, we are now in a position to show that the *ways* in which today's prophet opens our eyes are similar to the ways employed by his biblical counterparts.

1. He describes *what he sees*. Originally, the prophet was a 'seer'. Isaiah calls him the 'eye' of the people of God (29.10). Amos tells us what 'he saw concerning Israel.' Much of the New Testament revelation is an unfolding of visionary experience undergone by the apostles. Peter saw the 'catholic' Christ unfettered by Judaistic inhibitions; Paul saw the 'crucified' Christ now glorified and identified with his suffering body; John saw the 'cosmic' Christ, the 'Pantokrater' to whom all the kingdoms of this world submit. So today the prophet brings God's point of view to the Church. From him we learn that God's views are good news. He envisions the Church. His oversight ensures that God's plans are carried out. With prophetic insight he penetrates to the real issues that have to be resolved; with foresight he anticipates the changes that have to be made. Though subordinate to the authoritative word of Scripture, he nevertheless throws light on God's will and ways with the force and vividness of an eye-witness. His message is secondary but not secondhand because his source is the living God. Prophets not drugs unlock the 'doors of perception'.

2. He speaks *what he hears*. The prophet is the listening ear of the church. He is privy to the divine secrets, sharing in the divine council (Jer. 23.18). Isaiah eavesdrops on heaven's cabinet meeting. Abraham and Moses are prophets because they are the friends and confidants of God. Like them, the prophet today, is pre-eminently God's spokesman. He will tell us what God is saying. Who can doubt that this ministry is needed or is often sadly lacking.

   Commenting on a recent session of the General Synod of the Church of England which discussed the re-introduction of capital punishment, the Religious Affairs Correspondent of a leading daily newspaper noted that in the whole of the debate no one put forward any theological arguments, though strong such arguments, he conceded, do exist. This is tantamount to admitting that God did not get a word in edgeways, that his point of view was never represented. Instead, humanistic considerations prevailed. This is all too common in some sections of the Church where its so-called 'prophets', as we noted in an earlier chapter, are merely echoing what is being said by the world. In Francis Schaeffer's words 'when we listen to the religion that is largely preached in our generation, we hear the same thing the unbelieving philosophers and sociologists are saying. The only difference is that theological language is used'.[5]

A number of writers have pointed out that our bustling, over-stimulating technological society is a poor breeding ground for men whose primary need is silence, meditation and listening. Sometimes for this reason the prophet retreats into solitariness in order to hear God clearly once again, and to regain his sense of priorities. It is not tragedy but triviality which wears out the prophetic soul. In George Maloney's words 'the prophet studies to be quiet' before he speaks.

3. He shows *what he feels*. Having dealt with this in an earlier chapter, it is enough to emphasise briefly that the prophet represents the heart of God as well as his voice. Sometimes the emotions of God in him will conflict with his own natural feelings. Jeremiah's patriotism in face of national danger and Ezekiel's mourning in bereavement were both over-ridden in order to communicate God's own feelings to his people. The prophet embodies his message; he is not a Telex machine. He expresses the anger and anguish, the joy and compassion of the one who sends him. Yet for the same reason his own lifestyle can confirm or contradict his message. By his fruits of conduct and faith he is known.

4. *He asks questions*. 'The prophets,' as Heschel says, 'do not offer reflections about ideas in general. Their words are onslaughts, scuttling illusions of false security, challenging evasions, calling faith to account, questioning prudence and impartiality.'[6] The prophet will ask awkward questions to uncover the truth. 'Is it a time for you yourselves to be living in your panelled houses, whilst this house remains a ruin?' (Haggai 1.3). 'Will a man rob God?', asks Malachi as he finds the people withholding their tithes.

The Old Testament prophets 'searched intently and with the greatest care, trying to find out the time and circumstances to which the Spirit of Christ was pointing' (1 Peter 1.10). 'He will have a certain God-centred restlessness, a constant looking at things and asking how they could be better.'[7] A prophetic leader, filled with the same Spirit of Christ, will be the spiritual equivalent of a keen investigative journalist. He will inquire into the credibility gap between what we profess and what we are. He will expose the discrepancy between the ideal and the actual. He will ask whether opportunities have been deliberately ignored through cowardice or compromise on the part of the Church. He will probe possibilities for advance and progress that lethargy had overlooked. His searching questions prod the Church awake and keep the Church alive. Any community that responds negatively to such questioning by justifying or defending itself unthinkingly is fast on the way to becoming an institution. When the prophet is fended off in this way, then, to use Paul Tournier's phrase, 'the adventure is over'.[8] I use the word 'unthinkingly' because it is the role of the prophetic ministry to force the Church to think about what it is doing and why it is doing it.

5. *He brings the 'now' word from God.* Truth which is too generalised is ineffective. Even the word of God can be so systematised into concepts and doctrines as to lose its impact and thrust. If this happens then we have lost the sense of a Living Voice addressing us, confronting and consoling us. Ensnared in a routine of cyclic Bible studies, we almost imperceptibly lose the ability to know when God is actually speaking to us. In my own experience I found that a precondition of any renewal was to restore to the people the sense that God might actually be speaking specifically to them about certain definite things. It is this which the prophet brings home to the Church. His message, in Tozer's words, 'must alarm, arouse, challenge; it must be God's *present* voice to a *particular* people'.[9] So the prophet personalises and contemporises the timeless word of God. He challenges complacent assumptions based on previous revelation. So Amos warns that the Day of the Lord for which the people long may not turn out to be quite what they expect (5.18). Once God may have said 'peace, peace' but he is not saying it *now* and to believe that he is when there is no peace is to be lulled into a dangerously false sense of security. The prophet will not allow us to lock God's word up in the past, so that what God has once said makes us immune from what he is now saying. Because he brings the 'now' word of God the prophet may appear one-sided. This is one reason for the plurality of ministry described earlier. But even so to try to balance his message up too soon will blur its impact. Before we react by saying 'but, on the other hand' we need to hear God's voice clearly. Harry Blamires has pertinently compared the scholar with the prophet (or thinker). The scholar, he says, 'evades decisiveness; he hesitates to praise or condemn; he balances conclusion against conclusion so as to cancel our conclusiveness; he is tentative, sceptical, uncommitted'. But the prophet

'hates indecision and confusion; he is dogmatic and committed; he works towards decisive action'.[10] Jacques Ellul has neatly summarised the dialogue between a prophet and his hearer.

'Yes or no, this time, will you listen to this Word of God?
But I already heard it yesterday.
We are now living today.
It's all the same.
But you are not the same, you have to decide today'.[11]

6. *He evaluates the past.* 'The function of the prophet is to interpret to the chosen people the ways of God in history.'[12] It was prophets who wrote the history of Israel endeavouring to bring out the underlying purpose and outcome of God's dealing with his people (cf. 2 Chron. 9.29). Prophets trace for us the real movements of God and highlight their true lessons, by distinguishing them from all human traditions. Seemingly minor events are shown to have major significance. Behind such stories, in Jocz's words, 'is the prophetic conviction that the shaping of human destiny is in God's hands and that he does not depend upon an outward show of strength'.[13] Writing Israel's history the prophets pass over whole tracts of time, summarising a king's reign in a sentence as good or evil, measuring everyone small or great, against the yardstick of God's will. Today the prophet has the responsibility of being conversant with Church history. He will help us to see why the Church is the way it is and the world is the way it is. Knowing the Church's record of revival and declension, he applies the true lessons of the past to rouse God's people to be 'the generation that seeks God's face'.

7. *He leads the way forward.* There is much to suggest that in its earliest days prophets directed the Church's life under the inspiration of the Holy Spirit. In Luke's account of the Early Church 'prophets play a large part and determine the Church's most important decisions'.[14] As the analogy of Antioch implies, prophets take precedence in a local church in the direction of its affairs, especially its strategy and forward planning. Prophetic leaders point the way forward and then keep the church moving on its true course. Hosea reflects on the role of Moses as leader of Israel: 'The Lord used a prophet to bring Israel up from Egypt and by a prophet he cared for him' (12.13). In leading the Church

forward, the prophet may often have to break down what
obscures his view. Laying his axe to the root of sacred trees,
he acts as a true radical. But he tears down only with a view
to building again on clear ground. A true prophet is a man
of faith and therefore will never be a destructive critic or
disillusioned cynic. There are plenty of people who can tell
you what is wrong with the Church – it's not too difficult to
do so! Such people are not necessarily prophetic. A leader
with a prophetic ministry will not snipe from the sidelines.
He will be one with the people, leading them into new
experiences of the living God. This, incidentally, is why
prophets today, as they once did, should lead us in worship
and praise.

8. *He motivates.* The prophet opens the eyes of God's people
to strengths and achievements they scarcely feel capable of.
He is an exhorter. He does not show the vision and leave
you to it. When Zerubbabel and Joshua began to rebuild
Jerusalem, we read that 'the prophets of God were with
them supporting them'. Later it is recorded that 'the elders
of the Jews were successful in building through the prophesying of Haggai the prophet and Zechariah, the son of Iddo'
(Ezra 5.2, 6.14 NASB). It is said of Judas and Silas, themselves prophets, that they 'said much to encourage and
strengthen the brothers' (Acts 15.32). Our senior pastor at
home, Mike Pusey, has for long exemplified his 'patron
saint', Barnabas. Barnabas earned his nickname because he
was a Son of 'paraklesis' or encouragement. When we recall
that such prophetic encouragement was crucial to Paul in the
amazing aftermath of his conversion and was instrumental in
launching him into his own ministry, we will not underesti-
mate this aspect of the prophet's word. In Robert Brow's
fine words, 'It is not just a question of a little word of
building up and a few consoling thoughts. The building up
is lifting men and women out of the humdrum into the great
movement of God in history. The encouragement of real
'paraklesis' is the application of the Holy Spirit, the Paraclete
himself, to shake man to the very core and stand him on his
feet again to do exploits for God'.[15]

These, then, are the various ways in which, to his own measure,
today's prophetic leader can emulate his biblical predecessors. As
contemporary apostles lay a foundation, in every place, of life,
doctrine and obedience, so today's prophet lays a foundation
of revelation, vision and direction. As a result of its perpetual

introspection the Church is not short of opinions and answers. But as DeVern Fromke points out 'answers will never work where unveilings are needed'.

The prophetic ministry is needed at every level of the Church's life to preserve its integrity and freedom. Without the prophet the Church becomes a 'spiritless organisation' in which even apostolic work hardens into a new form of religious bureaucracy. Without the prophetic thrust, the teaching ministry perpetuates a cycle of timeless truth but is deaf to what the Spirit is now saying to the churches. Similarly, as Jim Wallis notes, 'without a prophetic voice challenging God's people to lay down their lives in the world, pastoral nurture can easily degenerate into self-serving group welfare or inward and unbiblical withdrawal'.[16] Evangelism, too, desperately needs to hear the prophet if its methods are to be as godly as its message, and if it is to avoid giving stereotyped answers to questions which people are not asking.

'I am sending you prophets' is a heartening promise from the Lord Jesus to today's church. *For too long conventional ministerial training colleges have been non-prophet making organisations.*But thankfully, and not before time, the Spirit is raising up a new breed of prophetic men. It is the burden of this chapter that such men are urgently needed. In my view prophets are a risk the Church must take.

23. Instructor

In the Scriptures a variety of fascinating metaphors is used to describe 'the word of God'. In particular it is interesting to note that the 'word' is likened not only to 'a seed' but also to the 'water' that nourishes the seed and causes it to grow. 'Let my teaching fall like rain', Moses prays in expectation (Deut. 32.2, cf. Isaiah 55.10–11, 1 Cor. 3.6). The word of God has to be sown deeply in men's lives. Once this is done, an ongoing ministry of the word is needed to water the seed of life and bring it thrusting through the ground. The teacher's aim is to nourish the life of God implanted in others until it blossoms into confident openness before God and the world, able to bear whatever fruit God intends it to produce. In short it is clear that in the New Testament the specific aim of the ministry of the word is to bring believers to maturity. Paul stresses this in writing to the Colossians. 'We proclaim him, admonishing and teaching everyone with all wisdom, so that we may present everyone perfect in Christ' (Col. 1.28).

Before we look at this we need to note three things.

(1) The ministry of the word is a 'stewardship from God' (Col. 1.25 NASB). God entrusts us with the message of salvation, with the very word of life, with the awesome task of interpreting the scriptures for our day. We are to be workmen who do not need to be ashamed, 'handling accurately the word of truth'.

(2) The steward's objective is that he 'might fully carry out the preaching of the word of God' (1.25 NASB). He is to 'make full the word of God'. The strong and exciting implication here is that by ministering the word we are actually fulfilling God's purpose in the world. Because the gospel is no gospel until it is received as good news and takes root in men's lives, the actual preaching of it is part of the saving plan. When we speak God's word we are not merely describing or even explaining something that has happened or is about

to happen. Speaking God's word is a truly prophetic activity in that it helps to bring into being what is being spoken of. We extend and prolong the gospel by the very act of declaring it.

(3) The subject of the steward's ministry is the 'mystery that has been kept hidden for ages and generations but is now disclosed to the saints' (1.26). It is a joy to be allowed to share open secrets (cf. Matt. 10.26–27). Even though men cannot grasp the meaning of our word without the intervention of the Holy Spirit we are still obligated to present clear and unambiguous revelation to them. Christian ministry is not a special branch of the secret service. A relative of mine recently heard a sermon on 'the beast' in the Apocalypse in which twenty-seven different interpretations of its identity were given. Now 'the beast' is in the Book and you may have to deal with it. But to leave your hearers with twenty-seven different ideas buzzing around in their heads is not teaching towards maturity! We are dealing with 'mysteries' but not with mystification! We live in an era in which God's purposes are manifest to us in a way that they were not even to the great heroes of faith of Hebrews chapter eleven. By grace we are 'in the know' and it is an exciting privilege to be called to communicate what we have been shown as faithful witnesses.

With these provisional points in mind, we turn to the various forms this communication takes.

Proclaiming Christ

Because the medium is part of the message when it comes to imparting spiritual truth, we need to watch that our methods are as godly as our message. This is why *proclamation* holds such a key place in God's economy.[1] It is no accident that God committed himself to saving the world through the preaching of the Cross. He has not done this because preaching was the only method available to him in an unsophisticated pre-media age. He chose this way quite deliberately. He has ordained that spiritual truth is ultimately transmitted by one man who, standing in the flesh in front of other men, communicates to them through his own personality and anointing the very word of life. This is simply a consequence of the incarnational principle which makes our gospel so distinctive in the world. To doubt the value of what is called 'propositional truth' – the view that truth can be put into words – is really to deny Jesus himself. For this was precisely what he did. As the unique embodiment of the word of God, he stood on the earth and spoke eternal truth to those who listened to him even if they did not always understand him. 'What we have heard' as well as seen, recalls the aged Apostle John, still wondering at the fact, constitutes the revelation of that Word of Life which was from the beginning.

So, Paul tells the Colossians, 'we *proclaim* Christ' (Col. 1.28). Not everyone who reads this will be in a position to be a proclaimer of the word. Some may aspire to be. There is no greater privilege for me than to be a man who is called to proclamation. 'Katangello' is the Greek word for it. It certainly does not mean to have a chat or give a little homily. To proclaim means 'to have the intention of celebrating, of publicly commending and openly praising'. This is what we do when we proclaim Christ. We celebrate him, openly and publicly, commending him with praise as Lord and Saviour and Messiah. This is the foundation of bringing believers to maturity.

'Preaching Jesus' is not the simplistic exercise some have made it. It is not merely an invitation to 'come to Jesus'. The kind of Jesus Paul is proclaiming he describes to the Colossians. The Christ is the firstborn of all creation, the image of the invisible God, who has reconciled all things by his blood and is now, as the first born to rise from the dead, the head of the Church, pre-eminent in everything. In order to bring others to maturity we need to present believers with the overall purpose of God and show them Christ's central place in it.

Those who minister God's word must teach this big view. They should teach the details as well, of course, for they are vital. But they should start with the big view. Young disciples often come to me and tell me how much they want this. 'We have all the pieces' they say; 'we have been taught forgiveness and the Spirit and authority and body-life and much more beside. What we want to know is how it all fits together'. A comprehensive view of God's strategy needs to be presented which shows how everything holds together in Christ. Understanding tactics is important but grasping strategy is the first priority. When I was a small boy my father often lifted me onto his shoulders at football matches so that I could have a good view of the whole match. As ministers of the word we have to do just this for those learning from us. Of course, we do need to get down to wash their feet, but equally we must lift them up and sit them on our shoulders, so to speak, giving them a vantage point from which they can survey the whole drama of redemption.

The 'now' word is important in ministering the word. But we do well not to neglect 'the whole counsel of God' which sets the 'now' word in its proper context and in so doing helps to make it true. I have watched my wife tackling a jig-saw puzzle. She starts by tipping all the pieces into an awful heap in the middle of the table. Then slowly she arranges an outer framework of edge pieces. All the time, while building the jig-saw, she is careful to do one other thing: and that is to keep referring to the picture on the box. So it is with us as we handle lives that are still being put together. Having given them an initial framework of truth, we need continuously to show them the picture on the box by proclaiming Christ to them as the one to whom all things are heading as their final conclusion. Instructed in how to talk and walk and fellowship with this Christ, growing believers will find him more than adequate to deal with all their needs and will start to become part of the answer rather than part of the problem.

Admonishing

Admonition is another form the word takes in bringing men to maturity. It operates on a smaller scale than proclamation and has to do with instruction at a personal and intimate level. To 'admonish' translates the Greek word 'noutheto' which means 'to set in the mind'. In our context it means to set truth in the minds of disciples with a view to changing their behaviour and attitudes in a way that will make them more mature.[2]

Unfortunately, admonition has acquired a very aggressive connotation. This ought not to be the case. For to set truth in someone else's mind is with a view to liberating them not dominating them. It is a truly prophetic function; one fulfilled by the prophets of the Old Testament who are said to have admonished Israel (Nehemiah 9.30). Nathan did this to David when he confronted the king over his sin against Uriah. In the parable of the ewe-lamb, Nathan set truth firmly in David's mind. 'You are the man, David'. This is admonition. It involves honest person-to-person confrontation. It is part of what is now fashionably called 'discipling'. Jesus did this quite naturally by talking with his disciples, being open with them, by turns encouraging, commending and correcting them, but all the time setting truth in their minds. We will never help people achieve maturity by sending memos to them. There has to be a consistent face-to-face, brother-to-brother admonition.

The subject of admonition is the same as the theme of proclamation. As proclamation presents the vision of Christ, so admonition seeks to set Christ clearly in the minds of those being instructed. In this way the preaching of the glory of Christ is broken down and applied practically to the believer's character and attitudes. Paul did this with the Philippians. He did not set out to deliver a major discourse on the pre-existence, humiliation and glory of Christ. He was initially dealing with a pastoral problem in Philippi of squabbling between certain members of the church there. What these believers need is to 'have the mind of Christ'. Though one with God he 'did not consider equality with God a thing to be grasped but humbled himself . . . ' (Phil. 2.6ff). 'Your attitude should be the same as that of Christ Jesus' is Paul's way of admonishing them. This is a consistent apostolic method. Is there trouble between Jewish and Gentile members of the Church? Then, they are admonished to 'welcome one another as Christ welcomed you'. When Paul wants a response to his famine relief appeal, his approach is the same. 'For you know the grace of our Lord Jesus Christ, that though he was rich, yet for your sakes he became poor, so that you through his poverty might become rich' (2 Cor. 8.9). Numerous other instances could be quoted (e.g. Eph. 5.1,25; Col. 3.13). What is happening here is that the Christ who is being proclaimed is also being set in the minds of disciples in order to produce mature and Christlike attitudes and actions.

There are important prerequisites to doing this.

(i) We must have a bridge of relationship with someone before we can admonish him. Too often Christians have fired words and hurled advice at one another as if admonition were a re-make of 'High Noon'. True exhortation involves 'paraklesis', a drawing alongside of others in a spirit of love and humility. A disciple is not a client, not even a counsellee, but a friend.

(ii) This implies that admonition is best given in the normal flow of life as men walk along together. Words of knowledge, wisdom, correction and encouragement can be shared quite naturally as we enjoy each other's company. Admonition does not have to be stored up for a fateful appointment in the diary. There is a certain kind of man with 'something on his mind' who wants to fix a time to meet you. Such men are invariably bad news! They usually only book to see you when they have a complaint to make. Their very outline through the front door glass is enough to make you groan. But true brothers have reached my heart when in the course of conversation, often while travelling together, one has said to me 'And by the way, Phil. . . .' 'That's right' has been my reply; 'that's good . . . you really feel that? . . . thanks for pointing that out . . . I really hear you on that.'

(iii) So admonition calls for a basis of understanding between us. It falls on deaf ears if given to what the Proverbs call a 'scoffer', a man too rebellious or too flippant to take anything seriously. But 'like an ornament of fine gold is a wise man's rebuke to a listening ear' (Prov. 25.12). Paul and Peter had a sufficiently deep understanding between them for Paul to rebuke his fellow apostle for inconsistency without losing his respect or friendship. 'I opposed him to his face' Paul writes, 'because he was in the wrong' (Gal. 2.11). Even in apostolic circles admonition has a part to play in bringing men on to greater maturity. It is a healthy sign when leaders give each other the right to intervene in this way in one another's lives. And the face-to-face aspect cannot be minimised or avoided. Some things are too important to be left to hints or inference. To want to manipulate change is very tempting but to walk in openness, speaking the truth in love, makes for maturity among all concerned.

(iv) We must never admonish unfeelingly or ungraciously. We cannot set Christ in someone else's mind if he is not first in ours. It is self-defeating to attempt to encourage Christlikeness by doing it in an unChristlike way. As we have had cause to note before, Paul admonished the Ephesians with many tears (Acts 20.31). Efficiency is returning to the Church and this is good. But the Church is not a business, nor can its affairs be conducted as if it were. As leaders in the body of Christ we are not marketing products but making people. Pastors soon find out that people are a lot less tractable than products, less cut and dried than principles. It is infinitely harder to change people than it appears on paper. For our admonition to be effective we will need to 'rejoice with those who rejoice and mourn with those who mourn' (Romans 12.15). Leaders cannot afford to apply even biblical principles coldly or legalistically.

(v) A prerequisite for admonition is goodness. 'I myself am convinced, my brothers, that you are full of goodness, complete in knowledge and competent to instruct one another ' (Romans 15.14). Before we can admonish others they need to be sure that we are out to do them good not put them down. Some men have approached me with advice which I might have needed but, suspecting that their intentions were to disqualify me rather than edify me, I disdained their counsel. At the same time I have accepted admonition from other men because I knew they were concerned for my best interests. This is at once a fatherly and brotherly ministry (1 Cor. 4.14; 2 Thess. 3.15) and both terms pick up the atmosphere in which it best takes place. At this point pastors need to be prophetic and prophets pastoral. Pastors whose sensitivity makes them loath to confront and prone to fudge the issue need the prophetic determination to set truth in people's minds in order to free them. Prophets eager to burst in with a 'thou art the man' rebuke, will check themselves and seek the tact and discrimination of the Holy Spirit. And because admonition is born of the goodness in a leader's heart he will serve it up with lashings of genuine encouragement and appreciation.

Before we leave the subject of admonition, there are several dangers attending it which needs to be mentioned.

(i) Don't allow those you admonish to become wholly dependent on you. Failure here breeds a new kind of priestcraft in which disciples become parasitic on the counsellor. Some counselling manuals open the way for this error by fostering the image of a professional consultant dispensing pastoral advice through acquired techniques. But our aim is maturity in others. And to be mature is to be so trained in righteousness as to be able to make accurate moral judgements of one's own (cf. Hebrews 5.14). One safeguard is to remember that though a pastor may be in the best position to give such counsel, true admonition is the responsibility of *all* the members of the body (Col. 3.16). No one has a monopoly of wisdom, and, as James Denney once commented, 'admonition is better than gossip'.

(ii) Don't admonish lightly or carelessly. Another danger is that admonition is offered without the framework of respect and humility it needs to bring godly results. Like the man who approached Jesus to ask for adjudication in a disputed matter, some people simply want their own decisions rubber-stamped by an authority figure. Others 'shop around' for the advice which fits their pre-determined plans. So admonition, as with all counsel, should not be offered indiscriminately.

(iii) Don't be domineering when admonishing. Admonition should never be coercive. 'I'll do it not because I think it's right but because you say so' is the kind of response which wise leaders will reject immediately. The mind, not the will, is the immediate target of biblical admonition. Understanding what the will of God is must be the primary incentive to change. Otherwise what is produced is a mere slavish adherence to 'rules taught by men' (Isaiah 29.13) which, as we have seen before, is the origin of dead traditions and formalism.

(iv) Don't offer unspiritual counsel. The danger for any leader is that merely out of his experience he can have something to say in every situation, whether or not what he says is worth saying. Professional talkers, especially in pastoral ministry, need to guard against the temptation to dispense advice to all and sundry or to have an opinion about every topic. That is not true admonition. Unless our admonition rests on the flow of light and truth coming both from the Bible and the Spirit, we shall rush in where even angels fear to tread and become interfering busybodies rather than pastoral counsellors. True counsel relies on the gifts of the Holy Spirit. Sometimes we shall need to keep our counsel and to allow the Holy Spirit himself to guide into all truth. We shall know when to stand back from a believer who is entering a time of testing, knowing that only our prayers not our prescriptions will see him through.

Teaching Everyone with all Wisdom

The third form taken by the ministry of the word in bringing Christians to maturity is 'teaching'. For a full Christian experience the Acts of the apostles needs to be supplemented by the epistles of the apostles! Continuing 'steadfastly in the apostles teaching' is the sure way to grow. Here again the theme is the same. 'Day after day in the temple courts and from house to house, they never stopped teaching and preaching the good news that Jesus is the Christ' (Acts 5.42). At a large celebration gathering, it is Christ who is proclaimed. When a group of disciples meet in a home they are 'put in mind of Christ' by scriptural admonition. In the teaching sessions of the church, it is no different; it is Christ who is the subject of the instructions.

In the current renewal of the Church there are those who rightly question the effectiveness of its teaching ministry. Larry Richards has questioned the *context* in which teaching takes place. How we teach and where we teach constitute what Richards calls the 'hidden curriculum' which determines attitudes and thought-patterns more than the words being spoken or taught. He questions whether the pulpit-pew arrangement is the best context for learning which is intended to lead to maturity. Certainly no one would measure the effectiveness of teaching by the number of sermons delivered. Of the traditional Sunday morning congregational meeting, Richards writes: 'This is the one function that through its hidden curriculum (that pattern of *how* things are done) 'teaches' them who they are as believers and what is expected of them.'[3] Discipling and cell-groups are suggested ways of remedying this, according to Richards. Others have called into question the actual *content* of teaching even that given in evangelical churches. For example, Kenneth E. Hagin argues strongly that lack of right teaching is the main reason for the immaturity of the Church. 'The Church', he contends, 'has been strong in teaching man his need of righteousness, his weakness and inability . . . but sadly lacking in bringing forth the truth of what we are in Christ, and of how righteousness and faith are available.' Hagin goes so far as to say that by treating believers as sinners, Christian teachers have undermined their faith. 'Our ministry, maybe unconsciously, has fed the congregations a psychology of unbelief.'[4] With these strictures in mind we look at the characteristic features of the New Testament teaching of Christ.

(1) To teach Christ is to teach *the Truth*. The gospel is the 'word of truth' which God desires all men to know and which sets men free (Col. 1.5, 1 Tim. 2.3, John 8.32). Truth, not sensations, brings liberation and builds maturity. Truth embraces true doctrine and genuine experience. It is a beautiful word. To the Greeks 'aletheia' suggests 'reality'. In the Old Testament 'truth' is always associated with the steadfastness and faithfulness and veracity of God himself. To attempt to define it is difficult. 'Truth is reliable reality' – is perhaps the nearest I can get to it. The world certainly needs reality it can rely on. The root cause of the corrupt society so graphically described by Paul when writing to the Romans is that it has 'exchanged the truth about God for a lie' (Romans 1.25). The devil, though neither everywhere-present, nor all-knowing, exercises such widespread influence as the Father of lies because he has conned the world into substituting false gods for reality. This is why we

are called so clearly to be ministers of revealed truth and why renewal of the mind is so vital a part of Christian maturity. Believers need to be taught clearly what God has accomplished for them in the atonement of his Son, what provisions are now available to them as a result, what strength and life is theirs in union with the glorified and interceding Christ on the throne of God, what the Spirit is doing for them and in them, and what is the nature of the warfare they are called to wage until Christ returns. All this is 'truth as it is in Jesus' (Eph. 4.21).

(2) Truth can be taught effectively only with the power of the Holy Spirit who is *the Spirit of truth*. The anointing that abides upon us is to teach us all things. We impart spiritual truth to spiritual men because the Spirit of God has brought wisdom from the depths of God to the depths of our own personality and understanding. 'We have not received the spirit of the world but the Spirit who is from God, that we may understand what God has freely given us. This is what we speak, not in words taught us by human wisdom but in words taught by the Spirit expressing spiritual truth in spiritual words' (1 Cor. 2.12–13).

(3) To teach the truth we must *combat error* and untruth. The apostles knew the positive value of being negative. Every apostle was concerned that the churches knew the truth, not in order to prove their orthodoxy but in order to know how to live godly and wholesome lives. If you believe wrongly, you live wrongly. The Colossians had drifted away from the truth of fulness in Jesus and had fallen for fancy speculation and specious philosophy. Paul gives this new thinking no quarter. Where he finds some Christians hanging onto old traditions of what should or should not be eaten and drunk, Paul goes on the offensive in his teaching. All forms of ascetism, ritualism and legalism must be rejected, he argues, because they lead to bondage and keep Christians in a spiritual babyhood. The pseudo-spirituality that puffs itself up with dreams and visions, private revelations and superior guidance and which is not unknown in charismatic circles, Paul combats relentlessly as unrelated to the Incarnate Christ, to his body and therefore to real living in it. So Paul teaches the humanity and glory of Jesus and roots all spirituality firmly in the reality of what he is.

(4) Truth must be taught as a *pattern of teaching*. 'But thanks be to God that, though you used to be slaves to sin, you wholeheartedly obeyed the form of teaching to which you

were entrusted' (Romans 6.17). True apostolic teaching is never random or arbitrary, but takes a definite and consistent shape. Christians mature because somewhere in the life of the church there is a form of teaching which is not optional but to which they are committed by virtue of their commitment to Christ in his body. Thankfully in the current renewal of the Church, Bible studies no longer exist just to tickle the ears of over-fed saints. God wants to write his laws of truth on our hearts.

(5) Apostolic teaching regularly *recalls Christians to first principles*. Frequently in the New Testament letters appeal is made to Christian beginnings as the ground of further exhortation. Are there difficulties hindering you progressing as believers? Let's go back to what happened when you were baptised into Christ. Did you die with Christ? Were you raised with Christ? How then can you go on sinning? This is a characteristically Pauline argument (Romans 6.1ff, Col. 2.12ff). All this lays stress on how important it is to have a radical and drastic start to the Christian life. Sadly some people pass through commitment classes in a very mechanical and heartless way. What emerges is like forced rhubarb which, though alive, is also limp, rubbery and tasteless! Paul wants the Colossians to go on in the same way they started. 'So then, just as you have received Christ Jesus as Lord, continue to live in him' (Col. 2.6). You started in freedom, Paul reminds the Galatians, why go on in any other way and lapse into bondage? (Gal. 3.1, 5.1–7). The problem the writer to the Hebrews faces is just this; that he cannot take his readers on to maturity as he would wish because their grounding in the foundation doctrines is so uncertain. Christians who by now ought themselves to be in a position to teach others are still in need of instruction in the ABC of the gospel. To counteract this we will need, from the beginning, as the apostles did, to spell out the consequences of our union with Christ.

(6) Teaching for maturity will *relate doctrine to life*. The apostles draw the most practical consequences from the most exalted doctrines. The opening section of most New Testament letters is often classed as 'doctrinal' and is separated from what is known as the 'ethical' passages with which they usually conclude. But true New Testament teaching makes a vital connection between theology and behaviour. Proclaiming Christ as central to all the purposes of God in redemption and history the apostles then usually go on to

draw out the immensely practical implications of knowing this for the every day life of believers. The word 'therefore' is the verbal hinge on which this life-giving logic turns. As someone has said, we need to teach what the 'therefore' is there for! Christian behaviour is not an arbitrary, irrational set of rules but the outflow of gospel truth. Because Christians have put on Christ in all his majesty and love, they can be expected to put off unforgiveness, lying and bitterness and to put on love, forgiveness and truthful speech. To teach this is to instruct everyone in all the ways of wisdom, which is true 'know-how'.(5) In this way those we are leading will learn how to behave in the household of God and grow to maturity in Christ. The teacher's aim will be to bring disciples to 'full assurance', to that 'freedom of mind and confidence that results from understanding Christ' (Col. 2.2), to the place where they are bold in worship and prayer, secure in who they are in the world, and living faithfully and joyfully to the glory of God.

To achieve this will require of the pastor-teacher two things. It will take a lot of *perspiration*. 'I want you to know how much I am struggling for you' Paul confesses to the Colossians (2.1). The pressure of hard work and the demands of intercession tax the resources of every shepherd and show us that the teacher's ministry is not for the faint-hearted. It will also need great *inspiration* if, as teachers, we are not to be hampered by reliance on our meagre natural resources and gifts but are to learn to draw on the 'energy which powerfully works' in us (cf. Col. 1.29).

All this – whether proclamation, admonition or teaching – seems an impossible task. And it is. For as preachers and instructors and teachers of God's word we are attempting to state the unstateable. But state it we must for there is no other way. When asked why she was a ballerina Pavlova is alleged to have replied: 'Do you think I would have danced if I could have told you?'

24. Coach

A sporting coach has a key role especially in team games. It is his job to rouse each team-member to play with total commitment. He will try to get the team to play together and with real purpose. He helps each individual to fulfil his potential and to fit into the overall pattern of play. He fires his team to perform with that special 'plus' which is more than the sum of its individual talents. Through its coach a team learns to overcome negative thinking and to become success-minded. With a top coach a team begins to believe it can win and therefore usually does.

Nehemiah is a good biblical example of a leader who performed this kind of role for the people of God. Returning home from the Exile with a God-given plan to rebuild the ruined Jerusalem, Nehemiah wisely does not immediately disclose his plans to anyone. Only after careful survey of the job to be done and having armed himself with facts to support his plan does he speak to the people. His first task is to raise their morale and to stir them to action. He soon convinces them of his dream and its practicality. Before long they are as enthusiastic as he is. 'Let's build the wall' is now their common aim. Nehemiah assures them of success.

Then he organises them for the task in hand, allotting various jobs to different groups and making sure each one has the resources they need. Once the work has started, he urges them on despite discouragement. He keeps them at it even when they are afflicted by self-doubt and voices are raised to point out how ridiculous the whole enterprise looks! He acts quickly to settle disputes which destroy unity and slow down the work. Constantly he motivates them to keep together and to allow nothing to divert them from their God-given priority. So they built the wall!

Success-minded

A leader in today's Church needs to be equally success-minded if he is to motivate the people to fulfil God's plans for them. He wants God's team to win. Christian leaders have often been content merely with having saved the Church from relegation. But this is not enough. It is not enough to settle for a safe middle-of-the-table position in the Second Division. Our aim is promotion and the championship.

It is significant to see what Paul was after as he planned to visit the church in Rome. Writing to the Christians there, he tells them what his aims are in coming to them.

1. He will make sure that every one is totally committed. The aim of his apostleship, he says, is 'to bring about obedience' in the lives of those he ministers to (Romans 1.5).
2. He will equip them with whatever they need. 'I long to see you that I may impart some spiritual gift to make you strong' (1.11).
3. He will motivate them. He wants to see them so that he and they 'may be mutually encouraged by each other's faith' (1.12). In motivating them, of course, he will be stimulated himself.
4. He wants to see results from working with them. 'I planned to come . . . so that I could work among you and see good results' (1.13 LB).

Apostles, prophets, evangelists, pastors and teachers are the basic *enabling* gifts in the Church. They are given by the ascended Christ to '*prepare* God's people for works of service' (Eph. 4.12). Another version speaks of the five-fold ministries as given 'for the *equipping* of the saints' (NASB). The Greek word translated 'equip' or 'prepare' is the word '*katartizo*'. It is an interesting word with a variety of uses.

1. 'Katartizo' is used of *repairing what is broken*. In medical writings it is used of '*setting broken bones*'. Apostles, prophets, evangelists, pastors and teachers maintain the hidden framework on which the Body of Christ is hung. They are concerned for the vital bone structure of the Church – for its doctrine, its vision, its reason for living, its discipline and good order. They seek to repair whatever is out of joint which makes the church unable to bear the weight of growth. They enable the Church to stand on its feet. 'Katartizo' is also used of '*mending broken nets*' (Mark 1.19). So the five-fold ministries seek to repair any breaches in love and fellowship within the church. Tangled or broken nets allow new fish to slip through and be lost. Evangelists have often been thwarted by bad churchmanship. The apostles for their

part are eager to untie knots in relationships. 'I plead with Euodia and Syntyche to agree with each other in the Lord' (Phil. 4.2). So Paul urges the Corinthians to be *'perfectly united'* ('katartizo' 1 Cor. 1.10). All the ministries devote much time to exhorting believers to 'love one another'. Each brother is to *'restore'* ('katartizo' – Gal. 6.1) his erring brother to full fellowship. Mending brokenness in individual lives, the ministries bring wholeness to the Church and thus make it fit for its ministry in the world. This kind of leadership eliminates shoddiness and trains the church for quality work in God's kingdom. 'By the grace God has given me, I laid a foundation as an expert builder, and someone else is building on it. But each one should be careful how he builds. For no-one can lay any foundation other than the one already laid, which is Jesus Christ. If any man builds on this foundation using gold, silver, costly stones, wood, hay or straw, his work will be shown for what it is, because the Day will bring it to light. It will be revealed with fire, and the fire will test the quality of each man's work. If what he has built survives, he will receive his reward. If it is burned up, he will suffer loss; he himself will be saved, but only as one escaping through the flames.' (1 Cor. 3. 10–15).

Making Bees Sting

One of Britain's most successful football managers is Brian Clough. He is noted for his ability to inspire great performances from modestly talented teams. But as he admitted in a newspaper interview, 'I couldn't motivate a bee to sting you if it didn't have the equipment. You can only bring out of people what they are capable of giving'.[1] Fortunately, neither the Church nor its leadership is limited to natural abilities.

2. 'Katartizo' means *'to supply a lack'*. Paul and his apostolic team of varied ministries are in no doubt about their intentions in visiting the Thessalonian church. 'Night and day we pray most earnestly that we may see you again and *supply* what is lacking in your faith' ('katartizo' 1 Thess. 3.10). Their deficiencies are in doctrine where they need apostolic wisdom about the Second Coming; in pastoral care where they are urged to love even more and to help the weak and timid; in behaviour where they need instruction in righteousness and sexual purity; in evangelistic awareness where some of them are so work-shy as to lose the respect of outsiders;

in prophetic understanding where they need teaching on how to use the prophetic gift in the body. The ministry team led by Paul aims to meet these needs when it comes and writes about them in advance. In a similar way we saw that Paul desired to visit the church in Rome in order to impart some spiritual gift. The Acts of the apostles reveals the apostles making good various deficiencies in the churches. In Samaria where the evangelist has been unsuccessful, the apostles make good the lack of the baptism in the Holy Spirit by laying hands on the new believers (Acts 8). Paul does a similar thing in Ephesus. Exposing the converts' needs, he fills in what is missing in their experience of the Holy Spirit (Acts 19). Such leaders help members of the body of Christ to know their gifts and calling, so that unused potential is identified and released. 'People get mixed up about themselves, they become bad judges of what they have to offer,' says football coach Brian Clough. 'I try to show them what they are really capable of and help them to give it.'[2]

So Paul who had been instrumental in equipping Timothy with the spiritual gifts needed for his work, later urges him not to neglect it but to stir it up and use it. Certain skills are taught and gifts given by the ministries, so that, grounded in the Scriptures, each 'man of God may be thoroughly equipped for every good work' (2 Tim. 3.17, cf. Heb. 13.21).

3. 'Katartizo' signifies *right ordering and arrangement*. [3] This is the likely shade of meaning in Hebrews 11.3 where the world is said to have been 'formed at God's command'. One commentator says that the words used here 'suggest a wise adaptation of part to part, and of the whole to its purpose'.[4] It is the task of the enabling ministries to help believers find their place, know their gift, and discover their ministry in the body of Christ. They seek to bring the best out of each member of the body. 'The purposes of a man's heart are deep waters but a man of understanding draws them out' (Proverbs 20.5). I have seen men released into the calling they sensed was deep within them by the significant prophetic word and sensitive insight of one of the 'Ephesians 4' ministries. With men like this around us one is not allowed to feel useless for very long. Such ministries will be as concerned to see the church set in order as Paul was when he told Titus what to do in the churches in Crete. 'The reason I left you in Crete was that you might straighten out what was left unfinished and appoint elders in every town as I directed you' (Titus 1.5).

As we have already noted, Paul stated that one of his aims was to bring about obedience in the church he visited. Without the enabling ministries the church will remain flabby and have as many fringe members as front members. But this will blunt its effectiveness in the world. So the enabling ministries aim for total commitment. They will be concerned in the same way to bring about a right relationship between leaders and led, between teachers and disciples. It is interesting that our word 'katartizo' is used in a statement of the Lord Jesus to this effect. 'A student is not above his teacher but everyone who is *fully trained* ('katartizo') will be like his teacher' (Luke 6.40). This means that spiritual progress has much to do with the relationship between the teacher and his disciple and that the disciple's rate of growth depends largely on his having a right and submissive attitude towards his teacher.

The ministries sent out to equip the church will also be seeking to bring about a *'wise adaptation of part to part'* by maintaining the unity of the church. Having a gift, you do not aim to compete with me but to complement me. So with Christ as head, 'the whole body, joined and held together by every supporting ligament, grows and builds itself up in love, as each part does its work' (Eph. 4.16). As 'praise is *ordained* ('katartizo') from the lips of children and infants', so harmony is achieved in the body of Christ. The ministries sent to equip the church are not the composers of the music which is the church's life and witness, but they are its arrangers. By this arrangement of the music, all the members are able to express themselves fully and at the same time, by submitting to one another, to make symphonies not solos.

In all these ways the ministry gifts of Christ equip his church to do her work in the world. The 'wise adaptation of part to part' is never at the expense of the wise adaptation of 'the whole to its purpose'. In Howard Snyder's words 'the church's task is not to keep Christians off the streets but to send them out equipped for kingdom tasks'.[5] 'Katartizo' carries with it the idea of effectiveness and efficiency for a result to be achieved. The equipment of the saints is for their work of ministry, for adult work in an adult world. It implies 'inner strength, whether of the community in its relationships, or of the character of its members: that is; their maturity as Christians'.[6] This relative 'perfecting of the saints' is for the benefit of the world. So apostles make the church apostolic, stirring the church to be outgoing and sacrificial in its lifestyle. Prophets make the church prophetic, a radical demonstration in word and deed, in song and purity, of what the living God is now saying and doing. Evangelists too, act first on the body before they act on the world. They aim to make the church evangelistic, with a heart for the lost, with good news to gossip and healing signs to follow the word. Pastors are there to make the church a caring community, where truth is spoken but in love. Teachers make disciples in the church, who are instructed in the ways of God, are apt to teach and able to give a joyful reason for the hope within them. The Father took immense care in preparing a body in which his Son could enter the world (Heb. 10.5 – 'prepared' = 'katartizo'). The Son himself for his part sends to us his ministry of gifts of apostles, prophets, evangelists, pastors and teachers. He sends them so that with equal care and zeal they might 'prepare' his spiritual body to be his means of self-expression on the world.

Moving Mountaineers

Most of a coach's work is done from behind the scenes in careful and thorough preparation. But this is not all. During Wimbledon I heard an interesting comment made by Gerald Williams, himself a Christian and the BBC's Lawn Tennis Correspondent. 'The best coaches', he said, 'do not tell you how to play a forehand or a backhand; they tell you what to think'. The battle is in the mind with many Christians. Men who can equip the Church for her ministry will be men who can motivate Christians. The best leaders are the best motivators. Moving mountains takes faith. But moving mountains is one thing; moving mountaineers is quite another!

In Watchman Nee's words, a ministry like this will 'create hunger for God in other people'. Like W. H. Auden's poet he will 'still persuade us to rejoice' even when the going gets rough. Like my friend and colleague Derek Brown, he will have the gift of faith which enables them to say 'go on . . . you can do it: come on . . . you can make it.' The coach is not an armchair observer. He is a man with his tracksuit on, a man to whom 'paraclesis' is second nature, a man who loves to get alongside his brothers and sisters and urge them on. In so doing such leaders will not only tell us to 'run in such a way as to get the prize' but will convince us by their faith and example that we can.

25. Troubleshooter

Apart from being the only living person ever portrayed by John Wayne in a movie, Paul 'Red' Adair has another claim to fame. He is the world's greatest expert at fighting oil-well fires. The methods he uses to do this are not superficial, as if the problem could be solved by pouring chemical 'water' on troubled oil! Instead he gets to the very source of the fire and attempts to cap the well even though it may be torching out flames at over two hundred degrees Fahrenheit. Not surprisingly his insurance premiums are high. But wherever and whatever the 'blow-out', 'Red' Adair is the troubleshooter most oilmen call on to set things right.[1]

The Church always has need of its own troubleshooters to resolve its internal difficulties. Paul bemoans the lack of such a man at Corinth. 'I say this to shame you. Is it possible that there is nobody among you wise enough to judge a dispute between believers?' (1 Cor. 6.5). A charismatic church, rich in spiritual gifts and exalted in knowledge, nevertheless lacked a wise man mature enough to bring peace and order to a confused and competitive group of immature Christians.

The qualities needed by a troubleshooter among God's people are foreshadowed clearly in Solomon, king of Israel. Daunted by the prospect of ruling the nation, the king is encouraged by the Lord to 'ask for whatever you want me to give you' (1 Kings 3.5). Feeling like a small child dwarfed by the greatness of the task and the number of the people, Solomon confesses that he 'does not know how to carry out his duties' (v.7). What he does know is what he needs from God in order to rule Israel and his request pleases the Lord. 'So give your servant a discerning heart to govern your people and to distinguish between right and wrong' (1 Kings 3.9). His prayer was answered in full measure. For 'God gave Solomon wisdom and very great insight and a breadth of understanding as measureless as the sand on the seashore' (1 Kings 4.29).

(1) *Wisdom* is the first gift a ruler needs. This is the ability to apply knowledge to bring practical solutions to men's needs. To know what our duties are is one thing: to know *how to* carry them out is another and this is wisdom. Such an ability is a divine gift and much to be prized, especially by Christian leaders. 'If any of you lack wisdom, he should ask God who gives generously to all . . . and it will be given to him' (James 1.5). Cleverly, Solomon placates Hiram, king of Tyre by commissioning him to provide raw materials for the new temple he is building. 'The Lord gave Solomon wisdom just as he had promised him. There were peaceful relations between Hiram and Solomon and the two of them made a treaty ' (1 Kings 5.12). The scope of the king's new found wisdom is amazing. 'He spoke three thousand proverbs and his songs numbered a thousand and five' (4.32). So adept did Solomon become at unravelling the complexities of everyday life that his words of wisdom became proverbial, greater than the folklore of the East, greater even than the wise sayings of Egypt to which they bear a superficial resemblance (4.30). Truly 'the words of the wise are like goads, their collected sayings like firmly embedded nails – given by one Shepherd' (Eccl. 12.11).

(2) *Discernment* is also needed if a man is to rule well. Solomon's first test as a troubleshooter was a big one. Two women brought a baby to Solomon and with it a terrible dilemma. Within a short space of time each of them had given birth to a boy. One child however had soon died. His mother then secretly swapped the dead baby for her friend's living one. The mother of the surviving child, initially suspicious, had become convinced that a substitution had taken place. Now, arguing bitterly over who was the true mother of the living child, they stood before Solomon to await his judgement. 'Cut the child in two and give half to one and half to the other' is the king's ruling! 'Yes!' agreed the false mother, 'for neither I nor you shall have him'. 'Please my Lord, give her the living baby!' pleaded the real mother: 'Don't kill him!' (1 Kings 3.16–28). For this discernment which distinguished truth from falsehood, Solomon was held in awe by the people. Able to make such practical distinctions to settle disputes Solomon had no difficulty in distinguishing the natural from the spiritual, the temple he was building from the real dwelling place of God (1 Kings 8.27). What is displayed here is the insight which gets beneath the surface to the underlying issues at stake. What

Solomon had was a 'hearing heart' not just a listening ear. He could pick up the reasons of the heart as well as the arguments of the mouth. 'People say: "You have understood me", when we have guessed what it is they wanted to say but could not bring themselves to put into words'.[2]

(3) *Breadth of mind* is a God-given asset in a ruler. A troubleshooter cannot afford to be small-minded, unable to see the wood for the trees. Faced with a dispute or unresolved issue he needs a sense of proportion and the ability to put things in perspective. He must not be a narrow specialist but able to trace the ways of God wherever they need to be found on the map of life. Solomon's interests were broad. He 'described plant life, from the cedar of Lebanon to the hyssop that grows on the walls. He also taught about animals and birds, reptiles and fish' (1 Kings 4.33). In applying the knowledge of God to the various predicaments of everyday living Solomon can ransack creation for parallels and parables. Speech patterns, family relationships, money matters, business affairs, eating and drinking, laughter and tears, love and laziness – all come within the scope of his wise judgement. For all of these areas there is a natural picture or analogy. Lions, sparrows, horses, dogs, ants, badgers, rabbits, locusts, lizards have their lessons for us. So too do clouds without rain, babbling brooks, deep water, and snow in summer. The way iron sharpens iron, the way butter is churned, the way water reflects a face, the way a bad tooth can't be bitten on – all these yield wisdom for those willing to learn. This breadth of mind makes Solomon a prophet, enabling him to envisage the incoming of the gentiles to the house of God (1 Kings 8.41ff). Further qualities which a troubleshooter needs are brought to light in Deuteronomy chapter one.

Judgements in the Household of God

On the verge of the Promised Land, Moses reminds the children of Israel how at one time they had proved too heavy a burden for him to carry alone. Moses recalls his feelings at the time. 'How can I bear your problems and your burdens and your disputes all by myself?' As we noted in an earlier chapter, Moses decided to delegate responsibility to other wise and understanding leaders respected by the people. He made clear what he expected of them.

(4) *Impartiality* is essential in a troubleshooter. 'Do not show

partiality in judging' (Deut. 1.17). Such a man will be fair
at all times and with all kinds of people. He will be wise
enough not to jump to conclusions, bringing no judgement
without hearing both sides. Solomon had a word for it:–
'He who answers before listening – that is his folly and
shame. The first to present his case seems right, till another
comes forward and questions him' (Prov. 18.13,17). He will
not judge without making a 'thorough investigation' (Deut.
19.18, cf. 21.2). Throughout the Scriptures, partial judges
are an abomination (cf. Prov. 24.13). So Timothy is charged
by Paul with keeping the instructions given to him by the
apostle 'without partiality and to do nothing out of favour-
itism' (1 Tim. 5.21).

Even between believers and unbelievers justice must be
seen to be done (Deut. 1.16). Once I was visited by a
deputation of neighbours complaining about the behaviour
of the children of one of our members. On this occasion
my judgement was that they were right and I took steps to
remedy the situation. I was moved to think that I might be
regarded as wise enough to settle a dispute in the
community; they were somewhat surprised to find that I
had taken so impartial a line with them. This incident stirred
me to believe that in a society where common justice is
becoming harder to find, wise men in the kingdom of God
might one day become the only arbiters and judges to which
a community can give its confidence. In the future, wisdom
may be justified by some strange children and evangelism
find some unusual new starting points. And all this is only
a training ground for the day when we judge angels!

(5) *Courage* is needed to be a wise man. 'Do not be afraid
of any man' Moses exhorts his judges (Deut. 1.17b). No
judgement should be brought, especially to a dispute, which
is forced upon us by emotional pressure. On one occasion,
I recall, I acted to discipline a brother too rashly, pressed
to do it by the emotions of other men. 'You really must do
something about that', I was urged. The fact that I took
along as a witness another brother who, though trustworthy,
did not share my view of the issue did nothing to help
resolve it and I lost my man. I decided that from then on
I would never react to a situation under the pressure of
other people's feelings. If for no other reason a 'wise man
keeps himself under control' and does not 'give full vent to
his anger' (Prov. 29.11).

Remaining aloof from threats or inducements, however

subtle, is simply the wise man's way of showing that the 'judgement belongs to God' (Deut. 1.17). Knowing the Lord's verdict through Agabus, Paul can hold to it amidst an emotional and sentimental upheaval that might have swayed a lesser man. Here again the 'fear of the Lord is the beginning of wisdom'.

(6) *Knowledge of his limitation* is vital for a wise man. 'Bring me any case too hard for you ' (Deut. 1.17). A wise man is wise enough to know when he is confronted with something he cannot handle on his own. He is humble enough to seek another's help and counsel. Once again plurality comes into its own for, as we have seen, 'in abundance of counsellors there is victory'. The issue may well be resolved provided I am not too proud to call in other men to cope with matters which I am not qualified or competent to deal with. Above all, as we noted earlier, the judgement which is needed belongs to God and fear of him is the beginning of our wisdom. Knowing this I am relieved of the burden or illusion of thinking I have all the answers. Faced with complex problems or disputes, I will turn to the Lord, seeking the gifts of the Holy Spirit, especially words of wisdom and knowledge. For this reason a true counsellor is a priestly man, who is concerned not so much with solving my problem as with bringing my case into the presence of God for him to throw his light upon it (cf. Deut. 17.8–9).

We can summarise what has been said so far.

1. Be wise, learning how to apply knowledge to practical needs, becoming as familiar with God's ways as his works.
2. Be discerning, ready to listen to the unspoken reasons of the heart, sensitive to the fact that even love needs discrimination.
3. Be broad in understanding (which is altogether different from being 'broad-minded' in the modern sense), never allowing the details to obscure the weightier more important aspects of the law.
4. Be disinterested, with no axe to grind except to know the truth and to set people free.
5. Be fearless, not by being aggressive but by being immune to the emotional manipulation of other people whether involved or not.
6. Be humble, recognising the gifts of others, and most of all remaining dependent on the gifts which only God can give.

The Foolishness of Wisdom

Anyone who makes mistakes in this area is in good company, though the scene of such failure may be more serious than our own. Gamaliel is such a case in point, as Luke makes clear in the fifth chapter of the Acts of the Apostles. The apostles are being threatened by a Sanhedrin which has lost all pretence at being an even-tempered assembly. 'They were furious and wanted to put them to death' is how Luke describes the mood. At this point a Pharisee, named Gamaliel, intervened to quell the rage. His intervention has all the marks of sweet reasonableness and for this reason has often had a good press among Christian commentators. But on closer inspection Gamaliel turns out not to be the model troubleshooter he at first appears to be.

Firstly he was *wrong in the caution he showed* (Acts 5.34–40). What appears to be masterful diplomacy is, in fact, political expediency born of uncertainty and indecision. 'If' and 'on the other hand' seem Gamaliel's keynote words. Alexander Maclaren's verdict is not unfair. 'How poor a figure this politic ecclesiastic, mostly anxious not to commit himself . . . cuts beside the disciples, who had chosen their side, had done with 'ifs' and went away from the Council rejoicing that they were counted worthy to suffer for the name.' Maclaren goes on: 'Who would not rather be Peter and John with their bleeding backs than Gamaliel sitting soft in his presidential chair, and too cautious to commit himself to an opinion whether the name of Jesus was that of a prophet or a pretender'.(3)

In this case 'where is the wise man?' is not God's invitation to the godly man to step forward but his ironic indictment of the best that unaided human wisdom can do (cf. 1 Cor. 1.20).

Secondly, Gamaliel was *wrong in the comparisons he drew* (5.36–37). Theudas and Judas were revolutionaries who flourished around the time Jesus was born. These were limited and patronising parallels to find. They showed that Gamaliel's reaction was not deeply rational, the product of thorough investigation. He did not take the trouble to look any further than weak historical precedent and so he obscured the truth. Both examples, of leaders whose movements soon petered out, show the underlying hope Gamaliel was entertaining. Like a bad smell, the early church would, he hoped, just go away!

Thirdly, he was *wrong in the criterion he used* (5.38–39). His arguments were carnal and ill-become a man of God. Since when have observable success or failure been a reliable guide to the godliness or otherwise of a people or a cause. Gamaliel should have known his own history better than this. Israel's own story gave the lie to his criterion for establishing truth. And the cross and resurrection of course had only recently demolished it altogether. For by the foolishness of dying and rising God had made a mockery of human pretensions and argument. Bonhoeffer may have overstated it when he said that Christianity is 'the sanctification of failure' but his words are altogether too true for the kind of glibness shown by Gamaliel to grasp.

Lastly, Gamaliel was *wrong in the conclusion he reached*. 'Leave these men alone' was hypocritical counsel when it involved flogging and beating the apostles. Some neutrality this was! It was dangerous counsel too, because leaving the apostles alone was just the invitation they needed to set the whole city ablaze with Jesus. It was impossible counsel to give for how can you remain aloof from Christ and his appointed apostles? Not to be for them is to be against them! As a troubleshooter Gamaliel caused more trouble than he was worth.

Firefighting

As we look now at what it means in practice to be a troubleshooter we may find 'Red' Adair a better guide than Gamaliel. If as leaders we have any responsibility for resolving issues and settling disputes among the people of God, we need to follow certain guidelines.

(1) *Act Promptly*. 'There's one thing about any blowout', says 'Red' Adair, 'They never get better; always worse. So the quicker you can bring them under control, the better off you are'. Fear of confrontation here only allows the situation to deteriorate. Attitudes harden and angry words settle into final arguments which everyone is too proud to retract.

(2) *Treat Each Case Differently*. The troubleshooter in the oil business has a warehouse full of standard fire-fighting equipment but he knows that each well has its own personality. A wise spiritual troubleshooter similarly will not pre-judge the issue, bringing to it a fixed solution. He will want to respond flexibly in a way that is appropriate to the person or occasion. Dealing with unreasonable people is an art. Answer a fool according to his folly and you make yourself like him. Yet it may well be right on another occasion to 'prick his conceit with silly replies' (Prov. 26.4; 26.5LB and cf. 2 Cor. 11.16, 12.11). David was wise enough not to presume that he had found a guaranteed method of victory

(2 Samuel 5). Asking the Lord a second time saved him from the disaster which preconceived ideas would have brought upon him. Direct assault brought victory the first time; but next time it was an encirclement which was the winning tactic.

(3) *Be Prepared to be Vulnerable.* 'Red' Adair's team once tried to use asbestos clothing to protect them when close to the fire. They soon discarded it because though very protective it proved to be too bulky to work in. Standard psychiatry has long advocated that the counsellor be dispassionate in front of his client, adopting a neutral emotional and moral stance towards him. By contrast, a Christian leader with a shepherd heart who is dealing with trouble will not want to remain clinical and aloof. He will help to take the heat out of a situation by taking some of it on himself. 'Who is weak and I do not feel for the weak? Who is led into sin and I do not inwardly burn?' (2 Cor. 11.29). Firefighters sometimes have to use explosives to clear away damaged surface equipment which is blocking the way to the source of the blowout. Initially a spiritual leader may have to use strong words and take drastic action to get hold of the situation before it gets out of hand. Sharp rebuke may be necessary to disperse the surface emotions and to bring the wranglers to a place where they are calm enough to discuss the real problems. Paul was not afraid to read the riot act to the Corinthians – even if it was 'in love'.

(4) *Treat Problems as Opportunities.* Acts 6 is a striking example of the creative uses to which disagreement can be put! What began in grumbling and dissension was resolved in a way that led to a fresh recognition of the gifts in the body of Christ and a major new apostolic thrust. In dealing with oil-well blowouts one method used is to dig relief wells some distance away to take the pressure off the main well which has blown. As in Acts 6 we can often take the pressure off by providing other and more godly outlets for the frustration or enthusiasm that has erupted. Locking a man up to his 'problem' is usually self-defeating. Finding another way for his gifts and zeal to be used – even while still dealing with his problem – usually helps resolve the issue.

(5) *Cover the Whole Situation with Love and Patience.* Oil-well blowouts are finally sealed by liquid mud and cement being poured into them. Blowouts in the church are finally resolved by love and much persistence. This is the love

which covers a multitude of sins not by condoning them but by nullifying their effects especially on others not involved in them.

My own record as a troubleshooter has been patchy. But on one occasion I was nearer to success than on others. Returning in euphoria from a particularly stimulating conference, I found a message telling me of a major blowout at one of our house groups in which two brothers, one of them the leader, had had a violent public disagreement. Immediately, though it was late in the evening, I telephoned the two men involved. I took charge of the situation, told them to 'cool it' and arranged to meet them at the earliest opportunity. I first saw each man separately. Then I sought God for specific wisdom on how to deal with the problem. Then, having received this, I presented to each man written instructions on how he should behave in the house group of God and secured each man's agreement as to the justice and and rightness of my counsel. I then showed each man the other's written direction. Then I got them together to accept each other's submission to my counsel and to one another. Prayerfully we committed the matter to God and in the weeks that followed I closely monitored the situation.

More remarkable and far more dramatic is Paul's handling of a serious crisis in the twenty-seventh chapter of the Acts of the Apostles. Luke's stirring account of the shipwreck and survival in which Paul was involved serves as a 'parable' of what happens when an apostolic troubleshooter takes charge.

Paul had embarked as a prisoner on an Alexandrian ship bound for Italy with 276 men on board. The ship soon hit bad weather, making 'slow headway', 'with great difficulty' so that 'much time was lost' and 'sailing had become dangerous'. Paul's advice at this point was rejected by the experts and democratic guidance was sought in a majority vote. Things only got worse. With more hope than judgement, more false assumptions than accurate estimates, more guesses than seamanship, the voyage drifted along. Nearly out of control, the ship was lashed together by ropes, a process known as frapping. Before long the cargo was jettisoned in a vain attempt to settle for less and make life bearable. Finally, all hope of being saved was abandoned (Acts 27.20). At this point Paul takes charge. 'The whole narrative,' in Rackham's words, 'throws into the strongest relief the personality of Paul. At the moment of utter despair he rises up in the midst and is found to be a rock on which all can trust, the inspirer of hope and the master-mind which is able to direct and command as the crisis requires'.[4]

A church making slow headway, having great difficulty, lagging well behind the times, at the whim of expert speculation or democratic guesswork, is in real trouble. Barely able to maintain itself, in danger of falling apart, it tends to jettison the things it once felt to be important as the reason for its living. Settling for less, it hopes merely to survive. Soon it lapses into resigned indifference with no confidence that matters will improve. Apostolic wisdom, though hard to take, will prove to be the only hope at this stage. Paul's first word in the crisis is a pointed admonition, the biggest 'I-told-you-so' in history (27.21). Secondly, he brings tremendous encouragement and clear, inspiring prophecy to stem the flow of despair and to restore morale. Then he takes his stand as a man with a vision of God and a purpose from God. Confident in belonging to God, in serving God and in believing God, he is able to master his own fears and to instill confidence in others. He is able even to face the fact that things may have to get worse before they get better! (27.26). Withstanding a sudden outbreak of selfish panic, Paul brings further counsel and prophetic encouragement (27.31–34). He even makes the upper deck an upper room and gives thanks to God by breaking what by now must have been very soggy bread. The ship then sank but not before every one on board had made it to the safety of the shore.

So, unconcerned that old church-structures are breaking up under him, the prophetic troubleshooter delivers God's people from the old order to fight another day.

Fire-raising

In case our earlier analogy proves misleading, it is worth saying that Christian leaders are not only in the firefighting business, but also in the fire-raising business. In every upsurge of the Spirit's activity, leaders will be faced with abuses and excesses usually from those whose maturity does not match their zeal. The wise man here will often have to judge and test and assess what is going on. But he will do this with extreme care, anxious not to 'put out the Spirit's fire' (1 Thess. 5.19). As James Denney notes, 'a fire smokes most when it is newly kindled. Very likely the smoke gets in the eyes; but the way to get rid of the smoke is not to pour cold water on the fire, but to let it burn itself clear.'[5]

In this way the foolishness of God confounds the wisdom of men and the sons of light prove wiser than the sons of this world!

26. Doorkeeper

In his helpful book 'Building Christian Communities', Steve Clark outlines three approaches to leadership in the Church. The first is what he calls the *status-orientated* approach. Here the leader is most concerned to maintain the order and stability of the organisation. He devotes his energies to preserving the traditions of the institution he serves, upholding its rites and ceremonies as essential to its life, and safeguarding its laws as vital for its existence.

Challenging this is what Clark calls the *functional* approach. Here the stress is not on office or position but on gift and ability. The functional leader is very pragmatic, and goal orientated. He is concerned most of all with getting a job done. Authority in this category is measured by competence and success. Such a leader tends to be the enemy of tradition and the advocate of change. He subjects everything to rigorous scrutiny with the question uppermost in his mind being 'does it work?'

It is worth noting here that in the renewal of the Church by the Holy Spirit there has been a welcome shift from the first type of leadership to the second. Much of what we are saying in this section of the book about the ministries in the Church comes within this functional category. But there is a third approach to leadership according to Clark. This he terms the *environmental* style of leadership. It is to this category, Clark maintains, that the biblical role of the elder belongs.[1]

It is this vital ministry of eldership that I now want to discuss. Clark's suggestion that an elder has an environmental approach to his ministry is a helpful one. He is less work-orientated and more 'value-orientated'. He gathers people and is concerned for their attitudes. How do they view one another? How do they value the group? Do they esteem one another? Are they growing in their relationships with one another? These are the questions an elder asks of those in his care. He is not pre-occupied with running its activities. He does not measure success by how well the Church does certain well-defined things. He is interested in its inner health, in the climate or environment in which the members live and which will so radically effect their growth and effectiveness.

The difference between the functional approach and the one we are now describing is a little like that between a production manager and a personnel officer. The former is chiefly concerned for the efficiency of the machinery, the smooth running of the assembly line, the competence and skill of the individual worker, and the quality of the product. The latter has the job of looking after the environment in which all this can happen. He may well find himself involved in sorting out disputes between workers, especially demarcation ones. What matters to him are the working conditions in the factory, its heating, lighting and air-conditioning; whether the workers have proper lunch breaks and proper protective clothing; whether they have problems in the family or difficulties over pensions or worries about redundancy. He knows that these things affect the success of the venture just as much as the skill of each worker or the efficiency of his machine. This is probably far too idealistic in today's rough industrial climate. But in the Church it is not. According to this analysis, an elder seeks to maintain the body as a life-support system for believers. He will have a 'feel' for the flow of life in the body of Christ, for how the body works and for how each individual is contributing to its atmosphere and climate. In words that Steve Clark has written elsewhere, 'the elders are not primarily responsible for activities going well but for how well the people themselves are doing'.[2] The fact that this wisdom comes from a Catholic source only serves to make it more interesting.

Robert Brow maintains that 'government by eldership is the oldest institution known to man'.[3] Certainly eldership has Old Testament roots which are worth considering. Originally elders were the heads of families, later called together as the representatives of Israel (Exodus 12.21ff, 18.1ff). Later, we are told, they 'sat in the gate' of each city, exercising a judicial and governmental function. They become 'doorkeepers' of each community, the regulators of its affairs, its effective and collective leadership (cf. Deut. 25.7–8, 1 Sam. 16.4, Ruth 4.1ff). When we come to the New Testament we find the elders in Judaism occupying a strong and prominent role in the opposition to Jesus, and elsewhere as the presidents of local synagogues.

In the early Church then there was precedent for the appointment of elders as the local leaders of the gathered community of Christ's people (Acts 11.30, 14.23, 20.17, 21.18). Their role was soon seen as essential if the new groups of believers were to be built up and strengthened. Paul tells Titus that the appointment of elders in the places he is sent to is part of the setting in order of the churches without which they would be in an 'unfinished' state (Titus 1.5 'that you might straighten out what was left unfinished'). Significantly, too, elders are mentioned in the plural in almost every case. Together they act as the leaders of local churches.

Overseen Not Overlooked

There is another term which in the New Testament is used synonymously with 'elder' ('presbuteros'). This is the word 'overseer or bishop' ('episkopos'). Since the research of J. B. Lightfoot it has been generally accepted that both these terms refer to the same man and the same role. 'Overseer' has more of a Greek history than 'elder' though it, too, can be traced in the Old Testament. In the Greek Old Testament 'episkopos' is used of Eleazer who had 'oversight' of the tabernacle (Numbers 4.16 LXX). Since it is God who has 'oversight' of the whole land, with his eyes continually on it, such men are his delegates who take care of what he cares for (cf. Deut. 11.12). God 'looks out' a people for himself; overseers are delegated to 'look after' them.

It is ironic that in current English, 'oversight' has come to mean the exact opposite of what it originally meant. Now it means 'failure to notice or pay attention to' and implies indifference and neglect! This usage is as far as could be from the early meaning of 'episkopos' which means one who takes care of others, who watches over them, looks after them. It is this supervision that is truly biblical. Incidentally, it is worth, at this point, countering another misunderstanding of 'oversight'. If it does not mean 'overlook', then equally it does not mean 'look over' as if it implied 'looking over someone's shoulder' in a threatening and oppressive way. My friend Stuart Reid suggested that a motto for Christians for the Orwellian year of 1984 might be 'Big Brother is watching you and really loves you!'.

Being Before Doing

Though 'elder' and 'overseer' are used synonymously in the New Testament, it has been suggested that 'elder' refers to what a local leader *is* while 'overseer' refers to what he *does*. Whether this distinction is true or not, what is clear is that the apostles set great store by the qualities of character which qualify men to be elders of the church.

Paul tells Timothy that a measure of maturity is the best recommendation for eldership. Is the man morally reliable? This seems a more urgent question to ask than 'what are his gifts?'. Little stress is laid at this point on a prospective elder's gifts though it is clear that he needs to be able to rule and apt to teach. The qualities listed by the apostle in writing to Timothy and Titus are to be seen less as legal requirements than as clear counsel to both men on what to look for in potential elders. Basically a man with eldership in mind must qualify on two counts. He must be able to *manage himself* ('temperate, self-controlled, not violent, but gentle, upright, holy and disciplined': 1 Tim. 3.1ff, Titus 1.6ff). He must equally be able to *manage his own household* ('husband of one wife, a man whose children believe and are not open to the charge of being wild and disobedient') for 'if anyone does not know how to manage his own family how can he take care of God's church' (1 Tim. 3.6). So the stress is on a man's character rather than his charisma. Because he is a leader in a given locality where people know him well, he must have a 'good reputation with outsiders so that he will not fall into disgrace' (1 Tim. 3.7). But immersed as he is in the affairs of the local church he must not become parochial or lose his vision for the wider Church and its calling in the world. Because he is called to plurality he must be able to work with other men in mutual submission as together they seek the will of God for the Church.

He is not, therefore, an autocratic manager of the people; not an academic teacher nor even a specialised counsellor. Nor is he a representative or delegate of some sectional interest in the church. He is with others a guardian, an overseer, a shepherd of the whole flock, who watches over the sheep, succours the weak and is alert to what threatens them (cf. Acts. 20.11, 28,21,35). The elder in short is a man who exercises a clear pastoral ministry.

There is no job-description of him given in the New Testament but fleeting glimpses of his work. He 'stands in front of others', is able to keep control, to manage, to take care of others. He is a ruler of the church. He implements heaven's rule on earth as an expression of his heavenly counterparts. Like them he rules best when he is a worshipper, at home in the throne room of God. If he 'rules well' he can expect financial reward (1 Tim. 5.17). Such is his respect that he is protected from trivial complaints made against him (1 Tim. 5.19). Such is his responsibility that his judgement is made public (1 Tim. 5.20). He is given oversight of the church's money which is perhaps why he is warned against greed and urged to be a man of scrupulous honesty (1 Tim. 3.3, Titus 1.7, 1 Peter 5.2). With the example of the 'overseer' Judas in mind this is timely wisdom for elders (cf. Acts 1.20).

He helps to maintain church discipline which is perhaps why he is not to be quick tempered or overbearing (Titus 1.7–8, 1 Peter 5.3). He needs to be a compassionate man with strong faith for he will be called upon to heal the sick (James 5.14).

Although not always a full-scale teacher an elder must nonetheless 'hold firmly to the trustworthy message as it has been taught, so that he can encourage others by sound doctrine and refute those who oppose it' (Titus 1.9). All this is enough to confirm that 'if anyone sets his heart on being an overseer, he desires a noble work' (1 Tim. 3.1).

The fact that such a man, made by the Holy Spirit, is appointed only in concert with apostolic ministry gives each church initial and additional confidence that it has got the right man (Acts 14.23, Titus 1.5). This practice is a safeguard for a local church against the abuse of eldership, giving it the right of appeal to another authority in the Church, and protecting it from self-appointed, self-perpetuating local leaders. In fact this three-way relationship between a local church, its elders and the apostles, is a vital one and is fast becoming a live issue in the Church today.

Open Doors

As the doorkeeper of the flock of God, the elder is obviously responsible for *closing the door* to false teachers and prophets who seek to infiltrate the local church. 'I know that after I leave,' Paul warned the Ephesian elders, 'savage wolves will come in among you and will not spare the flock' (Acts 20.29). Equally, an elder must *keep the door open* for genuine and God-sent trans-local ministries. It was tension between local and trans-local ministries which led the Apostle John to write with some grief to his friend Gaius. In what we know as his third letter, John is concerned to deal with the trouble caused to a local church by a man called Diotrephes. This man, it appears, 'loves to be first' and has arrogated to himself the leadership of the church. He is clearly proud, insubmissive, seeking to exercise authority without being under it, and overbearing to those beneath him in his care. What is most damaging to the church is his attitude to the Apostle John. 'He loves to push himself forward as the leader of the Christians there, does not admit my authority over him and refuses to listen to me' (3 John 9 LB). Diotrephes is closing the door to outside ministry and is rejecting apostolic covering and input. In doing so he deprives the church of the benefits of the other travelling ministries. 'He not only refuses to welcome the missionary traveller himself but he tells others not to' (3 John 10

LB). There is in this vivid glimpse of first century problems a very important principle. A local elder needs to open the door of the church to ministries bigger than his own. Too many church leaders today are manning the barricades against other men of God. Too many local elders are still shutting out the apostles, prophets, pastors, teachers and evangelists whom the Risen Christ is giving to enrich and equip the whole of his Church. But if an elder takes this course he locks his people into his own limited gifts and leadership. At worst he will become authoritatian, like Diotrophes; at best he will be a one-man band. Either way his people will lose something of the fulness of Christ which is in store for them.

Is this why it is so often urged that an elder should be 'hospitable'? (1 Tim. 3.2, Titus 1.8). There is more to this than meets the eye once we understand first century conditions for church life. The Church, in Sir William Ramsey's words, could not expose its members, whether journeying on public or private errands 'to the corrupt and nauseous surroundings of the inns kept by persons of the worst class in existing society'.[4] And not only the safety but the strategy of the Church was furthered by loving hospitality. For such hospitality implied an open door not only to the saints who arrived on your doorstep but to visiting apostolic delegates and trans-local ministries. Local elders like Diotrophes could make or break this strategy. G. G. Findlay goes so far as to say that on such a seemingly insignificant virtue as hospitality depended 'the communion of the churches generally, the maintenance of Apostolic authority and of unity in faith amongst them, and the continued propagation of the Gospel'!.[5] As he exercises this spiritual role, it will be said of the true elder, as was said of Eliakim, entrusted with divine authority, that 'what he opens no-one can shut; and what he shuts no-one can open' (Isaiah 22.22).

Perhaps an elder's best hope is in remembering that he is the doorkeeper not the door. The Pharisaic leaders of Israel had closed the door to God's kingdom to so many and thrown away the key. In Michael Hollings words 'a door cannot give itself more than by being open'.[6] Jesus is the Door. An elder's highest privilege is to attend this ever-open Door, to welcome all who come to it, and to encourage them not to linger on the threshold but to enter fully into the joy and facilities of the Father's house.

27. Trailblazer

Four times in the New Testament the term 'leader' is applied to the Lord Jesus.

He is the leader into life (Acts 3.15).
He is the leader in salvation (Acts 5.31).
He is the leader to glory (Hebrews 2.10).
He is the leader of faith (Hebrews 12.2).

The Greek word used in these instances is 'archegos'. As Philip Hughes notes it is a very interesting word but one which is difficult to translate satisfactorily. 'It signifies', he writes, 'one who is both the source or initiator and the leader, one who takes first action and then brings those on whose behalf he has acted to the intended goal.'[1] It carries with it the sense of founder or author, and suggests a certain princeliness as the different versions indicate.

Elsewhere in the letter to the Hebrews, Jesus is called the 'aitios' of salvation which points to him as the 'personal mediating cause' whose instrumentality makes him the 'source' of salvation to others (Hebrews 5.9). W. E. Vine says that 'aitios' describes 'one who takes a lead in or provides the first occasion of anything'.[2] Jesus is also designated our 'prodromos' or 'fore-runner' who like an advance party, has gone on ahead to open up the way for us, in this case into the Holiest (6.20).

To take our cue from him at this point will give a special colouring to our understanding of leadership. We shall be unable to rest easy in being defenders of the 'status-quo' or maintainers of a static institution. The view of Jesus we have sketched implies movement, progress, change and advance in his church. The kind of leadership appropriate to this will be that which is caught up in his momentum as a pioneer and trailblazer.

The writer to the Hebrews has Old Testament precedent in mind. Perhaps he is thinking of Joseph who was able to look back on his brothers' rejection as in the will of God. 'God sent me *ahead of you* to preserve for you a remnant on the earth and to save your lives by a great deliverance' (Gen. 45.7). He may be thinking of the Lord's words to Moses: 'Go and lead the people on their way so that they may enter and possess the land . . .' (Deut. 10.11). More likely he is finding a parallel to Joshua who was called, as leader, to '*cross over ahead*' of the people (Deut. 31.3f) – counsel which Joshua himself later passed on to the priests on the verge of Jordan (Josh. 3.6).

The leader's initiative here consisted in breaking new ground. This was in direct response to the initiatives of God himself who by fiery pillar and shady cloud 'went ahead' of his people to make their way straight. God goes before his people and the leaders who follow him and keep pace with him are the true leaders. Of the spies who went ahead to assess the land it was Joshua and Caleb who were the real trailblazers because they had the faith to follow the Lord without reservation. Defying giants of opposition they seized grapes of opportunity which would benefit and motivate those they were to lead. Adventuring so far ahead of the people they might have been tempted to disappear into the distance, into a privileged and private 'promised land' of their own. Leaders with prophetic gift especially need to resist this temptation. Some become so 'avante-garde' as to become élitist, inhabiting a rarified atmosphere, cut off from the needs and aspirations of normal mortals. Flying 'Concorde' they tend to arrive before the rest of us have started! Caleb and Joshua were not 'high-flyers' but pathfinders for the sake of others. They went further than the people in a spirit of faith, boldness, and prophetic foresight but they returned to where the people were in order to begin the more humdrum and frustratingly slow task of leading others into the good of what they had seen.

Settler or Pioneer

The difference between a settler- and a pioneer- mentality has become a familiar one in recent years. Slightly adapted, it clarifies the approach to leadership we are describing. In settler theology, the church is a courthouse. It is a symbol of security, law and order. In pioneer theology, the church is a covered wagon, always on the move, bearing the marks of life and always where the action is. Similarly, in settler theology, a leader is the sheriff, sent to enforce the rules. In pioneer theology, he is a scout, riding out ahead to find out which way the other pioneers should go. He lives the dangers of the trail and doesn't ask the pioneers to do what he hasn't done first. His spirit and courage serve as a model for all to follow.

True trailblazing prepares the way for fresh movements of God. In doing this the pioneering leader may have to hack his way through a jungle of traditions and accepted ideas. he will do this, however, not to prove how 'contemporary' he is, but in order to bring others on to clear ground. John the Baptist was a true radical, wielding an axe honed to sharpness on the very untrendy stones of repentance and righteousness. There is a faith and forthrightness called for here in spiritual leaders which is the indispensable prerequisite to revival. A pre-emptive strike by the prophets is only to pave the way for new advances in God. An axe needs to be laid at the root of every tree Father has not planted if room is to be made for God to move.

Nearly every major breakthrough in medicine and science has been achieved by pioneers who pressed through to new discoveries. Often ridiculed by a disbelieving world, mocked by patronising colleagues, they persisted in their research. They made mistakes, took risks, but had the passionate determination to break new ground. But, in Peter Marshall's question 'Why are there so few spiritual discoveries to match the progress made by science? The answer lies in lack of researchers. How many are willing to give themselves away to take risks in spiritual research?'[3] No man can press ahead in this kind of leadership and stay shy and retiring. Another New Testament word for leadership is 'prohistemi' which implies 'one who stands in front of others' (cf. Romans 12.8; 1 Thess. 5.12). A true leader is an upfront man whether in the church or in his own household (1 Tim. 3.4,5,12). Like an eastern shepherd he will lead the flock from the front not nag them from behind. This suggests the courage to take initiatives and make decisions.

While I have been writing this book the Labour Party in Britain has undergone a long, often tortuous process of electing a new leader. The smaller and newer political grouping, the Social Democratic Party, has experienced similar traumas. Ex-Cabinet minister, Roy Jenkins, has been a prominent figure in this debate within the SDP. Commenting on this, an astute political journalist, Antony Howard, noted how fashionable the 'democratic' or 'populist' approach to leadership has become, almost to the point of leadership by referendum. Howard ironically contrasted Mr. Jenkins' present attitude to this with what the latter had written years earlier of his political mentor, the British Labour leader, Hugh Gaitskell. 'He believed', Jenkins had once said of Gaitsksill, 'it was his duty to make up his mind *before* rather than *after* his followers. He always pointed the way and asked others to follow'.[4]

Heroes

The true spiritual leader is a man willing to find God's way and
to walk in it with such integrity and enthusiasm that others become
eager to follow him in it. He is prepared to stand up and be
counted, to accept the responsibility of being someone others look
to for direction, and up to in admiration.

Christians, especially, badly need heroes worth looking up to;
and living heroes not just dead ones at that! It is precisely this
lack which true spiritual leadership is intended to supply. The
principle of *imitation* in leadership is clear in the New Testament.
'Copy me as I copy Christ' Paul urges the Corinthians (1 Cor.
11.1 JBP). 'I implore you,' Paul exhorts his spiritual family, 'to
follow the footsteps of your father' (1 Cor. 4.16). 'You became
imitators of us and of the Lord,' he reminds the Thessalonians
(1 Thess. 1.6). The 'and of the Lord' is a vital qualification and
safeguard. It reminds us that while we make a man our model,
we must never make him our idol!

Behind this principle of imitation lies a basic strategy. As
leaders we ask others to imitate us because we are called to make
disciples. Formation not information is our aim. As leaders we
best achieve this not merely by speaking truth worth trusting but
by living lives worth emulating. As Charles Simpson has aptly
said; 'men need guides not just maps'.

The end product of this modelling for discipleship is tantalisingly
difficult to analyse. This is because we are not aiming to produce
standardised, carbon-copies of ourselves, complete with our warts
and all! In an interesting passage, the writer Robert Louis Stev-
enson, once attempted to define what is involved. 'To be a true
disciple is to think of the same things as our prophet, and to think
of different things in the same order. To be of the same mind
with another is to see all things in the same perspective; it is not
to agree in a few indifferent matters near at hand and not much
debated. It is to follow him in his farthest flights, to see the force
of his hyperboles, to stand so exactly at the centre of his vision
that whatever he may express, your eyes will light at once on the
original, that whatever he may see to declare, your mind will at
once accept'.[5]

Moral authority makes a man 'an *example* of what a believer
should be' (1 Tim. 4.12 Barclay). Titus, like Timothy, is called to
be a 'tupos', letting his 'life stand as a pattern of good living'
(Titus 2.7 JBP). Trailblazing, far from implying that a leader
zooms off into a stratosphere of his own advanced thinking, means
that he goes before the people in the down-to-earth business of

living, of speech, of love, of faith, of purity. Youthful leaders blaze a trail not by being eccentric but by being exemplary. Elders oversee the church not by being over-bearing, not by acting like 'little tin-gods' but by being examples to the flock (1 Peter 5.3 JBP).

Success Breeds Success

What this means is that a leader must be *believable*, a credible witness to what he is saying. William Branham was one of the most dynamic and prophetic healing evangelists of the 1950's. An interview with an angel launched him on his way! But what the angel said is interesting. 'If you will be sincere and can get the people *to believe you*, nothing shall stand before your prayer, not even cancer.' 'If you can get the people to believe you . . . ' seems a far cry from setting an example in speech and conduct. But at least it may serve to arouse us to the extra-ordinary possibilities opened up to us by a life of exemplary integrity. 'And the Lord said to Moses, "Behold, I shall come to you in a thick cloud, in order that the people may hear when I speak with you and may *believe in you* for ever" (Exod. 19.9 NASB). Men of faith, inherently trustworthy, will pioneer the supernatural and lead the Church into the promised Land of the miraculous. 'Have faith in the Lord' means to have faith in his prophets' (2 Chron. 20.20). And what is more, 'Have faith in his prophets and you will be successful'. People naturally follow successful men. Leaders who are going somewhere attract followers.

For this reason Paul exhorts Timothy to lead an exemplary life so that '*everyone may see your progress*' (1 Tim. 4.15). If a leader is moving on with God his people will go with him. If he is static they will have nothing to follow. This is more than merely being one step ahead of the people though every leader knows how desperately he has to strive to do this on occasions. The picture of the panic-stricken leader in the bathroom with his open Bible sweating to get a 'word' ten minutes before the house group arrives is too familiar to be funny. What Paul is stressing is that if a leader continues to make significant advances in his own Christian life he gives his followers something to copy.

Timothy is to be a pattern to the believers by showing them how to live the life in Christ.

(i) In exhorting them he is not to be a critic on the sidelines but someone who walks alongside them, liable, as they are, to make mistakes.

(ii) He is to stir up his own spiritual gifts. In this way he will rouse the people from sluggishness and stimulate them to rise to their own calling and fulfil their own God-given potential.

(iii) In ordering his life he has to settle on priorities for himself and the people. Totally devoted to these things he will show his people what to concentrate on. What a leader treats casually his people will treat lightly. Whatever a leader is absorbed in they will take seriously.

(iv) This means that, like Timothy, we are called as leaders to begin to live more open lives before the people – however risky this may seem. It is by considering the 'outcome' of our 'way of life' that others will respect us and come to imitate us (Heb. 13.7). In this it is an encouragement to know, as Larry Richards has said, that 'we are to be examples not of perfection but of a process.' For this reason, he adds, 'we can afford to remove the veils because we are being transformed; progress is being made'.(6)

(v) If, as Timothy was urged, we persevere in this, we will carry others along with us to greater maturity. 'Persevere in them, because if you do, you will save both yourself and your hearers' (1 Tim. 4.16).

Do You Want a Pilot?

The last New Testament term to consider in this chapter is 'kubernesis' which occurs in 1 Corinthians 12.28. 'And in the church God has appointed . . . those with the gift of *administration*.' It may at first seem strange to be treating administration as a sub-heading of trailblazing. How do we relate an apparently static picture of a neat and tidy office manager to the more dynamic image of a bold and adventurous trailblazer? Part of the answer to this is to discard preconceived ideas. I am all for efficient office management but I suspect that there is more to a New Testament administrator than this. 'Kubernesis' basically means a 'steersman' or 'pilot' who brings influence to bear to point something in a particular direction. The various translations of this word give their own flavour. It means 'good leaders' (JB), those 'given the power to direct others' or 'to guide them' (TEV, NEB). Barclay paraphrases it as 'those with the ability to administer the affairs of the church.' J. B. Phillips calls them 'organisers' and The Living Bible 'those who can get others to work together'.

(1) Overseers obviously need this ability and they have to

receive it from the Holy Spirit. Writing in the magazine 'Pastoral Renewal', Dr John Hesselink of Western Theological Seminary in Holland, Michigan tells of his fears at being invited to become President of the Seminary. After thirty years of missionary work, of preaching and teaching during which he had done very little administration, he felt unequipped for the new role he was adopting. 'My charismatic friends', he writes with good humour, 'along with others prayed for the healing of my eye when I had a detached retina in the fall of 1980; and I suspect others prayed that I might experience the gift of speaking in tongues. But none, as far as I know, prayed that I might receive the gift of administration or leadership, even though nothing would be more directly beneficial for me, given my present vocation.'[7] Dr Hesselink prayed for himself and has enjoyed ten years of administrative duties with the gifts and graces provided by the Holy Spirit for the task.

(2) Pastors need to recognise this gift in others if they are to promote body-life. Howard Snyder relates his experience as the missionary pastor of a small church in a growing, working class community on the edge of the city of Sao Paulo, Brazil. Living twenty miles away on the other side of the city and with many other responsibilities, he was able to visit the church only twice a week. Language and cultural barriers made his administrative oversight even more unsatisfactory. Then he noticed that at planning sessions one brother, Andrew, always took notes on a little pad. Andrew was a recent convert, not well educated who had been an alcoholic before turning to Christ. 'As I got to know Andrew better', recalls Snyder, 'I found he had a gift for organisation and administration. He knew how to bring people together around a common purpose and get a job done. He had not learned this anywhere; it seemed to be a gift of grace.'[8]

(3) Even worship leaders might aspire to this gift! The ability to steer the flow of charismatic worship is a priceless asset. It is derived both from careful preparation which gives a sense of purpose and an awareness of what the Spirit is doing as he plots his own course among a worshipping community. But then a pilot consults not only maps and chart, but wind, tide and current.

(4) Most important of all, growth ministries need this gift. Given originally in 'a period of fluid development'[9] it is especially useful as the Church looks to increase and

enlarge. The gift of 'kubernesis' is a vital part of a faith ministry. It provides the practical foresight which can anticipate in vision the consequences of growth and expansion and can begin in faith to make provision for them. It helps to blaze the trail for a new visitation from God. As David Womack has noted, 'Most churches are at the size for which they have conceived their image of church ministry and government.' But as he goes on to show, 'the church cannot substantially add to its numbers without expanding its base of operations. A pre-meditated development in the level of administration will often produce subsequent numerical increase'.[10]

This is a far cry from mere office management. A charismatic administrator is a man with *the gift of prophetic planning*. Bold initiators, faithful models of adventurous living, pioneers of uncharted realms of the miraculous, frontrunners and forerunners, and men with practical foresight and faith – all these in their own measure are trailblazers, preparing the way of the Lord.

Valour From his Eyes

We began by looking at Jesus. He is Leader of the leaders and we fulfil our calling by fixing our gaze on him. Sometimes what we are saying is less important than the direction in which we are facing. For it is to the Lord Jesus we look for inspiration in leadership.

'I have a captain, and the heart of every private man
Has drunk in valour from his eyes,
Since first the war began.
He is most merciful in fight,
And of his scars a single sight
The embers of my failing light
Into a flame can fan.'[11]

In settler theology, sin is breaking one of the town's ordinances. In pioneer theology, sin is wanting to turn back. At the risk of losing a reader or two, I confess my admiration for Edward Irving, that 'man ahead of his time' who pointed 'to things yet future for the great body of Christ'. He was a true, though much maligned, trailblazer of the Church's renewal and restoration. Of John the Baptist, Irving once wrote: 'It seems to me that the Baptist is a type of every herald of salvation. We have to do with the same over-grown wilderness of moral life. There are the same towers of pride and mountains of vanity to be brought low; the same hollow hopelessness and deep despair to be filled with consolation and assurance; the same rough asperities of character to be shorn smooth; the same crooked and intriguing policies to be made straight, that the gospel of Christ may have free course and be glorified; there is the same gate upon the heart to be lifted up; the same bolted, barred gates have to lift up their hearts, that the King of Glory may enter in.'[12]

In pursuit of this goal as leaders and to adapt Unamuno's prayer; 'may God deny us peace but give us glory.'

Finishing this book closes a chapter in my life. To be a leader is to break new ground for God, for myself and hopefully for others. This I must now do. What we gain by trailblazing is not always apparent. But what we have glimpsed so far we speak of with bated breath and without disillusionment. Perhaps this was how Kipling's 'Explorer' felt after he had spied out his 'promised land'.

'Have I named one single river? Have I claimed one single acre?
Have I kept one single nugget – (barring samples)? No, not I!
Because my price was paid me ten times over by my Maker.
But you wouldn't understand it. You go up and occupy.

Ores you'll find there; wood and castle; water-transit sure and steady
(That should keep the railway-rates down), coal and iron at your doors.
God took care to hide that country till He judged His people ready,
Then He chose me for His Whisper, and I've found it, and it's yours!'

Endurance is an unfashionable quality in a period when easy answers and instant solutions are expected. But to endure is necessary for all who are still 'towards' everything, even in their leadership. Our incentive as leaders is to follow our leader, and 'not lose sight of Jesus who leads us in our faith'. He endured the Cross for the sake of the joy set before him.

28. Starter for 10

Especially for beleaguered leaders, we summarise suggested ways of co-operating with God in effecting biblical changes in the Church.

1. Be Ready to Change Yourself

'You and I are incompatible', said the Lord to Bob Mumford, 'and I don't change'! As the man discovered who called the fire-brigade when shut in a telephone box, the door opens inwards. Change begins with us. Laying down the shield of professionalism, finding a new sense of identity and security, losing our fear of failure or criticism – these prepare us for leading others into change. Ezekiel was told to groan in the sight of the people. When I show genuine emotion others know I am not a plastic man, unaffected by the need for change urged on them.

2. Be Clear About Your Vision for the Church

Is it renewal of traditional church structures which I am after? Do I have a vision of the one Body which God has set his heart on, or will I settle for a pepped-up denominationalism? One thing is sure: if my trumpet blows an uncertain sound or my eye is not single the saints become confused and defensive. 'Where there is no prophetic vision among leaders the people will be scattered, unrestrained and ungovernable' (Prov. 29.18). Paying the price of the vision may involve being willing to lose the manse as Ezekiel did! (Ezek. 12.1ff). The leader who has nothing to die for has nothing to live for.

3. Repeatedly Teach and Affirm the Biblical Basis of the Changes that are Taking Place

'How dare you tell me how to worship! – I'll worship my way'. Such emotional reactions can be effectively withstood only be thorough teaching from the Scriptures on how God wants to be worshipped, so that we may do it his way. In most cases of hostility to change the Holy Spirit is taking the blame for the radical effect of the Word of God. The Apostles used the Old Testament to justify New Testament changes; so must we.

4. *Stress the Living Word of God*
Saturation preaching has made many evangelical Christians almost immune to the living Word of God. The idea that the Spirit may be saying something to our church about what God wants us to do today, comes as a shock to many. But God's Word in its sword-like thrust penetrates anything we are doing which does not have sound biblical foundations. 'Why do your disciples not walk according to the tradition of the Baptists (or Methodists or URC's, etc.) but sing their songs with upraised hands?' Such attitudes face the charge of invalidating the Word of God! Faith comes by hearing (not hearsay!) and hearing by the Word of Christ – not the traditions of men.

5. *Be Committed to all That God Wants to do*
Israel was accused of wanting God's work but not his ways (Ps. 95.9–10). So in every time of refreshing we are prone to want the fruits without the obligations inherent in the blessing of God. It is easy to settle for livelier worship with a new song book alongside the hymn book. But we can sing the songs the Holy Spirit has given while keeping the lid shut tightly on his other gifts. The changes he has in mind are more drastic than two 'choruses' slipped into the hymn-sandwich, fervently gobbled up by an eager minority and grimly tolerated by the rest! Enjoying the spin-offs of renewal without commitment to the restoration of the Church's structures is not only hypocritical but self-defeating.

6. *Lead From the Front not Behind*
'The people told me to' is a poor excuse for any leader – though both Aaron and Saul tried it (Exod. 32.31f; 1 Sam. 15.24). The Greek word used to describe the gift of leadership in the Church means 'to stand in front of' (Romans 12.8). I visited a church recently where the pastor is an older man not long baptised in the Spirit. I was so impressed just to see him doing what he was asking his people to do. He raised his hands, he spoke in tongues, he prophesied, he sang in the Spirit. The gentleness with which he did it only strengthened his authority as a man not afraid to lead from the front. Doing it before the Lord who is your audience will release you from self-consciousness – as it did David when he danced before the Ark. It will also enable

you to bear with criticism or misunderstanding. Meekness only adds to your authority here.

7. *Break With the Expectations of the People*

Jesus refused to be the Messiah the people wanted (Matt. 11.2; John 6.15). Do not be swamped by the pressures of what people think you should be doing. Listen to God. Jesus even let his best friend die rather than get out of line with Father's timing and plans (John 11.5ff). Let God give you a flock. You will know who they are because they will hear the Great Shepherd's voice in yours and follow you. Be prepared therefore, like Gideon, to lose the right people. Some help, as Ezra found, you can do without (Ezra 4.3). 'Why can't we have two services', I was asked once, 'one for those who like the old type service, and one for those who want to do these daft new things.' All I could say in reply was to ask who would be leading these alternative services. 'You would, of course'. To which I could only say that I was doing it the way I felt to be right already. Few organisations are indispensable either. You can start the process of change by refusing to support even as a figurehead any church activity you do not believe in. Bob Girard has put it well: 'Anything in the church programme that cannot be maintained without constant pastoral pressure on the people to be involved should be allowed to die a sure and natural death'.[1]

8. *Make Small but Significant Changes*

The prophets used symbolic actions to implement their word. To refer to this may sound like using a sledgehammer to crack a nut. But it is precisely the small, seemingly unimportant visible changes that most provocatively focus the preaching of the Word. Many who remain unmoved by prophetic preaching get immediately aroused when anyone does something different from the usual. Putting the chairs in a circle, raising the hands, using one loaf and one cup – these actions, among countless others, unimportant in themselves can, nevertheless, be very important in the context of a need to respond to what the 'now' word of the Lord is saying. Thankfully we do not have to go naked for three years, as Isaiah did, or hide our underwear in a ledge in the rock as Jeremiah did, or even lay on one side for three hundred days as Ezekiel did! Our actions, more modest in every way, may nonetheless like those of former prophets, become 'actions which under the hand of God initiate a movement of the Divine Spirit in the affairs of men' (G. A. Knight).[2] People will at least know you mean what you say, and so will be challenged to reach to the 'now' word because actual choices confront them.

9. Build Relationships with Other Men of God Both Within and Outside the Local Church

Make disciples as Jesus did, then what God is saying through you will become established truth and vision, no longer at risk if you get run over by a bus! Instead of your hobbyhorse which hopefully may go away soon, this vision can begin to create an alternative to the existing structures and system. In turn these faithful men – to whom you have committed yourself and your dreams – can teach others, thus eventually bringing the whole Fellowship into clarity and peace. In the same way it is good to get into responsible and regular relationships with other men of God in the area. Brothers like this, whom you can trust, are an incredible blessing from the Lord. Standing with you, at first privately then later publicly, they will re-inforce your own spiritual authority by showing that you too are a man under authority. In time, we can by this means begin to see more clearly just what we are in God, and come to recognise the apostles, prophets, shepherds, teachers and evangelists whom Jesus is raising up today in his Church.

10. Believe Your Own Prophecies

At the end of 'The Hobbit' Gandalf tells Bilbo the outcome of his incredible adventures. A wonderful restoration has taken place, better than anyone could have imagined. 'Then the prophecies of the old songs have turned out to be true, after a fashion?' said Bilbo. 'Of course', said Gandalf, 'and why should they not prove true? Surely you don't disbelieve the prophecies because you had a hand in bringing them about yourself?'.[3] A sober estimate of ourselves will save us from an inflated idea of our own importance. The Lord we serve, not us, is the author and finisher of our faith. But the joy set before us is no illusion. Why settle for less for the sake of a quiet life.

Notes

Chapter 1 – First Service
(1) W. E. Vine: An Expository Dictionary of New Testament Words. Pub. Oliphants. Article on Servant. A recent study of servanthood is Charles Swindoll: Improving Your Serve – Hodder 1983.

Chapter 2 – Double Fault
(1) Stanley Jones: The Unshakeable Kingdom and the Unchanging Christ. pp 141–42. Abingdon 1970
(2) Howard Snyder: New Winekins. pp 73–77. Marshall, Morgan & Scott 1977
(3) Quoted by Paul Rees: Don't Sleep Through the Revolution. pp121. Word Books 1969
(4) On two issues – the role of women in leadership and the outworking of authority – I find myself at odds with some influential opinion, notably Howard Snyder. I am unconvinced by his view that the 'headship' passages (1 Cor. 11.1ff and 1 Tim. 2.1ff) are not 'transculturally normative'. I feel, too, he comes close to setting up a 'man of straw' in his discussions of patterns of authority in the Church. For all this, Snyder has proved a stimulating 'guru' in recent years and his comments on the issue of authority, especially, will have to be reckoned with.

Chapter 3 – Undercover Agents
(1) John Howard Yoder: The Politics of Jesus. pp 174 Eerdmans 1977 and especially Chapter 9
(2) James Lee Beall: Your Pastor, Your Shepherd. pp. 132 Logos 1977
(3) Robert Schuller: Your Church has Real Possibilities pp. 51–52 Regal 1974
(4) Peter Wagner: Your Church Can Grow. pp 61–62 Regal 1976

Chapter 4 – Charisma
(1) James Dunn: Jesus and the Spirit. p 79 S.C.M. 1975
(2) John Taylor: The Go-Between God. p 5 S.C.M. 1972
(3) Samuel Chadwick: The Way to Pentecost. p.57–58 & 93 Hodder 1932.
(4) Arnold Bittlinger: Gifts and Ministries. p.18 Eerdmans 1973.
(5) James Dunn: Op. cit. p. 176–182

(6) Howard Snyder: Community of the King. p. 84 IVP 1977
(7) Howard Snyder: New Wineskins. p. 128 Marshall, Morgan & Scott 1977
(8) D. M. Lloyd-Jones: Preaching and Preachers. P. 328 Hodder 1971
(9) D. Guthrie: The Pastoral Epistles. p. 127 Tyndale 1964.
(10) Laurie Lee: I Can't Stay Long. p. 70 Penguin

Chapter 5 – Start Where the Buck Stops
(1) I first heard the gist of this story from Gerald Coates.
(2) Elizabeth Elliot: The Mark of a Man p.77ff Hodder 1981
(3) R. J. Rushdoony: The Institutes of Biblical Law p.342, 448ff Presbyterian and Reformed Publishing Company 1973.
(4) Steve Clark: Pastoral Renewal Vol. 5 No. 5Nov. 1980
(5) This theme is well covered in Leonard Verduin's 'Somewhat less than God' Eerdmans, especially chapter 2.
(6) Verduin: Op. cit p.28
(7) Derek Kidner: Proverbs p.43 IVP Tyndale Press 1964

Chapter 6 – The Music and the Call
(1) P. T. Forsyth: Christ on Parnassus p.225 Independent Press 1959
(2) George Maloney: Listen Prophets p.119 Dimension Books N.D.
(3) P. T. Forsyth: God The Holy Father p.110 Independent Press 1957
(4) P. T. Forsyth: Positive Preaching and the Modern Mind p.vii Independent Press 1967
(5) Quoted by James Stewart: The Wind of the Spirit Hodder 1968
(6) Kenneth Grahame: The Wind in the Willows

Chapter 7 – The Vision and the Dream
(1) Watchman Nee: What shall this man do? p.80 Victory Press 1962
(2) D. Kidner: Proverbs p.175 Tyndale Press 1962
(3) Judson Cornwall: Profiles of a Leader p.186 Logos 1980
(4) Easy access to this and other moving accounts can be had in Dr. Martyn Lloyd-Jones' commentary on Romans 8.5–17, 'The Sons of God (Banner of Truth) especially Chapters 25–27.
(5) Oswald Chambers: So Send I You p.33
(6) Campbell Morgan: Westminster Sermons Vol. 10 p.248 Pickering and Inglis

Chapter 8 – No Plastic Prophets
(1) Abraham Heschel: The Prophets Vol. 11 p.88 Harper 1975
(2) Richard Bazter: The Reformed Pastor p.106 1656 reprinted Epworth Press 1961

Chapter 9 – Man After God's Heart
(1) Leon Wood: A Survey of Israel's History p.260 Pickering and Inglis 1975

Chapter 10 – All the King's Men
(1) Herbert Kretzmer: Daily Mail – 7 Sept. 1981
(2) Kevin Perotta: Pastoral Renewal p.45 Vol. 5 No. 6 Dec. 1980
(3) P. T. Forsyth: The Soul of Prayer p.138–140 Epworth Press
(4) Kevin Perotta: op. cit. p.46
(5) E. M. Bounds: Power in Prayer. p.9

Chapter 11 – Two Are Better Than One
(1) Derek Kidner: A Time to Mourn and a Time to Dance p.50. IVP 1976
(2) Charles Blair: The Man Who Could Do No Wrong p.232 Hodder 1982

Chapter 12 – Without Fear or Favour
(1) A. W. Tozer: Of God And Men p. 15–16 Christian Publications

Chapter 13 – Alarm Bells For Leaders
(1) Charles Blair: The Man Who Could Do No Wrong Hodder 1982
(2) Judson Cornwall: Profiles of a Leader p.125 Logos 1980 cf. also Trevor Martin 'Kingdom Healing' p123f – Marshalls 1981
(3) ibid. Blair p.232
(4) ibid. Blair p.232
(5) F. F. Bruce: Men and Movements in Primitive Christianity p.48 Paternoster 1979.

Chapter 14 – Watergate In The Church
(1) cf. Clifford Hill: Towards the Dawn p.126ff Fount 1980
(2) ibid. p.130–131
(3) John Oman: Grace and Personality p.21 Fontana ed. 1962

Chapter 15 – Checkpoint
(1) Karl Barth: Fragments Grave and Gay p.116–17 Collins-Fontana 1971

Chapter 16 – Jesus: Clash With Leadership
(1) Campbell Morgan: Living Messages of the Bible Book 2 – p.243 Fleming Revell 1912 c.f. the perceptive study by John Stott 'Christ the Controversialist' Tyndale 1970
(2) John Howard Yoder: The Politics of Jesus p.40 Eerdmans 1977
(3) David Womack: The Pyramid Principle of Church Growth. Bethany Fellowship 1977

Chapter 17 – Jesus: His Model For Leadership
(1) F. B. Meyer: Joshua p.18
(2) Douglas Webster: Not Ashamed p.29 Hodder 1970
(3) Robert Murray M'Cheyne: Memoirs and Remains p.282 Banner of Truth reprinted 1966

(4) cf. James Lee Beall: Your Pastor, your Shepherd for a helpful study of the pastoral ministry today.

Chapter 18 – Jesus: His Lessons on Leadership
(1) A. B. Bruce:The Training of the Twelve p.15 First published in 1877
(2) Robert Coleman: The Masterplan of Evangelism p.43 Spire Books 1963. Coleman's book is a shorter, more modern treatment of the same ground covered by Bruce's work. His analysis is summarised in chapter 3 of his 'Evangelism in Perspective' pub. Christian Publications 1975.
(3) See article written by Goetzmann in Dictionary of New Testament Theology volume 2, p.247–256 (Paternoster Press 1976) for the latest attempt to unravel this parable by referring to contemporary Jewish law.
(4) On the general matter of the Pauline instruction on leadership qualifications, see the useful study book by Gene A. Getz 'The Measure of a Man' Regal Books, 1974.
(5) Coleman: op. cit. p.125

Chapter 19 – Jesus: His Legacy of Leadership
(1) For the implications of this see Peter Wagner's 'Look out the Pentecostals are Coming' Chapter 7. Coverdale 1973.
(2) See Armitage Robinson 'Ephesians' pp97, 181.James Clarke n.d.
(3) G. G. Findlay: 'Ephesians' Expositors Bible p.237 Hodder 1907
(4) A. Bittlinger: Gifts and Ministries p.25, 85 Eerdmans 1973
(5) Trevor Martin: Kingdom Healing p.117 Marshalls 1981
(6) cf. Bittlinger op. cit. p.65. cf. Gene Getz who advocates this, at least for the Early Church, in 'Sharpening the Focus of the Church' p.101. Moody 1974.
(7) Arthur Wallis: The Radical Christian p.184 Kingsway 1980

Chapter 20 – Father
(1) Juan Carlos Ortiz: Disciple p.111 Lakeland 1976

Chapter 21 – Master Builder
(1) J. B. Lightfoot: Galatians p.94 Zondervan reptd. 1962
(2) A. Bittlinger: Gifts and Ministries p.77 Eerdmans 1973
(3) Robert Brow: Twenty Century Church p.97 Victory Press 1968

Chapter 22 – Eye-Opener
(1) H. Ridderbos: Paul: an outline of his Theology p. 451 – SPCK 1977
(2) Arndt & Gingrich: A Greek-English Lexicon of the New Testament p.532 Cambridge 1957
(3) cf. G. E. Ladd: A Theology of the New Testament p. 93 – Eerdmans 1974
(4) ibid Ridderbos: p.451
(5) Frances Schaeffer: Death in the City esp. Ch. 4 IVP1969

(6) A. Heschel: The Prophets vol 2 p.xv Harper 1962
(7) James E. Byrne: Charismatic Leadership in 'As The Spirit Moves' p.210 ed by Kevin and Dorothy Ranaghan. Paulist Press 1971.
(8) Paul Tournier: The Adventure of Living p.36–7 SCM 1966
(9) A. W. Tozer: Of God and Men p.24 Christian Publications 1960
(10) cf. Harry Blamires: The Christian Mind p.50–51 SPCK 1963
(11) Jacques Ellul: The Politics of God and the Politics of Man p.50–51 – Eerdmans 1972
(12) Langmead Casserley: The Christian Community p.89 Longmans 1960
(13) J. Jocz: The Spiritual History of Israel p.130 Eyre & Spottiswoode 1961
(14) Edward Schweizer: Church Order in the New Testament p.72 SCM 1961
(15) Robert Brow: Twenty Century Church p.57 Victory Press 1968
(16) cf. Jim Wallis: The Call to Conversion p.128–9 Lion 1981

Chapter 23 – Instructor

(1) An extended treatment of preaching is not possible here. Helpful books on the subject from a variety of sources are:
P. T. Forsyth: Positive Preaching and the Modern Mind. Armstrong 1970 (a classic)
John Stott: I Believe in Preaching Hodder 1983
Colin Morris: The Word and the Words Epworth 1975
Watchman Nee: The Ministry of the Word CFP 1971
Dr. Martyn Lloyd-Jones: Preaching and Preachers Hodder 1971
(2) A lot of the credit for rescuing Christian counselling from the morass of pop-psychology must go to Jay Adams. Both his major books have been very influential.
Jay Adams: Competent to Counsel Baker 1970
Jay Adams: The Christian Counsellor's Manual Baker 1973
The one proviso I have is that Dr. Adams work needs to be supplemented by a greater recognition of the need for reliance on the charismatic gifts of the Holy Spirit.
(3) Larry Richards: A Theology of Christian Education p.277 Zondervan 1975
(4) Kenneth E. Hagin: Growing Up Spiritually p.91,93 Kenneth Hagin Ministries 1978
(5) Practical theology is what made many of the Puritans such masters of the spiritual life. The works of Richard Sibbes and Stephen Charnock are especially significant here. From widely different standpoints both Martyn Lloyd-Jones and Paul Tournier are adept at applying doctrine to pastoral needs. Dr. Lloyd-Jones' Spiritual Depression; its causes and cure' is a special joy even if it is not well-served by its title.
For wisdom on how to bring admonition and encouragement to cell groups nothing better has ever been written than by William Williams in his instructions to his class meeting leaders during the Revival in

Wales in the eighteenth century. These are available in 'The Experience Meeting' by William Williams, translated by Mrs. Lloyd-Jones, published by the Evangelical Press (1973).

Chapter 24 – Coach
(1) Brian Clough in an interview with Hugh MacIlvanny 'The Observer' – Nov. 18th 1979.
(2) ibid.
(3) W. E. Vine: An Expository Dictionary of New Testament Words. Oliphants Vol. 3 p.174 article on 'perfect'.
(4) Marcus Dods: Expositors Greek Testament p.353 vol. 4 Hodder 1912 edition
(5) Howard Snyder: New Wineskins p.115 Marshalls 1977
(6) Delling: Theological Dictionary of the New Testament: Kittel/Bromiley. Vol. (1) p.476 – Eerdmans 1965

Chapter 25 – Troubleshooter
(1) From an article in the Sunday Telegraph Magazine.
(2) Paul Tournier: The Person Reborn p.220 SCM 1967
(3) Alexander Maclaren: Expositions of Holy Scripture Hodder 1970
(4) R. B. Rackham: The Acts of the Apostles p.476 Methuen 1901
(5) James Denney: 1 and 2 Thessalonians p.236 Hodder 1892

Chapter 26 – Doorkeeper
(1) Steven B. Clark: Building Christian Communities p.111–145 Ave Maria Press 1972
(2) Steve Clark: Pastoral Renewal p.83 May 1978
(3) Robert Brow: Twenty Century Church p.73 Victory Press 1970
(4) quoted by G. G. Findlay: Fellowship in the Life Eternal p.15 Hodder 1909
(5) ibid. Findlay p.16
(6) Michael Hollings: I will be there p.35 Mowbrays 1975

Chapter 27 – Trailblazer
(1) P. E. Hughes: A Commentary on the Epistle to the Hebrews p.100 Eerdmans 1977
(2) W. E. Vine: Expository Dictionary of N.T. Words p.88 Oliphants 1961
(3) Peter Marshall: Mr. Jones Meet the Master Fontana 1954
(4) Antony Howard: The Observer Newspaper 1982
(5) quoted in 'The Greater Men and Women of the Bible' edited by James Hastings. Vol. 2 p. 364 (T & T Clark 1914)
(6) Larry Richards: A Theology of Christian Education p.142 Zondervan 1975
(7) Pastoral Renewal – September 1982
(8) Howard Snyder: Liberating the Church p.254 Marshalls 1983
(9) Beyer: Theological Dictionary of the New Testament Paternoster Press 1976 Vol. 3 p.1035

(10) David Womack: The Pyramid Principle of Church Growth p.73,79
     – Bethany Fellowship 1977
(11) Thomas Toke Lynch
(12) Larry Christenson: A Message to the Charismatic Movement p.39
     – Dimension Books 1972
The quotation from Irving is taken from 'Blinded Eagle' by H. C. Whitley
– p. 117 – SCM 1955

Chapter 28 – Starter for 10
(1) Bob Girard: Brethren Hang Loose p.73 Zondervan 1972
(2) G. A. Knight: Theology of the Old Testament p.185 SCM1969
(3) J. R. Tolkien: The Hobbit

'Towards Leadership' is a bulletin published six times a year on issues current in the Church and relevant to leaders. For fuller information and details of subscription, write, enclosing a stamped addressed envelope, to 'Towards Leadership', The King's Centre, High Street, Aldershot, Hants.